MEASURING MILITARY POWER

THE SOVIET AIR THREAT TO EUROPE

*Written under the auspices of the
Center for International Affairs,
Harvard University*

*A list of related works written under
the Center's auspices appears at the
back of this book*

MEASURING
MILITARY POWER
THE SOVIET AIR THREAT
TO EUROPE

Joshua M. Epstein

PRINCETON UNIVERSITY PRESS
PRINCETON, NEW JERSEY

Copyright © 1984 by Princeton University Press
Published by Princeton University Press, 41 William Street,
Princeton, New Jersey 08540

Library of Congress Cataloging in Publication Data will be found
on the last printed page of this book

ISBN 0-691-07671-5

Publication of this book has been aided by a grant from the
Whitney Darrow Fund of Princeton University Press

This book has been composed in Lasercomp Times Roman

Clothbound editions of Princeton University Press books are
printed on acid-free paper, and binding materials are chosen for
strength and durability. Paperbacks, although satisfactory for
personal collections, are not usually suitable for library rebinding

Printed in the United States of America by Princeton University Press
Princeton, New Jersey

DEDICATED TO
MY MOTHER LUCILLE, MY FATHER JOSEPH,
AND TO
SAM, MY BROTHER

CONTENTS

FIGURES

TABLES

ACKNOWLEDGMENTS

Beethoven once said, "Composers never finish their works, they just give up." While the same is doubtless true of authors and their books, this author would certainly have given up a great deal sooner without the support and encouragement he has received along the way.

Special thanks are due the Arms Control Project of the Center for International Studies at M.I.T. and the Ford Foundation for their financial support of the book's "first draft," my doctoral dissertation. I would also like to thank the Rand Corporation, where the dissertation was completed, for its generous support.

Working with the members of my dissertation committee, William W. Kaufmann, Ted Greenwood, and Stephen Meyer, was the greatest pleasure. For their energy, insight, and involvement, I will always be grateful. My gratitude to William Kaufmann goes well beyond both the thesis and the book; far more than anyone else, he has influenced the way in which I think about defense issues.

Though it may seem a roundabout way of getting from one end of Cambridge to the other, I returned from Rand to spend two stimulating postdoctoral years at Harvard, where the thesis became a book. The first year was spent at the Center for Science and International Affairs, the second in the Government Department's Center for International Affairs. To their directors—Paul Doty and Samuel P. Huntington, respectively—my sincere thanks. While indebted to all my colleagues at Harvard, I am especially grateful to Barry R. Posen and Steven E. Miller for their contributions to the book, and to the intellectual climate in which it was written.

I am also beholden to John Van Oudenaren for his computer assistance, and to Virginia Goss Livingston for her help in coordinating the manuscript's production.

The Council on Foreign Relations has my deepest thanks for an invaluable International Affairs Fellowship, during which the book was dragged (kicking and screaming) to read-ability by Princeton's superb editor, Elizabeth Gretz. Also, for their advice, I thank Sanford Thatcher, John Steinbruner, Richard Kugler, and Michael Mandelbaum.

Although they included criticism, editing, proofreading, and unflagging moral support, Melissa Healy's contributions to this project were, from beginning to end, of such variety that I am at a loss to do them justice—save to express my heartfelt thanks for every one.

All share in the book's "pluses"; for its "minuses" I alone bear full responsibility.

NOTE ON SOVIET SOURCES

The English translations for the titles of Soviet publications cited in the notes and bibliography are as follows:

Krasnaya Zvezda	Red Star
Znamenosets	Banner Bearer
Aviatsiya i Kosmonavtika	Aviation and Cosmonautics
Voyennyy Vestnik	Military Herald
Vestnik Protivovozdushnoy Oborony	Antiaircraft Defense Herald
Tekhnika i Vooruzheniye	Technology and Armament
Tyl i Snabzheniye Sovetskikh Vooruzhennykh Sil	Rear and Supply of the Soviet Armed Forces

The notes and bibliography use the following key to cite translation sources:

T1 Directorate of Soviet Affairs, Air Force Intelligence Service, *Soviet Press Selected Translations*

T2 Directorate of Threat Applications, Air Force Intelligence, *Soviet Press Selected Translations*

T3 U.S. Army Foreign Science and Technology Center, U.S. Army Material Development and Readiness Command

T4 Foreign Technology Division, Wright-Patterson Air Force Base

PREFACE

The single most fundamental assumption concerning the European military balance is that of Soviet conventional superiority. That assumption clearly conditions Western thinking on the need for theater nuclear forces; it represents the basic constraint on America's freedom to shift forces to other regions, such as the Persian Gulf; it dictates the bulk of U.S. and Allied defense spending; and it colors diplomacy at virtually all points of political competition between East and West. That the Soviets enjoy conventional superiority in Central Europe is among the most important assumptions, not merely in defense policy, but in world politics today.

Is that assumption warranted? The prevailing level of defense debate is inadequate to answer this question.

Everyone would agree that superiority entails the capacity to achieve concrete military goals such as the destruction of specific targets or the occupation of certain territory. Claims that the Soviets are superior, therefore, assert that certain tangible, statable military goals would be achievable by them were deterrence to fail. Superiority claims, in short, are claims about wartime effectiveness, about performance in the execution of wartime missions, about *outputs*.

Virtually the entire defense debate, however, concerns itself not with wartime outputs, but with peacetime *inputs*—static inventories of men and machines. Negligible attention is paid to the operational factors involved in taking those peacetime inputs (e.g., tanks, planes) and producing a wartime output—achieving any *specific* military goal.

In those rare cases in which basic operational factors (e.g., skill, flexibility, coordination, sustainability) are noted at all, they are usually left hanging, or are tacked on to an underlying "bean count." Very few attempts are made to *integrate* inputs (i.e., numbers of tanks, planes, etc.), technological factors, and operational factors in such a way that they can be brought to bear on output. Recognizing that each of these must be a component of analysis, their isolated treatment simply cannot come to grips with the real issue: *Given a specific Soviet threat (a postulated attack, or campaign) how does one arrive at a reasoned judgment as to its plausibility; is it plausible that the Soviets could successfully execute the postulated attack?*

This book tries to suggest a general approach to that question, a way of thinking systematically about it. It does so not by attempting to assess all conceivable Soviet threats, but by doing a close and careful job on one. The mathematical framework developed to analyze that threat, though it can be generalized, is not applicable to every other threat. But the considerations at work in devising and applying it are completely general. Those are the book's methodological contributions.

By their application, it offers an assessment of the Soviet offensive tactical air threat to NATO, now a critical aspect of the European conventional balance. The book thus takes an important step in the direction of a more meaningful, dynamic assessment of the balance of power in Europe, and hence, in the world at large. That is its military contribution.

Contrary to popular assumption, military analysis and political insight are not mutually exclusive. In fact, to assess Soviet capabilities in a rigorous way, one is compelled to examine Soviet politics in the military sphere. In arriving at its military judgments, the book reveals an intriguing and colorful side of Soviet politics that has received virtually no attention in the West—a Soviet "subsystem" whose military importance and political vibrancy make it a promising area for future research. That is the book's political contribution.

The discussion also raises some serious questions about the efficiency—indeed, the definition—of "Soviet defense production" and about the efficacy of Soviet military modernization more generally. At issue, finally, is the capacity of Soviet institutions to change, to adapt, when technological progress demands it. Or, as Marx himself might have framed the question, "Can Soviet *relations* of production evolve along with the *forces* of production themselves, or will there be deepening 'contradictions' between the two?"

Since, in this case, the productive output is military capability, one might conclude that such "contradictions of communism" must be an unqualified good for NATO. To be sure, Soviet problems present the Western Alliance with exploitable military vulnerabilities. But there is also a definite sense in which the Soviets' very deficiencies make them more, rather than less, dangerous militarily. Those deficiencies, the offensive (perhaps destabilizing) inclinations they inspire, and the deep Soviet dilemma they produce, are set forth in what I hope is a novel reading of Soviet military doctrine.

Returning to the book's main thrust, the assessment of current Soviet capabilities, it may avoid unnecessary confusion to address at the outset some of the common criticisms of contingency analysis (the assessment of concrete, specific threats) and the application of mathematics to it.

In the Introduction, a specific Soviet offensive air attack is presented for analysis: definite targets in NATO territory (air defense weapons, NATO airbases, communication nodes, etc.) are set forth, and their conventional destruction is posited as the immediate goal of Soviet tactical air operations.

As it happens, this is a contingency of widespread concern. But, presented with any such threat, it is always legitimate to ask: "How do you know that the threat you've posited is the 'right' one, the attack the Soviets would try to execute?" I don't know, and short of war itself, I cannot know, nor could I verify the "rightness" of any other attack that might be postulated. Indeed, one of the deeper ironies of this entire business is that, precisely in the event that our selection of contingencies, and our planning against them, *are* correct, we'll never "know" it, because they will have deterred war!

But, just for the sake of argument, suppose we did know precisely the attack the Soviets would attempt to execute were deterrence to fail. The current level of debate would still be inadequate to assess *that* threat. And since the Soviets are not in the habit of providing such intelligence, one is forced to postulate specific threats and assess their plausibility. If the threat before us can be analyzed, then the analysis can be expanded to include others, until the entire spectrum of plausible

Soviet threats is identified. Those who would prefer to begin that process with a different threat than the one analyzed here are welcome to do so. If this book succeeds, its methods will be equally applicable to that threat.

Nevertheless, the more "strategically" oriented would claim that contingency analysis—the focus on specific threats—is myopic and misguided per se. It misses the forest for the trees: "I don't care about specific threats," these critics will say, "I care only about the global balance of power."

So do I. I just don't know how to *evaluate* it without recourse to contingencies. Forests, after all, are made of trees; if one can be felled, maybe others can. This contingency may be the "wrong" one. But if its analysis proves to be possible, perhaps the same approach can be successfully applied to others—theater by theater, contingency by contingency—until the "global" spectrum of plausible threats is identified. As a start, the threat before us will suffice; the procedures developed will allow continuing on to other threats if that is desired. But the refusal to start anywhere (the "global-only" perspective) should certainly not be accepted as the equivalent of having finished.

Another evasion of military analysis has gained currency and deserves note. Its various formulations all reduce to the following claim: "Because the *perception* of Soviet capabilities is important politically, examination of the capabilities themselves may be dispensed with."

Certainly, perceptions of Soviet capabilities are important politically. But that rather unstartling observation hardly frees one from the problem of military analysis. On the contrary, precisely because perceptions matter, it is of the utmost importance to correct our perceptions if they are wrong. I don't know of any way to check the accuracy of our perceptions without examining their objects—the capabilities themselves —as rigorously as possible.

Obviously, diplomacy is not, and should not be, the slave of military analysis; military decisions cannot be made in a diplomatic vacuum. But that hackneyed admonition is no license to proceed with diplomacy in a haze of unexamined military perceptions, or to unquestioningly pander to erroneous ones.

The domestic political variation on the same theme generally runs as follows: "Defense decisions—with or without analysis —are politically (or economically) motivated, and since 'it's all politics' anyway, why go to all the trouble of analysis?" Because the outstanding question remains: which policy deserves to be advanced and supported in that political arena? Merely to observe that "it's all politics," or even to describe those colorful politics in bureaucratic detail, does not begin to address that more compelling question.

It wouldn't be as compelling were there some "invisible hand" to guarantee that the competing interests of politicians, defense industrialists, and the military services (to name a few) would somehow converge in a force structure that efficiently satisfies the nation's military needs. But there is no such mechanism in America's "marketplace of defense," and in its absence, there is no alternative to planning. In planning for deterrence, the first question is that of the potential adversary's capabilities—not his peacetime inputs, but his wartime outputs.

Lacking such assessments, the adequacy of one's own capabilities cannot be judged, locally or globally; deficits between wartime requirements and current capabilities, in turn, cannot be measured; and the relative attractiveness (politically as well as financially) of feasible corrective policies therefore cannot be gauged. In short, deterrent planning, defined as the derivation of wartime requirements, is not possible without threat assessment. It is toward that larger undertaking that this book, by both its methods and results, is directed.

While accepting these arguments for contingency analysis, many will still regard its quantification as a foredoomed quest for certainties in a world of chance. To be sure, anyone looking for certainty in this business would be doomed. But that is not the goal of quantification; mathematical statements are not presented as mathematical laws any more than judgments otherwise arrived at are presented as eternal truths.

Recall the question highlighted above: Given a specific Soviet threat, how does one arrive at a reasoned judgment as to its plausibility? The critical words are "judgment" and "plausibility." Obviously, the threat's execution is *possible*. Technically, any physical event is possible (i.e., there exists some probability). But not all possible events are *plausible*. If we did not draw this distinction all the time, we would live in constant terror of being struck by lightning, eaten by lions, or carted off to alien worlds: all possible, but none terribly plausible.

While it is possible that the Soviets' capabilities are literally boundless, none of us really finds this plausible either. No one who did could consistently advocate any expenditures on defense since, if the Soviets were perceived as literally and inalterably omnipotent, there would be no reason to spend a dime! Since no one is advocating that the Western Alliance stop spending, there must be a consensus that some upper bound on Soviet capabilities exists. If we agree—as in fact we do—on its existence, then how can we estimate it?

Needless to say, statistical confidence of a sort that might be obtained from a random sample of NATO-Warsaw Pact wars is (thankfully) unattainable. Though data exist on a variety of much narrower subproblems, *all macrolevel threat assessments rely on judgments of plausibility*.

The goal of quantification therefore is not to eliminate judgment; nor can any method ensure that judgments will be right. The goal is to ensure that judgments are *examined* against the most explicit criteria of plausibility that can be erected on the limited information base available. It allows one to ask clearer questions: "With what assumptions would this threat's execution be consistent? Are those assumptions plausible to me? What, in fact, am I assuming when I make a judgment on threats?" The approach allows one to identify and to pull out one's often unrecognized assumptions and look at them, ask others about them, and debate them. It does not purport to eliminate uncertainty, but to identify it in such a way that its consequences can be gauged and, where possible, its extent reduced.

The main point is that analysis seeks neither to preclude what is always possible nor to attain confidence in the statistical sense. Rather, it is condemned to the realm of plausibilities and, as such, is a tool of (and not a substitute for) judgment. Basically, the entire exercise is in the spirit of Socrates' dictum: "Know thyself." If you know yourself *better*—if your judgments are *more* reasoned—for having done it, then it was worth doing. In that sense, military simulation is a type of 'gedanken', or thought, experiment.[1]

Many of the usual qualms with quantification arise because the wrong goals are presumed (often by practitioners as well as critics). Other common criticisms of mathematics, however, rest on an unfair double standard, as Frederick William Lanchester observed:

> There are many who will be inclined to cavil at any mathematical or semi-mathematical treatment of the present subject, on the ground that with so many unknown factors, such as the morale or leadership of the men, the unaccounted merits or demerits of the weapons, and the still more unknown "chances of war," it is ridiculous to pretend to calculate anything. The answer to this is simple: the direct numerical comparison of the forces engaging in conflict or available in the event of war is almost universal. It is a factor always carefully reckoned with by the various military authorities; it is discussed *ad nauseam* in the Press. Yet such direct counting of forces is in itself a tacit acceptance of the applicability of mathematical principles, but confined to a special case. To accept without reserve the mere "counting of the pieces" as of value, and to deny the more extended application of mathematical theory, is as illogical and unintelligent as to accept broadly and indiscriminately the balance and the weighing-machine as instruments of

---

[1] A general mathematical structure for all such exercises is presented in Appendix D, with some general observations on the duality of threat assessment and force planning.

precision, but to decline to permit in the latter case any allowance for the known inequality of leverage.[2]

In other words, the bean-counting detractors of mathematics in fact *have* a mathematical model, namely, that the relative effectiveness of forces in war, f(r), equals their peacetime numerical ratio, r. Yet, without providing any compelling argument in support of *that* particular model, the bean counter feels no compunction in dismissing all competing models out of hand, merely on the ground that they are mathematical, when they are no more "mathematical" in principle than his own!

But, even granting all of this, there is one obvious question that deserves an answer: What about Soviet data? How does one obtain it? How can one proceed without it?

In some cases, reasonably trustworthy estimates are available. In many important cases, of course, they aren't. But, again, why jump to the conclusion that perfect measurements are necessary to address the problem at hand? What degree of precision is really required to do the job? The job is to establish a plausible *bound* on Soviet capabilities. To do that, it is sufficient to use values the Soviets are *unlikely to exceed*. Those may be the "wrong" numbers, but they will err on the side of favorability to the Soviets. If, on those assumptions, the threat is not plausible, then the "right" numbers would only render it less so.

Naturally the question arises, "How can you find numbers the Soviets are unlikely to exceed without knowing the real Soviet numbers to begin with?"

In the first place, it is possible to adduce the inequality of two numbers without knowing *either*. We do it all the time. We can say with confidence that Sam is taller than Ivan without knowing either's height. And, if we knew Sam's height to be six feet, we could say with equal confidence than Ivan was *less than* six feet tall without knowing his height. And so it is in this

---

[2] Frederick William Lanchester, *Aircraft in Warfare* (London: Constable and Company, 1916), pp. 46–47.

case. We often don't know Ivan's numbers, i.e., the Soviet numbers for certain variables. But we can often find an analogue for Sam, whose numbers we do know to a reasonable degree of accuracy.

For example, we do not have data for Frontal Aviation's[3] air-to-ground munition accuracy. But we do know the main factors upon which the value depends. They include the technology itself and the skill of the pilot, the latter being a function of training time and the quality of training, among other things. What we lack is an analogue for Sam. In this case, Uncle Sam will do.

There is no evidence that the United States is *behind* the Soviets in the relevant areas of technology, notably avionics and munition guidance. As for the determinants of pilot skill, the U.S. pilot flies roughly twice as much as his Soviet counterpart. Although shackled by various factors, U.S. pilot training is certainly no *less* realistic than Soviet. The former has incorporated the lessons of far more aerial warfare experience than the Soviets have logged since World War II. And, in retaining skills, the U.S. enjoys the benefits of simulators far in advance of those the Soviets are reported to possess; highly sophisticated computing and display technology, for example, is involved. Finally, Sam can learn from the winners in the Middle East, while the Soviets must glean their combat insights from the losers.

Where, in any of the areas that would determine accuracy, do the Soviets enjoy an advantage over the U.S.? In the technology? In any of the factors (training time, training quality) responsible for pilot skill? By what miracle of efficiency, then, would the Soviets come out with a value *higher* than the U.S. value? Is it *plausible* that they would? Not in my judgment.

So, in this case, Ivan is no *taller* than Sam. But, for bounding purposes, we'll assign Ivan Sam's height. It is not plausible that Soviet accuracy should *exceed* American. Thus, for bounding purposes, it will suffice to assign the Soviets the American

---

[3] Frontal Aviation, a separate Soviet service, is the offensive arm of the Soviet tactical air forces.

value. Indeed, we will begin by assigning Soviet Frontal Aviation an average hit probability of 0.75, a value that most American planners would regard as implausibly high for the U.S.

Is that the "right" Soviet value? Probably not. But is it unfavorable to the Soviets to use that value? Not in my judgment. And if, on assumptions of that sort, the Soviets still fail to execute the attack, then surely, on more "realistic" assumptions, they would fall even shorter of the mark.

This is why the book opens with a discussion of American tactical air modernization and its problems, so that enough American information is available to make this type of painstaking comparison for each of the Soviet variables where data is scarce. As a critique of the U.S. case, the chapter may be incomplete, but that is not its function in the book. Its function is to facilitate *Soviet* assessment by the above approach. While the book's interior chapters are of political interest in their own right, that comparative procedure is their ulterior motive, too; they are qualitative, but they perform a quantitative function and should thus be read on two different levels.

The numerical judgments thus made are then plugged into equations to produce curves of target destruction and force attrition over time. The equations *relate* inputs to outputs and capture one of the obvious features of the problem, one that escapes most discussions: its dynamic aspect. After all, we do envision *numbers* of planes (each carrying *numbers* of munitions, and supported by *numbers* of personnel), flying *numbers* of missions (sorties) per day for some *number* of days, all against some *number* of targets defended by some *number* of NATO combatants.

How do I "know" I've got the "right" equations? I don't. But, just as in the case of the Soviet numbers, why assume that the "right" equations are required to make a reasoned judgment on bounds? As long as they are not biased—by their algebraic form—against the Soviets, then they will suffice.

So, for example, the simulated Soviets enjoy perfect weather conditions (excluded from the equations), even though the real Soviets would be imprudent to assume them. No constraints on the range of tactical air planes complicate our bounding equations, though they might well complicate the Soviet planner's life. Aerial reconnaissance and damage assessment ("what's already been hit") are, by exclusion, conducted with perfection by the simulated Soviets. As we shall see, however, the real Soviets express serious concern about difficulties in each area.

Besides omitting many variables, others known to be time-dependent are held constant, and at very high initial values, in our equations. For example, the above-noted Soviet air-to-ground accuracy, initially set at 0.75, is impervious to degradation, even though precipitous deferrals of aircraft maintenance are sustained for days at sortie rates (missions per day) of six, higher than would be plausible in the U.S. case, and in a punishing wartime environment.

By their algebraic form, our equations also award the Soviets constant returns to ground support personnel in generating sortie rates, even though it is clear that at some point, diminishing marginal returns would set in.

These and a host of other such simplifying assumptions are made. Unrealistic? Yes. Unfavorable to the Soviets? Again, not in my judgment. Though the book's interior chapters provide evidence for those judgments, one may of course disagree. But let the methodological point be clear; as long as they err on the side of conservatism (i.e. favorability to the Soviets), then even the *wrong* numbers, applied in grossly approximative equations, will still address the *right* question: is the threat plausible?

If, on those conservative simplifying assumptions, it isn't plausible, then on more "realistic" assumptions, it should appear even less so. Or, to put it more pointedly, in order to discredit the conclusions it will not suffice to point out that "unrealistic" assumptions have been made; that is admitted. Rather, one has to show *where* those admittedly unrealistic assumptions have been unfavorable to the Soviets. How much more favorable to the Soviets would the assumptions *have to be* in order to alter the main conclusions? And are those assumptions, in fact, plausible?

Basically, the idea is to give the Soviets the benefit of the (often considerable) doubt, and see what happens. Certainty is a will-o'-the-wisp, judgment an ever-present hobgoblin, and so one does what hard-nosed common sense would indicate. In the face of imposing uncertainties, one makes assumptions explicit; with the available (often limited and imperfect) information, one tries to draw inferences that are consistent with those assumptions. The assumptions should then be varied (in sensitivity analysis), lest they prove wrong, as well they may, so that the *consequences* of irreducible uncertainty may be gauged. And, depending jointly on (a) the degree of uncertainty outstanding and (b) the sensitivity of one's conclusions to it, one buys hedges.

The method is not at all new and, in fact, it isn't "mathematical" in principle. It has claimed various epithets throughout history, but they have all been names for the same thing: facing up to the problem and trying to be rational.

MEASURING
MILITARY POWER
THE SOVIET AIR THREAT TO EUROPE

INTRODUCTION

The late 1950s were dark times for the Soviet Air Force. Resounding financial defeat to the emerging Strategic Rocket Forces was compounded by the subsequent transfer of a great many Air Force specialists, technical experts, and scientists into the fledgling nuclear missile forces. Insult was added to these fiscal injuries when, beginning in 1957 with the launching of Sputnik, Khrushchev and Marshal Vershinin expounded their view that the obsolescence of manned aircraft was imminent and that those children of Douhet would soon find themselves consigned to the air museums.[1] These developments, one assumes, reflected Khrushchev's willingness to place primary reliance on nuclear missilery, and even to undertake a general substitution of nuclear for conventional firepower. Financially, in terms of manpower, and in its doctrinal standing, the Soviet Air Force had certainly reached a low ebb.

Broadly speaking, the major change in Soviet military thought since Khrushchev has been the gradual reversal of that militarily confining preoccupation with nuclear weaponry, a rejection of Khrushchev's "one variant war." While the expansion and qualitative improvement of Soviet strategic and theater nuclear capabilities have been unremitting, the Soviets have clearly committed themselves to securing a far broader range of non-nuclear military options in Europe.

In no other service has this change been more starkly apparent than in Soviet Frontal Aviation, the tactical air arm and largest branch of the Soviet Air Forces. Formerly, Frontal Aviation was structured predominantly for air defense interception, and its operations were tightly bound to those of

---

[1] Brigadier General Giulio Douhet, early twentieth-century theorist of airpower, is discussed in Bernard Brodie, *Strategy in the Missile Age* (Princeton, N.J.: Princeton University Press, 1959). See also Asher Lee, *The Soviet Air Force* (London: Gerald Duckworth, 1961), pp. 159, 198.

the Red Army—more precisely, the Army Front Command (hence the name Frontal Aviation). In the course of the last decade, the mission structure of Frontal Aviation has swung dramatically in the direction of deep offensive interdiction (ground attack) and its supporting missions, while in the conduct of those missions, its operational independence from the Red Army has sharply increased.

New weapon systems, capable of operation at higher velocity, lower altitude, extended range, and greater payload have been introduced; the variable-geometry (swing-wing) Sukhoi SU-24 Fencer, SU-17 Fitter, and Mikoyan MiG-27 Flogger D series exemplify the trend. Tremendous impetus has been given to the development of low-altitude target acquisition systems, terrain-avoidance radars, automatic flight control, and other important areas of ground attack avionics. The range of environmental conditions (e.g., night, adverse weather) under which Frontal Air forces can operate has clearly expanded, while increasingly sophisticated and specialized air-to-surface munitions have entered its ground attack arsenal. New advanced weapon systems, the MiG-25 Foxbat and the multipurpose MiG-23 Flogger B, have powerfully enhanced the Soviets' capabilities in the allied missions of aerial reconnaissance and offensive counterair, respectively.

This very ambitious modernization program has been bolstered by the continuing modification of older planes for new forward roles. MiG-21s, long the workhorses of Soviet air defense, for example, have been reconfigured for armed reconnaissance, while the elderly Yakovlev Yak-28 Brewer E and even transport aircraft (Antonov AN-12 Cub) and bombers (Tupolev TU-16 Badger), have been turned into instruments of electronic warfare.[2]

---

[2] Two books that present the modernization of Frontal Air are Robert P. Berman, *Soviet Air Power in Transition* (Washington, D.C.: The Brookings Institution, 1978), and Phillip A. Petersen, *Soviet Air Power and the Pursuit of New Military Options*, Studies in Communist Affairs, vol. 3 (Washington, D.C.: Government Printing Office, 1979).

In comparison with its total eclipse by the nuclear Strategic Rocket Forces in the late 1950s and early 1960s, this resurgence of Frontal Aviation has been startling. Indeed, twenty years after Khrushchev's 1957 prediction that it would soon hold only antiquarian interest, Frontal Aviation's share of Soviet defense spending was roughly *twice* that of the entire Strategic Rocket Forces.[3]

Today, there is widespread agreement among Western analysts that Frontal Aviation has acquired the capability to execute—preemptively and very quickly, independent of the ground forces and by conventional means—large-scale offensive strike operations against NATO Theater Nuclear Forces and a wide range of NATO assets critical to the non-nuclear defense of Western Europe.[4]

More specifically, a two-phased operation is envisioned. Phase I, the so-called "independent air operation," is a preemptive, non-nuclear campaign aimed principally at the degradation of NATO's nuclear response capability.[5] Following the establishment of a corridor through NATO's air defense system, primary targets are assumed to include NATO Theater Nuclear Weapons (TNWs) and TNW storage facilities, C^3 (command, control, and communications) sites, and NATO tactical air bases (including nuclear-capable and nuclear-armed aircraft on quick reaction alert). Subsequent operations comprise Phase II and, in more direct coordination with the ground forces, would aim at consolidating the latter's gains and ensuring their broad maneuver. The conventional

[3] Central Intelligence Agency, National Foreign Assessment Center, *Estimated Soviet Defense Spending: Trends and Prospects* (Washington, D.C.: Government Printing Office, June 1978), pp. 3–4. The calculation is in rubles.

[4] According to Phillip A. Petersen of the Defense Intelligence Agency, for example, "The initiation of nonnuclear hostilities by the Soviets in Europe would unquestionably begin with a massive independent air operation against enemy nuclear forces, command posts, and airfields." Petersen, *Soviet Air Power*, p. 7.

[5] Its successful execution would also contribute to conventional air superiority.

interdiction of valuable mobile targets, in-theater NATO re-inforcements, lines of communication, and stockages is assumed to characterize this phase of operations.[6]

Now seen as integral to the Soviet ground advance, and as critical in degrading NATO's ability to redress conventional setbacks by nuclear means, Frontal Aviation is held to be the very linchpin of the Soviet non-nuclear offensive in Europe.[7]

This book addresses a very straightforward question: *Is it plausible that Soviet Frontal Aviation has acquired the capability to execute this two-phased conventional operation?*

This, it must be stressed, is a radically different question from that of whether the Soviets could destroy the same target set by other methods. This question we will *not* address, though the range of alternative approaches deserves note.

The use of nuclear weapons—the SS-20 missile or Backfire bomber, for example—on segments of the target set is among the possibilities. The Soviets might choose to withhold a cer-

---

[6] While general agreement exists regarding the new offensive capabilities of Frontal Aviation and regarding these overall features of its two-phased European mission, the reader looking for operational specifics will be sorely disappointed by the available literature. Unavoidably, we have had to make assumptions at the operational level in constructing the detailed elaboration analyzed in Chapter VI. A range of target sets is provided, as is the basis for innumerable variations on Frontal Air performance, manpower, and efficiency combinations, and on the NATO defense itself. A large number of those variations are, in fact, examined explicitly; however, if one's "favorite" has not been included, certainly all the data needed for its construction and evaluation are provided. Sources that, with varying degrees of operational significance, discuss the new Frontal Air threat appear with an asterisk in the bibliography.

[7] If the Soviet armored onslaught were successful, and NATO's theater nuclear forces could be *conventionally* suppressed, the Soviets—*without* crossing the nuclear threshold themselves—would have raised the spectre of "decoupling" in a very stark way, quickly forcing upon the United States the dread choice between conventional defeat and strategic nuclear intervention. To impose that choice on one's opponent may be the only meaning "escalation dominance" can have in an age of strategic parity. To impose it conventionally would be, in a unique sense, "elegant." Soviet Frontal Aviation would clearly be the core of any such attack, one—it should be noted—whose success would drive a wedge into NATO's deepest political fault line at the outset of hostilities.

tain number of nuclear-armed Frontal Air systems from the Phase I operation for use in Phase II, should the resources available for the latter's non-nuclear execution prove scarce. Employment of chemical munitions or long-range, surface-to-surface missiles are further possibilities, as would be the conventional participation of aircraft from the Soviets' Long-Range Aviation or Naval Aviation arms. Non-Soviet Warsaw Pact forces could, technically, function to supplement Frontal Aviation in the ground attack. Finally, parts of the target system could be made the responsibility of Soviet airborne assault forces rather than Frontal Aviation.

All sorts of tactical combinations of these and other alternatives are possible as well. Each has its own advantages and disadvantages, its promises and pitfalls. Major participation by the forces of Long-Range or Naval Aviation, for example, could jeopardize their primary missions, peripheral attack and maritime strike. Political constraints, on the other hand, could rule out the preemptive (Phase I) employment of non-Soviet forces. Intrawar deterrent goals could stay the use of nuclear weapons in such a capacity. The safe delivery of a large and self-sustaining airborne assault force could require such a commitment to fighter escort as to ultimately increase, rather than relieve, the burdens on Frontal Aviation, though the emplacement of Soviet ground forces behind enemy lines could be deemed worth the sacrifice. The confidence with which, and time at which, targets must be struck would further complicate the evaluation of each possibility.

None of these possibilities will be examined in this research. Here, attention is concentrated solely on what, in many ways, is the most classical and stylized attack of all. It also happens to be the attack of the most widespread concern. Even if it were not, however, our narrow focus would be justified. By limiting the analysis to Soviet Frontal Aviation's unassisted and *strictly conventional* capability, insight can be gained as to the likelihood that recourse to other methods would become necessary or attractive to the Soviets. The *extent* of any Frontal Air deficiency, the *types* of targets surviving, or the *time* at which force exhaustion occurs—such factors could well determine the subsequent options implemented by the Soviets.

While these factors can and will be estimated very carefully, no attempt will be made to determine the most likely Soviet response should Frontal Air fail, or to estimate either the probability or consequences of such a response. The narrow and fundamental task before us is formidable, revealing in its own right, and of overriding concern to Western analysts.

Logically, there are three steps to the assessment proper. The first is to develop a mathematical framework by which to conduct the analysis. The second is to obtain numerical values for the variables in those equations. Third, using those values, is to apply the equations in an evaluation of Soviet capabilities. All of this is done.

To have presented the material in this order, however, would have subjected the reader to a very abrupt and perhaps forbidding introduction to a rather specialized vocabulary and a complicated set of relationships. This would have been cruel and unusual punishment even for the mathematical stalwart, and might have presented an imposing deterrent to those less inclined toward such methods. The discussion, therefore, takes a more scenic route to the threat assessment that is its destination.

The first four chapters lay the groundwork for the program of "Ivan versus Sam" comparisons that was discussed in the Preface, and which is executed in Chapter V. While each chapter performs a definite function in the larger analytic scheme of things, each also has a life of its own.

Chapter I examines ground support and other problems the U.S. has encountered in its own tactical air force modernization. Those problems loom large in the "gold-plating" controversy, over whether the costs of American technological complexity have outweighed its benefits. In that intense debate, however, central terms such as "readiness" and "sortie rate" are often used so sloppily as to preclude any purposeful dialogue or—more important from our standpoint—any meaningful comparison with the Soviets. In order that the book's subsequent comparisons *be* meaningful, the first chapter therefore clears up some of those basic confusions.

Chapter II then challenges the prevailing wisdom on Soviet weapons "design philosophy," calling into question (a) its alleged distinctness from American practice, and (b) its even more dubious relevance to the Soviets' own maintainability problems (or "gold-plating" problems, if you prefer).

The Soviets themselves suggest that these are becoming quite serious in fact—that the Soviet ground support environment is having a hard time keeping pace in its skills and equipment with the advancing technology it must accommodate. Those problems in adjusting and adapting to new technology are, finally, systemic in nature and are the subject of Chapter III. Aside from being essential to the technical threat assessment, the discussion is revealing politically. In particular, the Soviet institutions (the Socialist Competition, the role and methods of the Communist Party, research, development, and state supply arrangements) within which military modernization takes place are shown to have reduced its effectiveness and to have impeded the Soviets in fully utilizing the technology they have acquired.

Turning from issues of Soviet efficiency on the ground, Chapter IV takes up questions of Soviet effectiveness in the air. The same, essentially political problems that have hampered the ground support system in accommodating new technology have adversely affected the Soviets in a wide variety of areas, including pilot training, reconnaissance, coordination in combined arms operations, and command and control. These problems, too, have impeded the Soviets in realizing the military potential promised by their advancing technology. Taken together, Chapters III and IV strongly suggest that Frontal Aviation suffers from a high degree of operational rigidity, making it a relatively inflexible instrument.

Many of those rigidities and operational limitations are "assumed away" in Chapter V. It is here that the *qualitative*, "art of war," insights accumulated in Chapters I through IV are applied in rendering the essential *quantitative* judgments, and in arguing that those numerical judgments are, in fact, conservative (i.e., not biased against the Soviets). A certain amount of further, and quite dry, accounting, however, is necessary to actually apply the equations (discussed shortly). While that ancillary bookkeeping is preserved in order that the technical analysis be duplicable, there was no reason to burden the text with it. Appendix A is its Elba.

To arrive at an assessment, the numbers thus derived are applied in equations. These, too, have been stayed from the general reader's path and are developed in Appendix B. In this book, of course, that mathematical framework is directed at the Soviet air threat. But, by suitable reinterpretations of its variables, it would be equally applicable in assessing ground force, transport, or naval capabilities. Terms like "sortie" and "flight time per sortie" are merely specializations of the more general notions, "operating cycle" and "real operating time per operating cycle," and so on. Underlying the analysis of Soviet offensive airpower, then, is a far more general framework for analysis, applicable not only to a wide variety of threat assessments, but also to the broad planning of Western forces.

In addition to its force planning and assessment applications, it is hoped that the mathematical framework might prove to be a valuable teaching tool in the area of defense policy studies. Designed to be as succinct and simple as its aims would permit, the system of equations that is developed below allows serious students with little mathematical training to get a grip on complicated defense problems, to obtain real results, and to expand the community of informed actors in this important area of public choice.

The numbers derived in Chapters I through V and Appendix A are applied in the equations of Appendix B, producing the threat assessment proper. That is offered in Chapter VI. Two main simulations are conducted and they yield the central military conclusions of the book:

First, it is *not* plausible that Frontal Aviation yet has acquired the capability to execute the two-phased (conventional) attack of primary concern to the West. Indeed, Frontal Aviation appears to fall far short of the capability to execute even Phase I of that attack, the independent air operation. In turn, any concerted attempt as its execution would be likely to preclude subsequent (i.e., Phase II) operations in direct support of the ground forces.

This is by no means to deny that the conventional offensive interdiction capabilities of Frontal Aviation have grown to significant proportions. They have, and Chapter VI discusses the potentially serious destruction of which Frontal Air is capable. That is, in addition to demonstrating the implausibility of prevalent assessments, the chapter addresses the further question: what *is* a plausible threat?

Finally, of the many forms which its attack might take, a furiously paced maximum mass attack is shown to yield greater returns to Frontal Aviation that an attack (by the same total force) from lesser *initial* mass, prosecuted at a more measured pace, and sustained (in echelons) over a longer period of time.

The last of the above findings is quite in keeping with Soviet military doctrine. That correspondence, and the more general convergence of Soviet doctrine and Soviet capabilities are also taken up in Chapter VI.

The stability of the basic military conclusion is demonstrated in the sensitivity analyses, presented with commentaries in Appendix C. The basic goal of a sensitivity analysis is, as the name suggests, to gauge the sensitivity of one's conclusions to changes in one's assumptions, as the latter are varied over the ranges of uncertainty in question. But, aside from their usefulness in that regard, the runs provided in Appendix C admit of at least three other interpretations.

First, many of the initial estimates are varied far beyond that bracket within which reasonable and informed people will disagree—beyond the range of uncertainty surrounding *current* (i.e., early 1980s) values. Once outside that (albeit blurry) bracket, the variations become a projective device: *ceteris paribus*, how might Soviet performance (*output*) change if some variable (e.g., Frontal Air inventory, an *input*) were to double, or triple, over the next decade?

Soviet trends are worthwhile topics. But the projection of some future bean count is no more conclusive than a bean count today. What do the apparent trends really mean? Would a doubling of the Frontal Air inventory double that force's destructive power; does "twice as big" (in inputs) mean "twice as strong" (in output)? As Appendix C demonstrates, the answer is no; *ceteris paribus*, there are diminishing marginal returns to Soviet numbers. With a framework that (a) relates inputs to outputs and (b) gives an assessment of output in some base period, the operational consequences of possible future developments can be evaluated. This is one use of Appendix C.

Second, the same variations can be interpreted as a catalogue—a "menu"—of assumptions *the Soviets* would have to make in order to enjoy confidence of greater current capability than our assessment indicates. This is among the attractions of a conservative, even a "worst plausible case" analysis. It allows one to turn the analytic tables and ask, "Is it plausible that *the Soviets* would make assumptions about their own prowess even *more* favorable than those that were made on their behalf? If not, how can *they* be confident of greater success than our estimates indicate?" Needless to say, in crises, under duress, when "provoked," people behave irrationally. But for that very reason, it is important to examine the degree of irrationality that deterrence will bear. What kind of assumptions would the Soviets have to make to perceive this attack as a "good bet"? How much rationality is enough, as it were, to hold in check the temptations that are borne of crisis?

Third, the variations can be useful in setting NATO's priorities, targeting priorities especially. I realize that, to the uninitiated, targeting may seem the most ghoulish of topics. But it is no more so than deterrence or the avoidance of war itself. At least in the conventional sphere, deterrence is, and always has been, based on the communication of war-fighting capabilities. Increasing NATO's efficiency, by enhancing the latter, can strengthen deterrence; it can also save money, at current prices a nontrivial matter in its own right.

Not all these interpretations and uses of Appendix C are explored there. But if they are kept in mind, the reader may discover oases in what—at first glance—might appear a desert of data.

Finally, the book's entire analysis is but a special case of a completely general abstract framework, sketched mathematically in Appendix D. That "science of the plausible," if you will, leads quickly to some basic insights on the duality of force planning and threat assessment. These are set forth as a formal critique—in three theorems—of "mirror-imaging."[8]

---

[8] Mirror-imaging is understood here as the assumption, implicit in much defense commentary, that matching the Soviets "tank-for-tank" and "gun-for-gun" is uniformly an intelligent planning criterion—equivalently, that failure to do so means inferiority.

CHAPTER I

PROBLEMS OF U.S. TACTICAL AIR FORCE MODERNIZATION

GENERAL TRENDS IN RELIABILITY, MAINTAINABILITY, AND COST

Among the most conspicuous features of technological change is the higher performance of new aerospace weapons.[1] Put simply, "the number of functions required of an individual aircraft has increased from one generation to the next." This trend has been reflected in the increasing complexity of major aircraft subsystems—power plants, navigation sets, weapons control systems, and the like.[2]

The disturbing fact, however, is that as their specified performance and attendant complexity have increased, the reliability of weapon systems has declined. In the words of General

---

[1] A systematic text covering the basics of reliability analysis is Bertram L. Amstadter, *Reliability Mathematics* (New York: McGraw-Hill Book Co., 1971). See also Igor Bazovsky, *Reliability Theory and Practice* (Englewood Cliffs, N.J.: Prentice-Hall, 1961).

[2] Thomas A. Blanco et al., *Technology Trends and Maintenance Workload Requirements for the A-7, F-4, and F-14 Aircraft* NPRDC TR 79-19 (San Diego, Calif.: Navy Personnel Research and Development Center, May 1979), p. 3. The most direct and commonly used index of system (or subsystem) complexity is the simple parts count. Measured thus, the trend of increasing complexity is nowhere more evident than in the area of military electronics. For the period 1949–1960, see E. F. Dertinger, "Funding Reliability Programs" in *Proceedings of the Ninth National Symposium on Reliability and Quality Control* (San Francisco, Calif.: The Institute of Radio Engineers, 1963), p. 29. For trends since, see Blanco et al., *Technology Trends*, p. 6, as well as Gene A. Kunznick, "F-15 Reliability Program Management," p. 156 and Samuel C. Phillips, "Keynote Address," p. 12, both in *Final Report of the Joint Logistics Commanders Electronic Systems Reliability Workshop*, Departments of the Army, the Navy, and the Air Force, 1 October 1975, (Washington, D.C.: Government Printing Office).

Samuel C. Phillips, former commander of the Air Force Systems Command, "Expanding requirements have increased complexity. Growing complexity has increased the number of parts; and as parts and components multiply, the reliability of the system as a whole tends to drop."[3]

This, of course, need not be the case theoretically. Indeed, a designer may increase the parts count, and thus the complexity of a system expressly to raise its reliability, the use of various sorts of redundancy being the most obvious case in point.[4] This and other methods of attempting to bolster reliability have been pursued by the United States. Nonetheless, as the sophistication and complexity of U.S. systems has increased, their reliability has decreased.

More disturbing still, since the 1960s, when the A-7 and F-4 were introduced, "the costs of modern aircraft have increased, in real terms, by a factor of four."[5] This, too, is an empirical relationship and does not mean that increases in cost must reduce reliability as a matter of physical law. But, as a matter

[3] Phillips, "Keynote Address," p. 12. See also Blanco et al., *Technology Trends*, p. 7. A distinction should be maintained between an increasing number of aircraft functions and a rising number of discrete aircraft parts. Microelectronics, as former Under Secretary of Defense for Research and Engineering William J. Perry contends, may allow functions (i.e., performance) and reliability to increase while complexity (defined as the number of parts) and unit costs decline; the hand-held calculator is his exemplar. See his review essay, "Fallows' Fallacies," in *International Security* 6 (Spring 1982) and William J. Perry and Cynthia A. Roberts, "Winning Through Sophistication: How to Meet the Soviet Military Threat," *Technology Review* 85 (July 1982), pp. 26–35.

[4] Logic diagram representations of the standard parallel and series redundant configurations are developed in Amstadter, *Reliability Mathematics*, ch. 7. Mean times to failure for the constant failure rate (i.e. negative exponential reliability) case are derived in Amstadter for various redundant configurations with various permissible failures on pp. 124–144 and in Appendices A.3, A.4, and A.6. A useful table summarizing the overall system reliabilities for the one-, two-, and three-branched parallel cases is provided in Richard H. Myers, Kam L. Wong, and Howard Gordy, *Reliability Engineering for Electronic Systems* (New York: John Wiley & Sons, 1964), pp. 44–45, while the shapes of the most common failure distributions and reliability functions appear on p. 20 of the same work.

of fact, the two have moved in opposite directions.[6] The reliability specified by contract, and assumed in the planning of forces, is, in a great many cases, far higher than the reliability that is actually delivered—actually demonstrated in the field.[7] As one Pentagon study put it, "You can argue, you can

---

[5] Department of Defense, *Annual Report of the Secretary of Defense for Fiscal Year 1980* (Washington, D.C.: Government Printing Office, January 1979), p. 184; Office of the Under Secretary of Defense for Research and Engineering, *Final Report of The Defense Science Board Task Force on V/STOL Aircraft* (Washington, D.C.: Government Printing Office, November 1979), p. 60; for a more extended discussion, see William D. White, *U.S. Tactical Air Power—Missions, Forces, and Costs* (Washington, D.C.: The Brookings Institution, 1974), especially pp. 39–50.

[6] For example, avionics now "account for nearly 30 percent of the total costs of fighter aircraft." Bruce E. Armstrong, *Avionics Data for Cost Estimating* P-5745-1 (Santa Monica, Calif.: The Rand Corporation, March 1977), p. 1. Here—notwithstanding the possibilities for microelectronics (see note 3)—the inverse empirical relationship between cost and reliability has been quite clear, as demonstrated in Howard P. Gates, Jr., "Electronics—X" in *Final Report of the Joint Logistics Commanders*, pp. 55–58.

[7] For example, among the reliability-related "guarantees" agreed to by the McDonnell Douglas Corporation in its contract to produce the F-15 was the so-called Air Vehicle MTBF (mean time between failures). This is the overall (unarmed) system MTBF and subsumes the engine, air frame, and avionics reliabilities. The contracted MTBF for the Air Vehicle was 3.5 hours. Kunznick, "F-15 Reliability Program Management," p. 143. Over its first six months in active duty service, January through June 1976, the demonstrated MTBF was 0.76 hours, off by a factor of nearly five. Although it experienced some reliability growth following its introduction into service, at the end of calendar year 1977, the F-15 Air Vehicle was demonstrating a field MTBF of 1.3 hours, still only 37 percent of the value specified by contract—and this a full three years after the November 1974 decision to enter full-scale production. Values are from Clarence A. Robinson, Jr., "Future Threat Guides F-15 Advances," *Aviation Week and Space Technology, Special Report: Tactical Air Command—Modernization and Management*, 6 February 1978, p. 72. Unanticipated problems with the F-100 engine have certainly made a major contribution to the F-15's reliability problem and have caused concern about the reliability that can realistically be expected from the F-16, which shares the troubled power plant. However, it is in the area of avionics where the divergence between the reliability specified by contract and the reliability demonstrated in active duty has been most consistently in evidence. See Gates, "Electronics—X," and Ben H. Swett, "The Avionics Reliability Study," in

threaten, you can cry, you can beg—but once the government is committed to produce the equipment, it is almost impossible to enforce a quantitative reliability requirement."[8]

These general trends in reliability do not, in and of themselves, dictate a decline either in the readiness of U.S. forces or in their capacity to generate and sustain very high numbers of missions per day, or sortie rates, as they are called. Even an extremely unreliable system—one that experiences failure very frequently—may attain very high availability (and activity) *if* upon failure it can be repaired quickly.[9]

As an everyday illustration of that principle, one's pencil point might break every few minutes; it might have a low "mean time between failures," in the language of reliability theory. But with an electric pencil sharpener (a maintenance system), one has hardly to stop writing at all in order to restore the pencil to peak performance and reenter the fray of composition.

A decline in reliability, then, can in theory be compensated for by a commensurate increase in maintainability. Unfortunately, however, in the U.S. case, the trend is in precisely the

---

Final Report of the Joint Logistics Commanders. Swett describes "where Air Force Logistics Command got their 10-to-1 'rule of thumb' that says 'field MTBF will be about 1/10 of specified MTBF'" in this area on pp. 85–86. For thoughts on why specified and field reliability diverge in the American case, see Joshua M. Epstein, *Political Impediments to Military Effectiveness: The Case of Soviet Frontal Aviation* (M.I.T., Ph.D. diss., 1981), p. 94. The MTBF is defined in general and derived for the constant failure rate case on pp. 123–126 of Amstadter, *Reliability Mathematics.* A simpler treatment, along with a few interesting military historical examples appears in Gilbert Kivenson, *Durability and Reliability in Engineering Design* (New York: Hayden Book Company, 1971), pp. 83–89. See ch. 12 of Amstadter for an interesting presentation of reliability growth models and of difficulties encountered in predicting reliability growth. Especially interesting is section 12.2 on achieving reliability growth through a process of alternating tests and design changes.

[8] Swett, "The Avionics Reliability Study," pp. 85–86.

[9] The term "repaired" is understood to include all those activities required to restore the system to its specified level of performance. Recalibrations and the removal and replacement of defective modules would be among these, for example.

TABLE 1.1
Complexity-Maintainability Trend

Aircraft Group	Group Average MMH/FH
F-5A, B, E	18
A-7B, C, E	23
F-4B, D, E, J, N	38
F-14A, F-15, F-111A, D, E, F	48

Highest: F-14A = 59.97

Lowest: F-5A, B = 16.0

SOURCE: MMH/FH for the F-5A, B, and E, the F-4D and E, and the F-111A, D, E, and F were provided in 1979 by the U.S. Air Force, Doctrine and Concepts Division, Deputy Directorate for Long Range Planning, Directorate of Plans. For the A-7B, C, and E, the F-4B, J, and N, and the F-14A, the source is Blanco et al., *Technology Trends*, p. 26. The F-15 figure is from Clarence A. Robinson, Jr., "Future Threat Guides F-15 Advances," *Aviation Week and Space Technology*, 6 February 1978, p. 72.

opposite direction. As their complexity has risen, the reliability of American systems has decreased, and they have become more difficult to maintain.[10] Among the standard indices of aircraft maintainability in peacetime is mean maintenance manhours per flight hour (MMH/FH). By that measure, the data in Table 1.1 should suggest the overall trend.

[10] A mathematical discussion of the relationship between reliability, maintainability, and availability is given in Epstein, *Political Impediments*, pp. 48–53. Some implications for deterrence when these are misperceived are discussed there. The fact that field reliability has proven to be less than expected has, in many cases, resulted in maintainability also being less than expected. For example, spare parts levels are planned to meet planned, or expected, failure rates. Since failure rates have been higher than expected, the demand for replacement parts has also risen to higher-than-anticipated levels—levels exceeding the supply of spares, resulting in maintenance problems. For one example of this, see Richard Halloran, "Combat-Readiness of F-15 Questioned," *New York Times*, 11 December 1979.

Returning to the pencil analogy, there are two corollaries that bear on the Soviets. First, pencils are very inexpensive. Therefore, rather than invest in a sophisticated maintenance "infrastructure"—an electric pencil sharpener—many of us just keep a big mug of pencils on the desk (i.e., near the "theater" of intellectual war). When the pencil we're using wears down, we don't even try to restore it to service. Without lifting our heads from the paper, or breaking our concentration at all, we casually toss the dull pencil aside and pull a presharpened one from the old school mug. As long as pencils remain cheap, that's a perfectly sensible procedure.

By all accounts, the Soviets used to have the same approach to aircraft. They were relatively cheap, and when a plane broke down, it could be set aside too. Rather than attempt to restore it to peak performance right there in the theater of war, the Soviets could simply "plug in" a new plane drawn from their "old school mug": Stalin's defense industry.

But, impelled by technological competition with the West, Soviet aircraft have become increasingly complex; the "pencil" is no longer that cheap.[11] And the Soviets—for a variety of reasons—are turning away from their traditional "old school" solution. Given current costs and complexity, the Soviets cannot simply "throw away" an advanced weapon and bring in a new one every time one breaks down. As we shall see, they are being forced to develop a true maintenance strategy in the Western sense. But they are having a hard time adapting the "old school" institutions—political, economic, and military—to the new requirements.

The second point to bear in mind is that, even granting Soviet weaponry higher reliability (itself open to question), it does not follow that the Soviets enjoy higher availability; that, as noted above, is determined only jointly by reliability *and* maintainability. As we shall see, there is reason to seriously

---

[11] William Perry holds that "in fact, the latest generation of Soviet tactical aircraft is more complex than its American counterpart." Perry and Roberts, "Winning through Sophistication," p. 32.

doubt the ease with which the Soviets can maintain their new advanced weapons.

Within the American trend of increasing overall maintenance manhour requirements, important additional effects are observable. In order to understand these, and as a basis for Soviet-American comparison, the organization of U.S. ground support must be sketched.

Maintenance as well as logistic support for U.S. air forces is conducted at three different maintenance levels (MLs): organizational, intermediate, and depot.

Organizational Maintenance (ML_1)

This is maintenance of the flying unit's (the "user organization's") own equipment and is performed by personnel of that organization—hence the name "organizational" maintenance. Tasks would include the inspection, servicing, adjusting, and lubrication of equipment as well as the removal and replacement of parts, minor assemblies, and subassemblies, as indicated by on- and off-aircraft diagnostic and test equipment. "Personnel at this level usually do not repair the removed components, but forward them to the intermediate level," as would be the procedure in the case of any repair falling outside the organization's own capacity. Accordingly, "the least-skilled maintenance men" are utilized at this level. The refueling and rearming of aircraft would normally be performed at ML_1. Given the combat requirements for speed in all of the above-mentioned "turnaround" operations, organizational maintenance is afforded "minimum time . . . for detailed maintenance or diagnostic checkout."[12]

It is very important to note that the rapidity with which organizational ground support can conduct the required maintenance (as well as rearming and refueling) essentially determines the feasible sortie rate. If the so-called "turnaround" can

[12] Benjamin S. Blanchard, Jr. and E. Edward Lowery, *Maintainability* (New York: McGraw-Hill Book Co., 1969), pp. 93 and 91.

be completed quickly, there will be little time between sorties and a greater number of sorties will be performable per day. Consequently, an aircraft designer charged with the task of ensuring the capability for high sortie rates should "expect to find limited personnel skills and related support at this level and should plan equipment maintenance and servicing requirements accordingly."[13] Accurate field reportage and designer sensitivity to field maintenance problems are therefore essential if technological change is not to outstrip the capacities of ML_1 and result in lower than desired sortie levels. Whether or not the Soviet designer has, in fact, been sensitive to that problem is a topic to be discussed at length below.

Intermediate Maintenance (ML_2)

Intermediate—or "field"—maintenance is generally performed at fixed installations established to support a number of lower-level (i.e., organizational) maintenance units within some specified geographical area. In the case of carrier-based tactical aircraft, for example, field maintenance is primarily shore-based while organizational maintenance would be conducted on the carrier or other ships in its task force. "Assigned work includes calibrating, repairing, or replacing damaged or unserviceable parts, components, and assemblies, modifying material, and providing technical assistance to user organizations."[14] Intermediate maintenance facilities are staffed by more highly skilled personnel and have a larger complement of more sophisticated test equipment than would be found at ML_1. Since maintenance of a more detailed nature is conducted there, it is only natural that rapid turnaround time be less imperative at the intermediate level than at ML_1.

---

[13] Ibid., p. 93.

[14] U.S. General Accounting Office, *Productivity of Military Below-Depot Maintenance—Repairs Less Complex Than Provided at Depots—Can Be Improved*, Report LCD-75-422 (Washington, D.C.: Government Printing Office, July 1975), p. 1.

Where repair is feasible at ML_2, it is conducted on a return-to-user basis. Where it is not, defective equipment is forwarded to the depot level.

Depot Maintenance (D)

Depot level maintenance is conducted at what are essentially industrial facilities. These "are generally located remotely from individual theaters of operation and provide services for several such theaters."[15] The most highly skilled specialists as well as maintenance equipment of extreme bulk and sophistication are available at the depot level, whose tasks would include the complete overhaul, modification, and rebuilding of equipment. Reworking and repair of subsystems and components requiring complex actions would also be conducted here. Occasionally, parts not otherwise available may be fabricated using the depot's extensive shop facilities and expert personnel.

Depot operations are not conducted on a return-to-user basis. Rather, repaired components and other depot products are returned to the theater supply systems from which they came.[16]

In contrast to this three-tiered American structure, the Soviet system is essentially two-tiered, and lacks a comparable intermediate (ML_2) "cushion" between the critical flightline (ML_1, where the wartime turnaround must be accomplished quickly) and the remote depot (where time-consuming industrial queues await the damaged plane). Therefore, in the Soviet case, if its maintenance problems outstrip the skills and equipment available at the organizational level (in their case, the Air Regiment), the aircraft—if it is to return to combat at all—will have to return via depot, and may not see action for a very long time.

---

[15] Blanchard and Lowery, *Maintainability*, p. 94.

[16] For more on this, see Ray A. Dunn, Jr., "U.S. Air Force—Total Force Overview and General Purpose Force Manpower Requirements Issues" in *The Total Force and Its Manpower Requirements Including Overviews of Each Service*, vol. 2, Defense Manpower Commission (Washington, D.C.: Government Printing Office, May 1976), p. D–25.

In order to estimate the Soviet Air Regiment's capacity to generate and sustain high wartime sortie rates (missions per day), it will be necessary to gauge its adjustability to technological advance. As a basis for that estimate, some important additional effects of modernization should be noted on the American side.

As shown in Table 1.1 above, *aggregate* maintenance man-hours per flight hour (MMH/FH) has increased; the *sum* of the organizational, intermediate, and depot values has risen. Equally important for our purposes, MMH/FH has risen "*at each* maintenance level."[17] Again, in theory this need not be the case. Modernization could, for example, have resulted in an increase in MMH/FH at ML_1 alone: malfunctions of the type organizational maintenance is designed to handle could simply have increased in frequency. Had this been the only effect, aggregate MMH/FH ($ML_1 + ML_2 + D$) would have risen, as observed, but without increasing MMH/FH at either the intermediate or depot levels. In fact, however, not only have "ML_1-type" malfunctions increased in frequency but maintenance tasks beyond organizational capabilities have expanded as well.[18] Nor has an increase in MMH/FH at ML_2 succeeded in containing the problems, which have overflowed to swell the demand for depot-level resources as well.

Indeed, and this is the second point, modernization, while producing across-the-board increases, has dramatically altered the pattern in which the total maintenance burden is *distributed* among America's three maintenance echelons. For example, the aggregate MMH/FH for the relatively simple A-7E

---

[17] Blanco et al., *Technology Trends*, p. 25.

[18] That ML_1-type malfunctions have increased in frequency can be deduced from the following two facts: first, as pointed out in ibid., p. 20, data "clearly show that automatic diagnostics onboard an aircraft have the effect of reducing MMH/MA [maintenance man hours per maintenance action] at the organizational level ... ." But, as pointed out, MMH/FH have increased at each ML, including ML_1. Clearly, since MMH/MA have fallen, but MMH/FH have risen, their ratio (MMH/FH)/(MMH/MA) must have risen. But their ratio is just maintenance actions (MA) per flight hour (FH)—thus the frequency (per FH) of system events (failures) requiring maintenance has risen.

is 24.01. Of this total, 69 percent (or 16.58 MMH/FH) is conducted at the organizational level, with depot MMH/FH representing only 14 percent (or 3.36 MMH/FH). By contrast, of the total of 59.97 MMH/FH absorbed by the highly sophisticated F-14A, organizational capabilities can accommodate only 52.6 percent (31.57 MMH/FH) while depot work as a percentage of the total is 29.3 percent (17.57 MMH/FH).[19] Depot requirements, then, as a percentage of the aggregate, are more than twice as high for the F-14A as they are for the A-7E. And, it should be noted, the actual depot MMH/FH demanded by the F-14A (17.57), in absolute terms, is over five times the corresponding figure for the A-7E (3.36).

Rising complexity, then, has not only increased the sheer *volume* of maintenance required (per flight hour) at *each* maintenance level, but it has sharply increased the demand for higher *skills*—notably, depot skills—as a proportion of that rising total.[20] As will become evident, the Soviets are facing similar problems.

Merely as a rough indicator of the associated costs on the U.S. side, it is worth noting that in outlays, Operations and

---

[19] Blanco et al., *Technology Trends*, p. 26.

[20] A discussion of these trends in relation to American "black-boxing" of integrated avionics systems is available in Epstein, *Political Impediments*, p. 95. The distinguishing characteristics of integrated avionics systems and of the associated flightline, intermediate, and depot maintenance functions are described in Polly Carpenter-Huffman and Bernard Rostker, *The Relevance of Training for the Maintenance of Advanced Avionics* R-1894-AF (Santa Monica, Calif.: The Rand Corporation, December 1976) and in Polly Carpenter-Huffman, Bernard Rostker, and John Neufer, *Analysis of the Content of Advanced Avionics Maintenance Jobs* R-2017-AF (Santa Monica, Calif.: The Rand Corporation, December 1976). Of USAF personnel in Central Supply and Maintenance (which covers depot operations and maintenance), over 80 percent are civilian. This is noteworthy because in most Soviet-American manpower comparisons, direct- and indirect-hire civilians are neglected on the U.S. side, while their uniformed functional equivalents are counted in the Soviet total. U.S. Congress, Senate, Committee on Appropriations, *Department of Defense Appropriations for Fiscal Year 1980, Part 3—Operations and Maintenance: Hearings before a subcommittee of the Committee on Appropriations*, 96th Cong., 1st sess., 1979, p. 739.

Maintenance (O&M) has repeatedly overshadowed every other appropriations title in the Air Force budget.[21] Nor is that situation unique to the Air Force. In outlays, over the entire defense budget, O&M exceeded every other title in fiscal years 1975 through 1981, and has since been outweighed only by the procurement account. At well over 40 billion dollars per annum since fiscal year 1980, operations and maintenance of military equipment is, in fact, a national priority.[22] More sobering still, O&M figures systematically underestimate certain real costs of unreliability and equipment maintenance because many of the budget's non-O&M lines (e.g., personnel, RDT&E, procurement, and military construction) contain very substantial expenditures directed at reliability and maintenance problems.[23]

---

[21] See, for example, U.S. Congressional Budget Office, *Resources for Defense: A Review of Key Issues for Fiscal Years 1982–1986* (Washington, D.C.: Government Printing Office, January 1981), p. 112.

[22] U.S. General Accounting Office, *Defense Spending and Its Relationship to The Federal Budget* (Washington, D.C.: Government Printing Office, June 1983), p. 118.

[23] Procurement, for example, includes government purchases of specialized test and maintenance equipment. Replenishment spares, essential to corrective maintenance, are paid for out of the procurement budget, as are the simulators used in the training of maintenance personnel. System modifications that may be called for explicitly for reasons of unreliability (e.g., the F-15's F-100 Engine Diagnostic System) are paid for out of procurement. The RDT&E (Research, Development, Test, and Evaluation) budget is more O&M explicit, including expenditures for "test and evaluation, including *maintenance . . . and operation* of facilities and equipment" (emphasis added). Executive Office of the President of the United States, *The Budget of the United States Government: Fiscal Year 1980, Appendix* (Washington, D.C.: Office of Management and Budget), p. 310. Again, specialized on- and off-aircraft test equipment, developed specifically to enhance maintainability, absorbs RDT&E funds. R&D-funded activities in materials science include the development of new composites to increase component reliability. Even Military Construction underwrites all the costs incurred in building the machine shops and other facilities basic to the maintenance infrastructure. For further O&M expenditures outside the O&M budget see any recent Appendix to *The Budget of the United States Government* or the relevant hearings (procurement, etc.) of the Defense Authorization and Appropriations Committees of the Congress.

The costs, in short, are staggering. What are the benefits? What, for example, is the readiness of U.S. equipment?

READINESS OF EQUIPMENT

A readiness rating system seeks to register unit capabilities to carry out assigned missions. Since weapon systems are "man-machine" systems, the assessment of unit readiness perforce includes judgments about the capabilities of personnel to perform their assigned functions. While it is generally agreed that personnel readiness depends upon training, flight time, the realism of exercises, and other factors, there is no general law relating these to actual wartime performance. Any assessment of combat readiness thus faces uncertainties concerning the readiness of people. While there is uncertainty concerning material readiness as well, it is clear that if only fifty percent of a unit's *weapons* are ready, then no more than fifty percent of the *unit* will be, even if one hundred percent of its people are. Current readiness of fully combat-equipped aircraft, then, while it is only part of any overall readiness status, represents an important upper bound on unit readiness. It is here, in the area of material readiness, that the reliability-maintainability problems reviewed above are most clearly in evidence.

As complexity has increased, reliability has generally declined. At the same time, no compensating increase in maintainability has been forthcoming, despite vast expenditures. Predictably, the net result has been a general decline in readiness as suggested in Table 1.2. In order to draw reasonable inferences about the Soviets, it is critical to interpret these data correctly. While a troubling inverse relationship between American complexity and readiness is clear, there is a fundamental distinction that is missed by most of the popular horror stories about American readiness.

The basic question is this: for planning purposes (or for purposes of threat assessment), does one define readiness merely as the force that can be *put* in the field; is it just initial deployability? Or should one build in to one's definition, and readiness rating system, some checks that the force can be *kept* in

TABLE 1.2
Mission Capability Trend

Relative Complexity	Aircraft over Which Average Is Computed	Percent Not Mission Capable
Low	A-10,A-4M	30.15
Medium	A-7D, A-7E, F-4E, F-4J	35.90
High	F-15, F-111F, F-111D, A-6E, F-14A	46.70

SOURCE: Computed from data presented in Benjamin F. Schemmer, "Pentagon, White House, and Congress Concerned over Tactical Aircraft Complexity and Readiness," *Armed Force Journal International* (May 1980), p. 28.

the field long enough to execute its assigned mission? Surely, it only confuses matters to measure American readiness against the latter, more demanding standard and then compare it against Soviet "readiness," defined merely as the initially deployable force. In order to avoid that very common error, the meaning of these "Not Mission Capable" data should be clarified.

First, "Not Mission Capable" is a peacetime index. As such it reflects a number of restrictions that, while they may be binding in peacetime, would likely be dispensed with in war. For example, aircraft may be classified as "Not Mission Capable Supply" due to peacetime prohibitions on spare parts cannibalization and on the drawing down of war reserve material stocks. However, according to former Assistant Secretary of Defense Thomas B. Ross, "in wartime, there would be unrestricted use of war reserve spares and unrestricted cannibalization."[24] Similarly, aircraft might be grounded as "Not Mission Capable Maintenance" in accordance with peacetime flight safety or performance requirements, requirements that would relax considerably in a combat environment.

[24] Benjamin F. Schemmer, "Pentagon, White House, and Congress Concerned over Tactical Aircraft Complexity and Readiness," *Armed Forces Journal International*, May 1980, p. 30.

Reflecting as they do such peacetime restrictions as these, the readiness ratings given above would tend to understate the force that could actually be brought to bear initially. Indeed, according to former Assistant Secretary Ross, "by the standard that truly reflects combat availability—the number of planes that could carry out their missions in time of conflict—the overall readiness rate is close to 80 percent for the Air Force and 70 percent for the Navy." Mission Capability rates like those cited above may reflect, as Ross suggests, "another standard—virtually flawless functioning of all parts and components at all times."[25] Needless to say, this is a far more stringent standard than deployability per se.

While it would be mistaken to interpret "Not Mission Capable" as indicating literal nondeployability, it might be imprudent to accept mere "deployability" as adequate preparedness for war. At issue, finally, is the acceptable balance between initial wartime deployability and wartime sustainability at specified levels of activity and performance. The issue, more succinctly, is what one understands to be the "mission" of those forces being rated.

For example, as Mr Ross suggests, unrestricted wartime cannibalization might, in fact, raise initial wartime deployability rates to levels considerably higher than the Mission Capability figures above. But, as former Secretary of Defense Brown cautioned, "cannibalization is a particularly inefficient use of resources in which... skilled manpower is wasted on the removal and reinstallation of two pieces of equipment instead of one." This raises turnaround times, reducing sortie rates. In addition, aircraft may be cannibalized to the point of inoperability—or, as Brown put it, "aircraft bought to fight the enemy are turned into grounded 'hangar queens.'"[26]

Thus, if the "mission" dictates sustaining a high percentage of one's force (allows few "hangar queens") at high wartime sortie rates (demands low turnaround times), then a dependence on cannibalization would represent a serious risk.

[25] Ibid., p. 29.
[26] Ibid., p. 30.

Peacetime "Not Mission Capable Supply," therefore, might be interpreted as a *projected* wartime over-reliance on cannibalization, a reliance representing an unacceptable risk to the wartime "mission," broadly understood.

Likewise, if "Not Mission Capable Maintenance" (NMCM) represents even a modest divergence from, as Ross puts it, "virtually flawless functioning of all parts and components," consider how quickly that divergence could grow in war. While initially, an NMCM aircraft might be capable of performing most of its essential functions with, for example, degraded avionics, the high failure rates and long repair times associated with current levels of complexity could quickly reduce performance to less-than-acceptable levels. The lower the level *at* deployment, the more quickly will performance degrade beyond acceptable limits—particularly at the sustained high sortie rates that may be called for in wartime.

As in the case of "Not Mission Capable Supply," then, a peacetime status of "Not Mission Capable Maintenance" may be interpreted as a wartime projection—something akin to a probability—that the aircraft, though perhaps deployable, would suffer unacceptable performance degradations in an unacceptably short time if operated at the sortie rates dictated by the "mission."

In short, all Mission Capable aircraft are deployable, but the converse is not true. Demanding peacetime criteria (i.e., definitions) of "readiness" are, among other things, an attempt to hedge against nonsustainability in war. The U.S. Air Force (USAF) falls a good deal short of meeting those criteria, and the shortfall, as indicated above, has only increased with aircraft complexity. But the utility of those criteria as wartime projectors explains their use by the United States, as against the far less restrictive deployability rates for which they are often mistaken, and against which they are generally (and erroneously) compared on the Soviet side. In this book, we will not make that mistake.

A further necessary condition for sustaining high performance weaponry at high sortie rates is, of course, an efficient support system on the ground: a cohesive team of highly skilled, well-equipped technicians, trained to diagnose and re-dress the aircraft's maladies under combat conditions.

SORTIE RATES, VIRTUAL ATTRITION, AND FLIGHT TRAINING

Within the Tactical Air Command (TAC), the reforms insti-tuted to meet that standard have focused on organizational maintenance (ML_1), whose efficiency, as noted earlier, is the critical factor in determining the sortie rates that can be gen-erated and sustained at peak aircraft performance.

The Black Flag initiative, incorporated in USAF Regulation 66-5 on October 17, 1977, is the heart of TAC's effort and is designed "to organize and train TAC units in a manner closely simulating the way they will be required to perform in a com-bat environment." According to TAC Headquarters, "What we're doing is formalizing what has always happened in a com-bat situation."[27] Black Flag has an organizational and a scheduling component.

The organizational reform is called POMO (Production Oriented Maintenance Organization). POMO divides main-tenance manpower into three groups. The aircraft generation squadron is the element providing direct flightline mainte-nance support to the wing. "The aircraft generation squadron is divided into aircraft maintenance units (AMUs) of about 200 people each that work three shifts seven days per week *directly on the flightline.*" The aircraft generation squadron for a four-squadron wing would contain four AMUs, "each correspond-ing with its matching tactical fighter squadron." This gives *to each squadron* of aircraft its own direct organic maintenance support element and follows from TAC's emphasis on "training the way we fight. We don't deploy wings, we deploy squadrons, and the ideal organization is a separate mainte-nance capability for each squadron."[28]

---

[27] "Black Flag Readies Maintenance Crews," *Aviation Week and Space Technology*, 6 February 1978, p. 129.

[28] Ibid., pp. 131 and 129. Emphasis added.

This decentralized approach contrasts with the former TAC organization still used by the Strategic Air Command (SAC) and Military Airlift Command (MAC). Under the old TAC approach, the wing's entire complement of line manpower would be held in a single pool and dispatched centrally. The nature of their missions, which dictate relatively few sorties each of relatively long duration, relieve SAC and MAC of the pressure to design ground support for maximum sortie rates. TAC, for which this is of critical concern, has found that the POMO reforms have cut turnaround times. For example, each AMU develops an acquaintance with its aircraft that "enables it to turn aircraft around faster in combat conditions without reference to computer records." In addition to its aircraft generation squadron of four AMUs, each TAC wing has a component repair squadron of 400, and an equipment maintenance squadron of roughly 550, neither of which is broken down into squadron-specific subunits like AMUs.[29] They are manned by specialists who, for example, would make use of organizational (and, if necessary, intermediate) shop facilities in performing what component or weapon system reworks are feasible below depot level.

While technological advances have demanded increased skill at each maintenance level, POMO has attempted to minimize those inefficiencies deriving from over-specialization. "Line, specialist and weapon system personnel are integrated and cross-trained to perform all tasks effectively.... Instead of the specialist simply waiting, he can accomplish many other tasks." Nor has cross-training and the engagement in simple but time-consuming operations detracted from productivity within the specialist shops. On the contrary, "one result is a faster shop turnaround time" and "an overall increase in knowledge and capability, and a greater appreciation among maintenance personnel of what others do."[30] (It is worth noting, however, that cross-training does *not* take place between pilots and maintenance personnel.)

[29] Ibid., pp. 133 and 131.
[30] Ibid., pp. 129 and 131.

Finally, a devolution of authority and greater flexibility in its distribution have been introduced. POMO has "given control of the work force to the man on the flight line who runs the aircraft maintenance unit." "If a man can manage, he can manage outside of his own narrow specialty... any specialist can become top man on the flight line."[31]

Under the Black Flag initiative, then, POMO has instituted (a) a decentralization of manpower to squadron-organic AMUs, (b) increased flexibility and reductions in narrow specialization through cross-training of maintenance personnel, (c) a devolution of authority to flightline personnel, and (d) less rigidity in the chain of command generally. All of these have increased combat realism and flexibility overall and have reduced turnaround times as part of the effort to maximize sortie rates under combat conditions. As will become evident, this decentralized, flexible approach stands in sharp contrast to Soviet procedures.

Even so, American sortie rates, surged with the express purpose of attaining the maximum, generally fall well short of TAC's European goal of three sorties per day.[32]

The Air Force, naturally, presents isolated countercases.[33] And, in fact, the term "maximum sortie rate" is every bit as vague as the term "readiness." Just as the Air Force doesn't

---

[31] Ibid., pp. 129 and 131.

[32] Philip J. Klass, "Operational Procedure Shifts Yield Major Gains," *Aviation Week and Space Technology*, 6 February 1978, p. 235.

[33] For example, Coronet Eagle (conducted 2–30 October 1980) apparently convinced General Creech, Commander of the USAF Tactical Air Command, "that the F-15 can fly five sorties per day in combat," even though (a) "the German hosts restricted flying to daylight hours for noise abatement," (b) the reduced (thus overmanned? overstocked?) squadron of eighteen planes was not engaged in realistic air combat exercises (e.g. Red Flag), and (c) it is quite unclear whether the planes involved actually recorded a sortie rate of five in any case. For the above quotes, and a more favorable account, see Lt. Col. Walter Kross, USAF Draft Document 1854A, Archive 0220A, 13 May 1982. The same exercises are discussed in U.S. Congress, Senate, Committee on Armed Services, *Department of Defense Authorization for Appropriations for Fiscal Year 1982, Part 5—Preparedness: Hearings before the Senate Committee on Armed Services on S.815*, 97th Cong., 1st sess., 1981, p. 2451.

plan to go to war with merely deployable planes, so, it does not plan to fly mere sorties. Rather it plans to fly *effective* sorties, and in a very punishing environment. The real issue, therefore, is not sortie rates per se, but again, the amount of performance (per sortie effectiveness) one must sacrifice in order to *sustain* a high sortie rate.

Beyond a certain level (between 1.0 and 1.5 for advanced U.S. fighters), higher sortie rates are feasible, but only if maintenance is deferred.[34] At some point, maintenance simply cannot be deferred any more. The number of failed components and subsystems begins to multiply; defects cumulate and ramify. The final effect is either virtual attrition (e.g., effective inoperability, mission aborts) or such losses of function as to dramatically increase vulnerability, any and all of which could require nothing less than depot level maintenance. The latter, given the two-year depot repair times logged by U.S. F-4s in Vietnam, is a form of virtual attrition in its own right.[35] The more complex and sophisticated the aircraft, the more pronounced are these effects and the more quickly do they set in.

Maintenance deferral is rather like banking. The plane is willing to extend "credit" for a certain amount of maintenance. The more sophisticated the plane, the stingier; that is, the shorter is the term of the loan, and the higher is the "interest rate," so to speak. The F-15 will let one pay on an "installment plan" (do some maintenance after each sortie, though less than the full requirement) which cuts the sortie rate, or it will let one accrue pure debt (sustain a very high sortie, and hence deferral, rate) and pay a much higher bill at the depot when the term of the loan comes due.

---

[34] For example, using equations developed in Appendix B, the sortie rates feasible for the F-15, assuming that *no* maintenance is deferred, are 1.08 (assuming two hour sorties) and 1.44 (assuming ninety minute sorties). In turn, the same methods indicate that, assuming two hour sorties, a full 64% of the F-15's peacetime maintenance (total MMH/FH) would have to be deferred in order to push the entire F-15 wing (72 planes) up to 3.0 sorties per day. The methods of Appendix B are applied to the peacetime American modernization experience overall in Epstein, *Political Impediments*, ch. 1 (for the above numbers see pp. 75–76).

[35] Schemmer, "Pentagon, White House, and Congress Concerned," p. 30.

That fact explains the cyclical nature of the Tactical Air Command's other reform, the Production Oriented Scheduling Technique (POST), which complements POMO. Under POST, a wing will "surge" sorties for two consecutive days each work week (40–45 hours). On those surge days, maintenance units "support a simulated combat flying schedule.... Every usable aircraft is turned around as fast as possible."[36] But the maintenance thus deferred must be made up. The weekly two-day surges require heavy maintenance work on the other three days of the work week; on those days, sortie rates fall to very low levels.

For example, operating within POST's cyclical framework, the 67th Tactical Reconnaissance Wing—a dual-based thirty-nine plane wing flying the relatively simple reconnaissance version of the F-4, the RF-4C—records the "typical monthly schedule for its thirty-six available aircraft" shown in Table 1.3. It is very doubtful that the Tactical Air Command's surge norm in fact approaches its goal of three sorties per day; rather, according to Black Flag managers, "the 1.5 rate may be the 'magic number.'"[37] But the more important point is not debatable in any event: high sortie surges require maintenance deferrals, and sustained operations at those sortie rates run up a maintenance debt. Beyond a certain point, the line of credit simply closes down. When it does, you have virtual attrition. By satisfying tough definitions of "readiness" (e.g., Mission Capability), one may forestall its onset. But the problem is there, and must be accounted for in any assessment of capabilities.

To account for these dynamics on the Soviet side, a few basic ingredients are required: one needs an estimate of the full

[36] "Black Flag Readies Maintenance Crews," *Aviation Week and Space Technology*, 6 February 1978, pp. 129 and 133.

[37] Ibid., p. 133. Obviously, there are deviations from this. For example, in December of 1977, forty-eight F-15s, in three days of surged flying, logged 109 sorties (day 1), 115 sorties (day 2) and 122 sorties (day 3), for sortie rates of 2.27, 2.40, and 2.54, respectively. "Langley F-15 Group Deployed to Korea," *Aviation Week and Space Technology*, 6 February 1978, p. 241. Such performances, however, are very rare, and the duration over which these rates (still less than the TAC goal of 3.0) are sustained is short.

TABLE 1.3
POST Cycles

Day	Total Sorties	Sortie Rate
Monday	14	.39
Tuesday	12	.33
First 3 Wednesdays	54	1.5
First 3 Thursdays	54	1.5
Friday	2	.06

SOURCE: Computed from data presented in "Black Flag Readies Maintenance Crews."

peacetime maintenance absorbed by frontline, advanced Soviet planes, that is, the full maintenance load with *no deferrals* whatever. By the methods of Appendix B, it is then quite easy to compute the percentage of that total *peacetime* maintenance (in manhours per flight hour) that must be deferred in order to surge up to a specified *wartime* sortie rate. As a function of the number of sorties flown at that sortie rate—equivalently, at its required level of deferral—one can estimate the corresponding probability of virtual attrition. That, along with estimates for actual attrition (Soviet planes shot down per sortie) will yield a curve of Soviet air attrition (actual and virtual) over time, one essential component of the analysis.

As attrition proceeds, of course, the Soviets will be destroying targets (NATO airfields, theater nuclear forces, etc.). The extent of that destruction, and the rapidity with which it is visited on NATO will depend not only on sortie rates and their sustainability from the ground, but also on the skill of the Soviet pilot in the air. The two—the ground and the air—are intimately related. To clarify the connection, and as a reference point in gauging Soviet pilot skill, certain features of the U.S. experience as seen "from the cockpit," as it were, deserve note.

First and foremost, inadequately trained people won't get the most out of the technology at their disposal and the most sophisticated aircraft and mission equipment (e.g., missiles) will not be effective. In fact, the more advanced and complex the aircraft, the more skill is required to fly it effectively and reap its promised benefits in effectiveness. In turn, to develop and then retain those more advanced skills, a greater number of sorties is required for training.

For example, wings of the simple A-10 reach their highest— Category 1 (C-1)—level of aircrew readiness in their primary mission (close air support/battlefield interdiction) only if they fly 6,054 training sorties within a six-month period. For F-15 wings, the corresponding figure is 6,416—higher, as one would expect (and on a per crew member basis, the difference is considerably greater).[38] But precisely where the demand for training sorties is highest, the supply is lowest, as demonstrated in Table 1.4.

If the F-15's readiness rate were higher, of course, the peacetime monthly sortie rates required to meet pilot training demand would be lower (more planes would be flying, so each one could fly less) and the demand-supply gap might be closed. But aircraft availability is constrained to inadequate levels by the underlying reliability-maintainability problems that have come with increased complexity. As a consequence, American pilots don't fly enough to meet the Tactical Air Command's

---

[38] Edward H. Kolcum, "Difficulty of Challenge Determines Credit in Grey Flag," *Aviation Week and Space Technology*, 6 February 1978, p. 194. The difference on a per crew member basis is significantly greater since the "USAF-proposed wartime tailored aircrew ratios needed to support the maximum sortie generation efforts required in combat" are 1.77 for the A-10 and 1.34 for the F-15. Ibid., p. 195. In terms of sorties per man, then, C-1 readiness for A-10 crew personnel requires

$$\frac{6{,}054 \text{ sorties}}{1 \text{ wing}} \cdot \frac{1 \text{ wing}}{72 \text{ planes}} \cdot \frac{1 \text{ plane}}{1.77 \text{ men}} = \frac{47.5 \text{ sorties}}{\text{man}},$$

and for the F-15

$$\frac{6{,}416 \text{ sorties}}{1 \text{ wing}} \cdot \frac{1 \text{ wing}}{72 \text{ planes}} \cdot \frac{1 \text{ plane}}{1.34 \text{ men}} = \frac{66.5 \text{ sorties}}{\text{man}},$$

or 40 percent greater than the A-10 requirement. Again, the more sophistication, the more demanding the training.

TABLE 1.4
The Demand-Supply Gap

	A-10 Wing	F-15 Wing
Sorties/mo. required for C-1 aircrews[a]	1009	1069
Available (fully or partially mission capable) planes/wing[b]	49	40
Resultant demand in sorties/mo./available plane	21	27
Actual supply in sorties/mo./available plane[c]	19.6	16.3
Supply as percent of demand	93%	60%
Demand-Supply Deficit	7%	40%

[a] The six-month totals divided by six.

[b] The standard wing numbers 72 planes. The entries are equal to 72(1 − NMC), where NMC is the respective Not Mission Capable rate reportedly issued (in February 1980) to the services in former Defense Secretary Brown's "Consolidated Guidance." For the A-10, NMC = 0.326; for the F-15, NMC = 0.443. See Schemmer, "Pentagon, White House, and Congress Concerned," p. 28. Since aircraft are either Fully, Partially, or Not Mission Capable, 1 − NMC is the fraction falling into the first two categories.

[c] Franklin C. Spinney, "Defense Facts of Life," unpublised paper, Office of Program Analysis and Evaluation, Department of Defense, December 1980, Slide 34.

highest standards of combat proficiency. Problems of ground support (aircraft readiness and sustainability) are thus passed on to the pilot. The Soviets, as we shall see, have not eluded the same vicious cycle.

It is worth stressing that, in this connection, the issue is not whether the F-15, for example, can be "cranked up" to five sorties a day in some more or less realistic exercise. It isn't even whether the plane could be held (in peak performance) at such sortie rates for a week or two, although that is doubtful. Rather, the question is whether, over the entire training year, the aircraft is providing a steady-state (average, over all POST cycles) peacetime sortie rate sufficient to meet the Air Force's own standards for high pilot skill. The answer would appear to be no.

Flight simulators, to be sure, have become very sophisticated. Realistic video displays of aerial combat in three dimensions are enhanced by computerized inducement of bodily acceleration effects (through manipulation of the pilot's inner ear). Moreover, although American air-to-air missile firings have been too few, the real skill lies less in firing the missile per se than in maneuvering the aircraft to an advantageous firing position. Since simulators can substitute for a certain amount of such flying, it can be argued that they may, in turn, substitute for a certain number of live firings.

Few would argue, however, that simulators are filling the gap in actual flying time, least of all American pilots themselves, who rate inadequate time aloft as the primary deficiency in American training—and many of them quit the Air Force for that reason.[39]

The direct manner in which inadequate (and inadequately realistic) training degrades effectiveness is easily illustrated: "the AIM-9J Sidewinder infrared-guided air-to-air missile, which had demonstrated its effectiveness when fired from McDonnell Douglas F-4s, did not perform well when fired from the McDonnell Douglas F-15s." Why? Pilots converting from the F-4 to the "far more maneuverable F-15" were "over-leading" the target, resulting in misses. Put simply, pilots converting to the F-15 from the much slower F-4 were "flying past" their targets in much the same way as a quarterback, suddenly endowed with a much stronger arm, might over-throw his receivers. Once the problem was diagnosed, TAC's efforts turned to "training pilots flying the F-15 not to try to aim so far forward on the target."[40] But, at roughly one missile firing per year—another casualty of cost growth in the more sophisticated weaponry—and with serious deficits in training sorties, the practice required to realize the weapon system's

---

[39] This is by no means the only factor underlying America's pilot retention problems; pay and benefits are factors as well. Aircrew testimony to the effect that it is one of the primary factors is reviewed in Franklin C. Spinney, "Defense Facts of Life," unpublished paper, Office of Program Analysis and Evaluation, Department of Defense, December 1980, slides 31–33, and pp. 12–13.

[40] Klass, "Operational Procedure Shifts," p. 234.

potential may not be possible in the near term; if present trends continue, it may not be possible at all.[41]

The situation, moreover, is not unique to the F-15; indeed, the F-15 is probably not the worst offender (more likely, the swing-wing F-111D is). Its problems are just part and parcel of a much deeper, and quite pernicious syndrome whose profile—albeit blurry at various points—is clear enough.

SUMMARY

In broad strokes, as their complexity and *potential* effectiveness have increased, American tactical air systems have become less reliable, less maintainable, and less ready. There is reason to doubt their capacity to generate the specified sortie surges under all but the most artificial conditions. And there is every reason to believe that, at *peak* performance, they would prove exceedingly difficult to sustain at those sortie rates in any case. Their year-round peacetime sortie rates, moreover, have fallen significantly short of those required to meet the Air Force's highest standards of pilot (i.e., aircrew) proficiency, impeding the development of precisely those skills needed to realize the planes' potential (and exacerbating American problems in retaining those who *have* acquired them). All the while, the systems have become much more expensive to buy, much more expensive to arm, and much more expensive to fix when failure occurs (which happens more often now than ever).

All of that said, there is one fact that cannot be dismissed: in the hands of a skilled pilot, the F-15—when operating at peak performance—is among the best air superiority weapon systems in the world. Indeed, given that, in the Lebanon conflict of 1982, they lost over *eighty* Soviet-made fighters (most of them more advanced than the MiG-21) to the Israelis'

---

[41] Dept. of Defense, *Annual Report of the Secretary of Defense, Fiscal Year 1980*, January 25, 1979, p. 192, and "F-15 Deployment to Netherlands Nears," *Aviation Week and Space Technology*, 6 February 1978, p. 233.

none,[42] I wonder how the Syrians would answer James Fallows's pointed question: "Consider a confrontation between an F-15 and six MiG-21s. Would you rather be the pilot of the F-15 or one of the six MiG pilots?"[43]

Some believe that the drawbacks of American modernization have outweighed its undeniable benefits in enhanced performance *per* plane, the result being a net decline in military strength. The less sensationally inclined, while admitting serious inefficiencies, believe the extreme "gold-plating" thesis to be overdrawn.

Since the abundant technical data available on the U.S. side has not afforded a resolution of the celebrated "gold-plating" controversy, the much less abundant Soviet data cannot be expected to support yet firmer conclusions on their side. But the evidence is more than sufficient to open the neglected question, and to submit that the Soviets are, in fact, running into very deep problems in managing their military modernization and reaping the benefits promised by their own advancing technology.

Have the Soviets avoided problems of the type and/or severity of those the U.S. has encountered? Where, in Soviet weapons "design philosophy" (Chapter II), in the Soviet ground support environment (Chapter III), or in Soviet pilot training (Chapter IV), is there evidence of a Soviet advantage in avoiding such problems? Beyond those America has come up

---

[42] "In all, in the course of the first week's fighting in the war, a total of 86 Syrian planes, all first line, of the MiG-21, MiG-23, and Sukhoi-22 types, were shot down without the loss of one Israeli plane." Chaim Herzog, *The Arab-Israeli Wars* (New York: Random House, 1982), p. 348.

[43] James Fallows, *National Defense* (New York: Random House, 1981), p. 43. Of course, Soviet pilots are probably better than Syrian, and U.S. pilots are probably not as good as Israeli. Granted; but let us pursue this. Speaking very loosely, suppose the Soviets are "twice as good" as the Syrians. Then, *ceteris paribus*, the Lebanon exchange ratio "halves," let us say, to 40:1. In turn, suppose U.S. pilots—in the same "back of the envelope" sense—are only "half as good" as the Israelis. Then the ratio drops, again by half, to 20:1. But, "back of the envelope" or not, it is still over *three* times the 6:1 brandished by Fallows.

against, do the Soviets have further modernization problems of their own; owing to the peculiarities of their military system, are there respects in which technological advance is even harder for them to manage? Are the usual assumptions about Soviet force structure (e.g., interoperability, standardization) themselves warranted?

With the U.S. experience as background, these and other questions will be taken up en route to the threat assessment of Chapter VI.

CHAPTER II

SOVIET WEAPONS DESIGN AND THE RELATIVE NATURE OF THE "GOLD-PLATING" PROBLEM

American maintenance problems have increased dramatically in the course of modernization. As we have seen, this has adversely affected the sortie rates that advanced U.S. tactical air forces can generate and sustain. If one is to assess the Soviet Frontal Air threat, it is likewise essential to estimate the sortie rates which that force might generate and sustain. In turn, it is only reasonable to begin with the question of Soviet maintainability and the manner in which modernization may have affected it. In order to think clearly about that relationship, much of the conventional wisdom regarding Soviet weapons design—its distinctness from American practice and its bearing on the maintenance problem altogether—must be reassessed.

"Simplicity," "commonality," and "design inheritance" are features of Soviet weapons design that are very familiar to all students of Soviet weapons acquisition. These, for a host of economic, institutional, historic, and other reasons, are said to "dominate the designer's thinking" and are generally agreed to be the outstanding features of Soviet "design philosophy."[1] For reasons that will be made apparent, commonality and design inheritance will be discussed first.

---

[1] Heather Campbell, *Controversy in Soviet R&D: The Airship Case Study* R-1001-PR (Santa Monica, Calif.: The Rand Corporation, October 1972), p. 38; Arthur J. Alexander, *Weapons Acquisition in the Soviet Union, United States, and France* P-4989 (Santa Monica, Calif.: The Rand Corporation, March 1973), p. 7.

As defined by Arthur J. Alexander, commonality means "multiple use of subsystems, components, and parts across equipment of the same vintage, together with repeated use of the same subsystems in succeeding generations."[2] As an example of this "sharing of design features among different aircraft," Dr. Alexander notes that "the same guns, radars, and pumps are found in a wide variety of aircraft." He points out that "the SU-7 (ground attack and tactical air cover) and the SU-9 (all-weather interceptor) had common fuselage, tails, and (originally) engines, whereas the wings, armament, and equipment were chosen for their different roles."[3] Commonality is evident not only in tactical aircraft, but as well in such areas as transport aviation, tanks, air defense systems, and naval design, as Dr. Alexander has documented.[4]

"Design inheritance is similar to commonality, but it is inter- rather than intra-generational." It is evident, Dr Alexander continues, "in the long series of models and modifications of the MiG-21 (first designed in the mid-1950s), which have incorporated new versions of engines, armaments, radars, and aerodynamics as they have become known and available."[5] Design inheritance, also termed incrementalism, "has the tendency of confining development to proven techniques. Innovation takes place in small increments. The large uncertainties of large jumps in technology are avoided."[6]

Overall, Dr. Alexander observes that in the Soviet case, "technological change and improved weapons result primarily from the process of cumulative product improvement and evolutionary growth.... Designs with no known antecedents are rare. However, even in these systems, many of the subsystems are based on proven components" adapted from sys-

---

[2] Arthur J. Alexander, Abraham S. Becker, and William E. Hoehn, Jr., *The Significance of Divergent US-USSR Military Expenditure* N-100-AF (Santa Monica, Calif.: The Rand Corporation, February 1979), p. 29.

[3] Arthur J. Alexander, *R&D in Soviet Aviation* R-589-PR (Santa Monica, Calif.: The Rand Corporation, November 1970), p. 22.

[4] See Alexander et al., *Significance of Divergent Expenditure*, pp. 29–31.

[5] Alexander, *R&D in Soviet Aviation*, p. 22.

[6] Alexander, *Weapons Acquisition*, p. 9.

tems in being. "The all-new system, with newly developed sub-systems is rare .... This," he stresses, "is in *sharp contrast to American behavior* where the 'weapon system' concept dominated development practices for at least two decades."[7] Before turning to question the operational significance of these features of Soviet design practice, it is important to examine whether the contrast is as sharp as Dr. Alexander has suggested.

First, the extent to which a series of weapon systems, combat aircraft, for example, exhibits commonality or design inheritance, depends upon naming. If the U.S. renamed the F-4B after every block number, or even airframe, change, the resulting sequence of systems would exhibit remarkable commonality indeed, as indicated in Table 2.1. We would have exactly the same arsenal, but it would appear to exhibit far greater incrementalism in design.

Second, even under the current naming, the extent of the contrast is open to question. To use one of Dr. Alexander's examples, aircraft guns, the General Electric M-61A1 Vulcan 20 mm cannon is "the standard internal armament of most high-performance combat aircraft produced in the United States today."[8] It is mission equipment for the elderly F-104, F-105, and F-106 forces, the F-4E Phantom, A-7D, and A-7E aircraft, as well as the current F-111, F-14A, F-15, and F-16 fleets.[9]

Neither does Dr. Alexander's example of the SU-7 and SU-9—"common fuselage, tails, and (originally) engines"— establish the contrast since the same (indeed greater) commonality is observable between, for example, the F-4G (suppression of electro-optical surface-to-air systems) and the F-4E (interceptor). The former are "converted F-4E Phantoms," the principal difference being that in the F-4G, the F-4E gun is

---

[7] Alexander et al., *Significance of Divergent Expenditure*, pp. 30–31. Emphasis added.

[8] Tom Gervasi, *Arsenal of Democracy: American Weapons Available for Export* (New York: Grove Press, 1977), p. 161.

[9] Ibid.

TABLE 2.1
Evolution of F-4 Airframe

Block Number	Corresponding Series of Aircraft Bureau Numbers	F-4B	F-4N	No. of Aircraft	Aircraft Service or Airframe Changes (ASC/AFC)
6f	148363f-148386f	X		24	
7g	148387g-148410g	X		24	AFC 86
8h	148411h-148434h	X		24	ASC 42
9i	149403i-149426i	X		24	None
10j	149427j-149450j	X		24	None
11k	149451k-149474k	X		24	None
12L	150406L-150435L	X	X	30	ASC 17/78 AFC 160
13m	150436m-150479m	X	X	44	ASC 92/115/133
14n	150480n-150651n	X	X	42	ASC 125
15o	150652o-150653o	X	X	2	ASC 69 AFC 151/305
	150993o-151021o	X	X	29	
16p	151397p-151426p	X	X	30	ASC 139
17q	151427q-151447q	X	X	21	None
18r	151448r-151472r	X	X	25	ASC 153 AFC 158/190
19s	151473s-151497s	X	X	25	ASC 186 AFC 176/216
20t	151498t-151519t	X	X	22	AFC 162/178/217
	152207t-152215t	X	X	9	

21u	152216-152243	X	X	28	AFC 262
22v	152244-152272	X	X	29	AFC 165/173/174/193
23w	152273-152304	X	X	32	AFC 202/213/241/267
24x	152305-152231	X	X	27	AFC 203
25y	152965-152994	X	X	30	AFC 172/220/273/317
26z	152995-153029	X	X	35	AFC 218/227/274
27aa	153030-153056	X	X	27	AFC 249/252/263
28ab	153057-153070	X	X	14	None
	153912-153915	X	X	4	

SOURCE: Thomas A. Blanco et al., *Technology Trends and Maintenance Workload Requirements for the A-7, F-4, and F-14 Aircraft* NPRDC TR 79-19 (Santa Monica, Calif.: Navy Personnel Research and Development Center, May 1979), p. 19.

NOTE: Although there are over 550 AFCs, those after number 317 are not identified with blocks of aircraft bureau numbers.

"replaced by sophisticated electronic equipment."[10] Fuselage, tails, and engines are identical. The same commonality, moreover, is evident between the F-4D (interceptor) and RF-4C (reconnaissance), as well as a number of aircraft pairs within the A-7 series.

Moving beyond such isolated examples, a May 1979 report published by the Navy Personnel Research and Development Center examined avionics, mission, and support equipment "to determine commonality among the A-7B, A-7E, F-4J, F-4N, and F-14A aircraft. To be included in the analysis, items had to be sufficiently significant to merit an official identifying nomenclature and essential for weapon system support."[11] The Navy found 165 items to satisfy those criteria. The comprehensive list includes major weapons, electronic countermeasures (ECM), flight control, radar and navigation equipment, as well as displays and guidance computers all the way down to cameras and a survival radio.

It is important to understand the method used in computing the commonality between any two aircraft. For example, the F-4J was found to contain 69 of the items on the list. The F-4N was found to contain 64. No fewer than 63 of these were also among the 69 F-4J items. That is, 63 of the items on the 165 item list were common to the F-4J and F-4N. Of the 69 with which the F-4J is equipped, the 63 items common to both represent 91 percent. Of the 64 items with which the F-4N is equipped, the 63 items common to both represent 98 percent. The percent commonality differs, therefore, depending upon the accounting. But however one does the accounting, the result is 91 percent commonality or higher. These figures, as well as the corresponding data for the A-7B/A-7E commonality are given in Table 2.2.

Looking only at avionics on board the A-7 "as it evolved from the B to the E series" is also revealing.[12] Ninety-three

---

[10] United States Air Force, Tactical Air Command Public Affairs Office, *F-4 Wild Weasel Fact Sheet* (Langley Air Force Base, Virginia).

[11] Blanco et al., *Technology Trends*, p. 7.

[12] Ibid., p. 14.

TABLE 2.2
Intragenerational Commonality

Aircraft Pairs	Common Items	% Commonality
A-7B (71) vs. A-7E (80)	55	A-7B, 77%; A-7E, 69%
F-4J (69) vs. F-4N (64)	63	F-4J, 91%; F-4N, 98%

SOURCE: Blanco et al., *Technology Trends*, p. 14.

avionics subsystems and major avionics items were drawn from the 165-item list for use in the analysis. Fifty-three of them are present in the A-7B while the A-7E avionics suite contains 76. The common avionics items number 36, 68 percent of the A-7B's or 47 percent of the A-7E's, as illustrated in Figure 2.1.

While this indicates a high degree of continuity, the actual commonality "is considerably greater than 68% since the significant number of electromechanical subsystems and the airframe itself, which are continued unchanged between series, were not considered." The Venn diagram below, moreover, depicts the situation in 1968–1971, when the A-7E was first

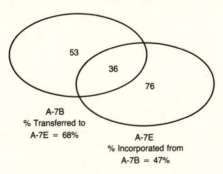

FIGURE 2.1 Venn Diagram of the Intersection of A-7B and A-7E Avionic Suites
SOURCE: Blanco et al., *Technology Trends*, p. 17.

introduced. Since that time the A-7B has been upgraded (though not renamed) "to include items originally installed on the A-7E." Not only, therefore, does the diagram understate the degree of commonality in 1968–1971, but, while the names have remained the same, the commonality has in fact grown. And the situation is by no means unique to the A-7 series. Rather, "there is major technological continuity within any aviation system type and model."[13]

Further research would appear to be called for regarding the "sharp contrast" claimed by Dr. Alexander. Its precise nature and, in turn, its extent, seem unclear at the intra-generational level, that is, *within* either the F-4 or A-7 series. At the intergenerational, or design inheritance level, the same lack of clarity is evident. The complete ordering, giving the inter- and intragenerational commonality, and using both the more and less advanced aircraft as the reference point, is shown in Table 2.3. Dr. Alexander is no doubt correct in writing that, in the Soviet case, "the all-new system, with newly developed subsystems, is rare."[14] However, in this respect per se, no "sharp contrast" with American experience emerges from the data. On the contrary, among the major conclusions of the Navy study cited above is that, in the U.S. case, "the most striking characteristic of technological change is its essential continuity across generations of aircraft."[15] At both the intra- and intergenerational levels, then, the widely as-sumed contrast between Soviet and American practice is open to serious question.

In assessing Soviet capabilities, however, the operationally significant issue is neither commonality nor design inheritance in any case. The U.S. evidences very high commonality, design inheritance, and technological continuity across generations of aircraft. Has this prevented required maintenance from rising dramatically across those same generations of aircraft? No. But isn't this the important issue from an operational stand-

---

[13] Ibid., p. 17.

[14] Alexander et al., *Significance of Divergent Expenditure*, p. 30.

[15] Blanco et al., *Technology Trends*, p. 7.

TABLE 2.3
Intra- and Intergenerational Commonality

Aircraft Pair[a]	Common Items	% Commonality
F-4J (69) vs. F-4N (64)	63	F-4J, 91%; F-4N, 98%
A-7B (71) vs. A-7E (80)	55	A-7B, 77%; A-7E, 69%
A-7E (80) vs. F-4J (69)	43	A-7E, 54%; F-4J, 62%
A-7E (80) vs. F-4N (64)	43	A-7E, 54%; F-4N, 67%
A-7E (80) vs. F-14A (91)	42	A-7E, 53%; F-14A, 46%
A-7B (71) vs. F-4J (69)	38	A-7B, 54%; F-4J, 55%
F-4J (69) vs. F-14A (91)	38	F-4J, 55%; F-14A, 42%
A-7B (71) vs. F-4N (64)	36	A-7B, 51%; F-4N, 56%
F-4N (64) vs. F-14A (91)	37	F-4N, 58%; F-14A, 42%
A-7B (71) vs. F-14A (91)	34	A-7B, 48%; F-14A, 37%
Range:	34–63	37%–98%

SOURCE: Blanco et al., *Technology Trends*, p.14.

[a] The number of avionics and mission equipment items installed in each aircraft is shown in parentheses.

point? The Soviets' capacity to execute the attacks of concern to the West hinges precisely on the sortie rates they can generate and sustain. We have seen that these in turn are determined largely by the efficiency of the ground support environment—its manpower, its facilities, and its expertise. Commonality per se is not the issue. The operational question is the adjustability, the adaptability, of the ground support environment to a *change* in aircraft technology, i.e., to a decrease in commonality.

If the Soviet ground support environment is less adjustable to such changes than the American, then even less radical (more incremental) changes in aircraft technology could result in increases in maintenance manhours per flight hour (MMH/FH) requirements as great as those the U.S. has experienced, and, in turn result in equally severe problems in the critical areas of sortie generation and sustainability. It is argued below that the Soviet ground support environment is, in fact, less adjustable than America's. As will be demonstrated in Chapter VI, this fact has important implications for the Soviet threat itself and for the efficacy of the Soviet air modernization program generally.

Before proceeding, it is important to add that the relative technological simplicity of Soviet aerospace systems may not bear on the issue either. This third pillar, if you will, of Soviet design philosophy Dr. Alexander defines in the following way: "Simplicity means uncomplicated, unadorned, unburdened, the performing only of what is required and no more."[16] Needless to say, "what is required" changes as missions change. As a significant ground attack/deep interdiction capability has come to be required of Soviet Frontal Aviation, "what is required" has evidently come to include more sophisticated avionics, terrain avoidance (and "shoot-down compatible") radars, increased automation of flight control functions, and variable geometry wings, for example. Regardless of whether or not the introduction of a new technology requires "high level political intervention," once the Soviets have decided that "what is required" is a new technology, we can agree with Dr. Alexander that they will attempt to make it as simply *as possible;* they may even do so at the expense of some performance.[17]

The SU-17 Fitter swing-wing is an excellent case in point. In the U.S. case, the F-111's armament is hung from a wing that hinges, for all intents and purposes, *at* the fuselage. Hinging at the fuselage allows for a maximum reduction in lift when the wing's angle to the fuselage is a minimum. However, as

[16] Alexander, *R&D in Soviet Aviation*, p. 21.

[17] Alexander et al., *Significance of Divergent Expenditure*, pp. 30–31. Regarding the introduction of new technology, Dr. Alexander argues that "the design philosophy of incremental change, marginal advance, and design inheritance, if followed rigidly, would eventually lead to technological stagnation" (*R&D in Soviet Aviation*, pp. 24–25). Suspension of these ingrained procedures is therefore necessary where "discontinuous change" (ibid., p. 25) or the introduction of "new in principal" weapons is sought. In these cases, high level political intervention has been characteristic. Dr. Alexander's fullest elaboration of the institutional setting within which such interventions occur is presented in Arthur J. Alexander, *Decision-Making in Soviet Weapons Procurement*, Adelphi Papers nos. 147 and 148 (London: The International Institute for Strategic Studies, Winter 1978/79).

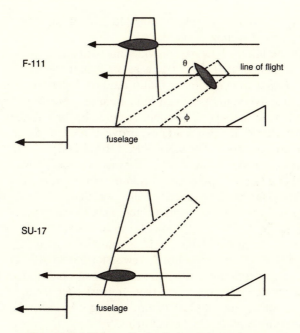

FIGURE 2.2 U.S. vs. Soviet Swing-Wing Schemes
(Overhead View)

that angle varies, servomechanisms and other devices must
vary the angle of the armament if it is to be released tangent
to the aircraft's instantaneous line of flight. These servomechanisms and other subsystems increase the complexity of
the American system. (See Figure 2.2.)[18]

The Soviet SU-17 wing hinges farther from the fuselage. The
armament is hung from the immovable portion of the wing
between the hinge and the fuselage, thus avoiding the U.S.
requirement for a system compensating the armament's initial
direction for variations in the wing's angle to the line of flight.
In this respect, the system is simpler. But performance is traded

---

[18] For more detailed drawings of Soviet swing-winged aircraft, see Bill
Sweetman and Bill Gunston, *Soviet Air Power* (New York: Crescent Books,
1978).

away in the unavoidable, or nonreducible lift imparted by the larger fixed section of the wing.

None of this, however, provides an adequate basis for concluding either that the SU-17 is easier than its predecessor for the *Soviets* to maintain, or that it requires fewer Soviet maintenance manhours per flight hour than the *American* maintenance manhours per flight hour required by the F-111, or any other aircraft for that matter. It provides *no basis for concluding anything* about the SU-17's MMH/FH in *Soviet* manhour terms. But this is the type of number we need if we are to evaluate Soviet capabilities. It is important to be clear on this.

Some far more advanced civilization than our own might find the F-111 to be "simple" and easy to maintain. Would this make the F-111 any easier for *us* to maintain? Would this change the fact that the F-111 is harder for us to maintain than the F-5? Of course not. Likewise for the Soviets. The fact that Soviet systems are, by some measures, simpler than U.S. systems does *not* mean that they are easier *for the Soviets* to maintain; at most, it means that they might be easier for us to maintain than are our own systems.

Presumably, this is what is meant by reports that "the MiG-25 is unsurpassed in ease of maintenance."[19] Perhaps so; unsurpassed (by comparison to U.S. systems) in the ease with which *U.S. technicians* can maintain them. But it is not U.S. technicians who will be maintaining them! How much harder than its Soviet predecessor is the MiG-25 to maintain for Soviet personnel, personnel to whom the technology *is* new? Are *Soviet* maintenance skills adjusting quickly enough to advances in *Soviet* technology? This is the issue. And it has little to do with whether or not new Soviet planes are simpler than new U.S. planes from some purely technological perspective. The point is that they are more complicated than their *Soviet* predecessors. Unless the Soviet maintenance base can adjust with sufficient rapidity to the new technology, Soviet mainte-

---

[19] Arthur J. Alexander, *The Process of Soviet Weapons Design* (paper prepared for Technology Trends Colloquium, U.S. Naval Academy, Annapolis, Md., 29 March–1 April 1978), p. 7.

nance manhours per flight hour will rise. In principle (see Chapter V) they could rise to levels even higher than those the U.S. records for its most advanced systems.

The entire matter, in short, hinges on *relative* rates of change: the rate of Soviet technological advance with respect, not to U.S. technology, but to the Soviet ground support environment. If the latter—its skills, its equipment—keeps pace with the technology, maintenance problems are held in check; if it doesn't adjust with sufficient rapidity, and falls behind that technology, a "maintenance gap" opens and maintenance problems proliferate, sustainability suffers, and capabilities fall short of potential—even short of prevalent Western assessments, perhaps.

In order to make a reasoned judgment on Soviet capabilities, therefore, it will be necessary to gauge the adjustability of the Soviet ground support environment to advances in Soviet aircraft technology. It is to this question (formalized in Chapter V) that the next chapter is devoted. Once sortie *effectiveness* issues (e.g., pilot skill, command and control, flexibility) are discussed in Chapter IV, the stage will be set for the full threat assessment that follows.

CHAPTER III

SOVIET EFFICIENCY ON
THE GROUND

The Soviets provide little data on most of the issues to which the following two chapters are devoted. Therefore, it is difficult to judge exactly how significant the problems are. In addition to the paucity of hard data, the problem of judgment is made more difficult by the exhortative functions of much Soviet writing, compounded perhaps by an understandable conservatism evident among militaries generally—the tendency to worry about one's capabilities.

Nevertheless, if the problems literally did not exist, it is hard to understand why the Soviets would be exhorting their correction, in some cases, for the last fifteen years. The high frequency with which the same concerns are repeated makes one doubt, moreover, that these are isolated occurrences. Virtually identical problems, furthermore, are reported in the journals of administratively separate and, by all accounts, rather insular bureaucracies, from the Air Force monthly, *Aviatsiya i Kosmonavtika (Aviation and Cosmonautics)* to the Rear Services' journal, *Tyl i Snabzheniye Sovetskikh Vooruzhennykh Sil (Rear and Supply of the Soviet Armed Forces)* to the Ministry of Defense publication, *Tekhnika i Vooruzheniye (Technology and Armament)*, to name only a few. Such remarkable consistency would be difficult to comprehend unless the problems discussed so frequently were widespread. Widespread problems of long standing and frequent occurrence may still be denied the attention of high-ranking individuals. These problems, however, are not denied their attention. On the contrary, they evidently merit published and widely disseminated commentary from within the very highest political and military offices of the Soviet state.

The accounts "ring true" for other reasons as well. For example, as will be noted at various points, the appearance *in print* of many Soviet modernization problems closely follows the appearance *in the field* of the technologies themselves. More important, perhaps, is the surprising frankness of the Soviets' accounts. They are quite specific in describing their difficulties, and in many cases offer thoughtful and convincing analyses of their own shortcomings—not at all the sort of ritual fare one might expect.

The Socialist Competition

The Soviets have long recognized the need to keep maintenance resources in pace with advancing aircraft technology. But since the early 1960s, the Soviet Air Force (SAF) has faced increasingly severe problems in doing so. Perhaps as a consequence of high-level decisions taken in the late 1950s, the SAF lost out in its competition for resources with the nuclear Strategic Rocket Forces (SRF). Its defeat in the fiscal arena was compounded by the subsequent transfer of many of the SAF's maintenance and other technical specialists to the SRF and to the expanding civilian fleet, Aeroflot.[1]

However, while the resource constraints tightened, aircraft modernization proceeded.

> In particular, aircraft CAE [communications, armament, and electronics] systems were being improved and modified. This in turn meant that the volume and complexity of maintenance work also increased, necessitating both quantitative and qualitative changes in maintenance resources.

Increases in the maintenance labor force, intensification and upgrading of labor force training programs, and an adequate flow of modern, state-produced aerospace ground support

---

[1] Andris Trapans, *Organizational Maintenance in the Soviet Air Force* RM-4382-PR (Santa Monica, Calif.: The Rand Corporation, January 1965), pp. 21–22.

(AGS) equipment were all required. None of these was forthcoming. By the period 1964–1965, the resultant "maintenance gap" had "attracted the critical attention of many Soviet military writers and an urgent search for means of improving aircraft maintenance was under way." The search had two main thrusts. First, since the state was not forthcoming with an adequate supply of maintenance equipment, the deficit would have to be made up through the efforts of local innovators. That is, deployed forces, civilian technicians, and other local craftsmen would have to design and build the required equipment themselves, making use of whatever materials and production facilities were locally available. As early as 1965, the fact that a significant portion of its maintenance equipment was "locally jerry-built," was noted as "a particularly striking aspect" of the Soviet ground support environment. This practice has witnessed a dramatic expansion since that time.[2]

The second main thrust at closing the maintenance gap attempted to raise the productivity of the tightly constrained labor force already in existence. Reorganizations—"rationalizations"—of ground support activities and their management have been the primary areas of experimentation.

Both the innovation (local design and manufacture) and rationalization drives were to be fueled by the "Socialist Competition." Its system of individual and group incentives, bolstered by a fraternal and vigorous competitive environment, would marshall all the creative forces available and harness them to the task of pulling the maintenance base up to stride with the advancing aircraft technology. All of this would take place under the expert and vigilant guidance of the Communist Party organs, the "bottleneck eliminators" of the entire process.[3]

The approach has not been successful. In fact, it has resulted in serious adjustment problems and in large part, it further accounts for the extraordinary confusion and inefficiency evident in the day-to-day conduct of ground support activities.

[2] Ibid., pp. 21, 13, and vi.
[3] Ibid., p. 24.

Conflicting goals and a self-defeating system of incentives and rewards have contributed much to the shortcomings of the Socialist Competition. The Communist Party's attempts to address these "internal contradictions" by the imposition of ever more detailed and stringent regulation accounts for the unique coincidence of absolute rigidity and considerable disorganization that characterizes the entire Soviet ground support process.

AREAS OF LOCAL R&D

All of the Soviet Armed Forces are actively involved in local research and development.[4] "The overwhelming majority of the military collective groups in our Armed Forces ... have made higher Socialist pledges in innovation and rationalization this year."[5] The preponderance of this work has specifically to do with maintenance, training, and logistics.

For example, a wide variety of simulators are designed and built within operating forces. The deputy commander-in-chief for combat training of the Soviet Air Force notes that

in recent years the tactical radius of aircraft and their ordnance load have increased greatly; radar navigational equipment, on-board electronic suppression equipment, and automated control systems have been improved.

As "conditioned particularly by the complexity of new aviation equipment," he continues, "in a great number of cases only on simulators can one master the functions which for flight safety

---

[4] In general, "local R&D" stands for non-state R&D, R&D conducted outside the structure of Industrial Ministries and the national economic planning (GOSPLAN) framework. Primarily, we will be concerned with regimental R&D.

[5] "The Mass Character of Technical Creativity," *Tekhnika i Vooruzheniye*, no. 6 (1978), pp. 2–3. T3, 1979, p. 7. So-called "Socialist pledges" are commitments taken yearly by individuals and units. One might pledge to work on a certain innovation, or to improve his performance of certain duties. Units might pledge to increase the percentage of specialists 1st class to some level, for example.

considerations are impossible to master in actual flight." While few, if any, simulators are listed under the USSR in Western compendia, one finds that a great many have been designed and built within Soviet operating units. "An original simulator which allows pilots to master the combat application of the new on-board radar navigational system" is one such.[6] As reported by the chief of the Department of Invention in the Ministry of Defense, another "example of such equipment is the stand-simulator designed and produced in one *chast'* [unit]. It includes ... air and ground situation and weapons application results displays."[7] Such simulators are said to occupy "a special place" in the training of combat personnel, "especially during familiarization with new equipment."[8]

The Soviets repeatedly stress that "the wider the range of tactical application of an aircraft, the more complicated its systems, the greater is the importance of proper technical servicing." Since only the "dependable operation of service equipment" itself "insures aircraft readiness and ... enhances flight safety," adequate training in the use of new aerospace ground support equipment is of the utmost importance to the Soviets.[9] However, "the complexity [of this equipment] is no less than that of [the] aircraft" itself.[10] Hence the large volume of locally constructed simulators directed at the training of ground support personnel. Working models of aircraft subsystems are used in training of assembly and disassembly tasks, and a variety of simulators have been built locally for training in the

[6] General-Col. of Aviation P. Kirsanov, "Enhancing the Training of Aviators," *Tekhnika i Vooruzheniye*, no. 8 (1976), pp. 1–5. T1, November 1977, pp. 284; 287; 286; 287.

[7] Major General-Engineer A. Safranov, "The Creative Activity of Innovators' Thematic Contests," *Tekhnika i Vooruzheniye*, no. 11 (November 1978), p. 36. T3, 1979, p. 122.

[8] Kirsanov, "Enhancing the Training," pp. 286 and 287.

[9] "Military Engineer and Equipment: Efficiency—A Demand of the Times" (unattributed), *Vestnik Protivovozdushnoy Oborony*, no. 4 (1978), pp. 68–71. T3, 1979, p. 103.

[10] Lt. Col. Yu. Olenev, "Competently Maintain and Efficiently Ready the Ground Flight Support Facilities," *Tyl i Snabzheniye Sovetskikh Vooruzhennykh Sil*, no. 9 (1978), pp. 72–75. T3, 1979, p. 112.

use of automated fault-isolation and diagnostic equipment. Fault isolation, the Soviets report, today represents a full 80 percent of aircraft repair time.[11]

The design and manufacture of maintenance equipment by far surpasses all other areas of local R&D. It vastly outweighs simulator construction and spans virtually the entire gamut of ground support technologies, from the so-called "minor mechanizations" to specialized diagnostic and electrical repair instrumentation, encompassing even heavy machine tools and powered assembly equipment. Small and specialized tuning, measurement, calibration, and adjustment tools, carriages, stands, and minor spot-checking equipment are among the many locally fabricated items falling into the "minor mechanization" category. Heavier equipment for the drilling, cutting, and bending of all sorts of rolled steel also emerge regularly from the regimental TEChs.[12] Even heavier items include metal rolling equipment itself, as well as power hoists and jigs used in the inspection and repair of weapon systems.[13] Local design and manufacture of CAE maintenance equipment, however, seems to absorb the greatest proportion of innovative effort, as it did even in 1965.

Shortages of state supply in this area, moreover, have been exacerbated by the immobility of what instrumentation has been forthcoming from industry. Of the mid-1960s, one reads that

> flightline maintenance personnel had to dismantle equipment and lug it to the regimental TECh for checking, since only this work center had the equipment needed;

[11] Major-Engineer V. Yulin, "The Use of Precision Charts When Servicing Radio-Electronic Systems," *Vestnik Protivovozdushnoy Oborony*, no. 5 (1976), pp. 65–69. T3, 1976, p. 113.

[12] TECh (*Tekhniko-ekspluatatsionnaia chast'*). This is the regimental facility in which scheduled aircraft maintenance is performed. It would house the more sophisticated and less mobile AGS equipment as well as whatever heavy machinery the regiment might possess.

[13] See, for example, Major General of Technical Troops (GSFG) K. Yefremov, "Mechanization of Labor-Intensive Work," *Tekhnika i Vooruzheniye*, no. 6, (1978), p. 40. T3, 1979, pp. 108–110.

indeed, . . . CAE and other equipment had to be laboriously dismantled, checked and installed again—not by choice but by necessity, since there simply was no portable CAE testing apparatus.

And, since "industry provided only a part of the testing installations . . . maintenance personnel built the rest themselves."

> What seemed to be lacking was power-driven mobile equipment in general, and portable instruments for testing and calibration of CAE systems in particular; accordingly, the efforts of local innovators were focused chiefly on these areas.[14]

The same problems not only loom large today but, impelled by the Soviets' continuing interest in operation from austere fields, the Ministry of Defense (MoD) has strongly stimulated innovative effort in the broader logistical arena.[15]

In rare instances, the Ministry of Defense, through one or more of its Main Directorates, may announce a nationwide competition among local innovators to fill some particular need. Among the "thematic tasks" (the rough Soviet equivalent of a U.S. military "request for proposal") of this sort specified in 1978 was to "build a better airmobile technical maintenance *chast'* to carry out organizational repair and recycling under field conditions."[16] The chief engineer of the Air Forces writes that in response,

> specialists in the leading technical maintenance *chasti* are moving in the direction of increasing the mobility of the instrumental laboratories and are building small, mobile laboratories designed to do maintenance and repair work under any engineering conditions.[17]

---

[14] Trapans, *Organizational Maintenance*, pp. 5 and 14.

[15] Yefremov, "Mechanization of Labor-Intensive Work," p. 110.

[16] Major General-Engineer A. Safranov, "Innovators Share Their Experience," *Tekhnika i Vooruzheniye*, no. 6 (1978), pp. 38–39. T3, 1979, p. 103. *Chast'* is a general Soviet term for "unit." As in this case, however, it may also refer to the regiment's complement of certain facilities and equipment.

[17] General-Lt. Engineer V. Skubilin, "In the Interests of Combat Readiness," *Tekhnika i Vooruzheniye*, no. 8 (1973), pp. 1–3. T3, 19 February 1974, p. 8.

Units in the Group of Soviet Forces, Germany (GSFG) are reportedly among them.[18]

Another logistical area of local R&D is the manufacture of spare parts for weapon systems. For example, an "appliance for rolling in 4–16 mm diameter copper, copper alloys, aluminum, and steel tubing" is used to "repair pneumatic and hydraulic systems when new tubing must be [locally] manufactured."[19] Another "proposal helped provide ... parts that were in short supply" for the "ZMZ-53 and 'Moskvich' engines."[20] In the area of radar, units are strongly reminded that

in preparing to carry out repairs on the equipment, one must not forget the reserve supplies. They must be created from assemblies and units taken off used equipment and which has undergone centralized repairs. At the same time, even now it is essential to start manufacturing attachments which correspond to the repair specifications.[21]

In addition to combat and support simulators, logistics, and (predominantly) maintenance and repair equipment, even subsidiary weapon system R&D is occasionally conducted locally:

Announced by the Main Directorate for Land Forces Combat Readiness and the editors of the magazine *Tekhnika i Vooruzheniye* is a contest "to develop automatic target control systems for tank (small arms) fire quality and for combat vehicle driving quality."[22]

---

[18] Safranov, "Innovators Share," p. 103. While no detailed specifications of the airmobile *chast'* appear to be available, a detailed diagram of its ground forces analogue may be found in Epstein, *Political Impediments*, pp. 188–190.

[19] In each issue of the monthly journal, *Tekhnika i Vooruzheniye*, is a feature section called "The Innovator's Relay," devoted to the presentation of innovations. This one appears in that section of issue no. 6, 1978, pp. 42–43 and is one of a dozen innovations presented in the issue. T3, 1979, pp. 116–117.

[20] Lt. Col. A. Zenushkin, "The Contribution of the Rationalizers," *Tekhnika i Vooruzheniye*, no. 6 (1978), pp. 38–39. T3, 1979, p. 106.

[21] Lt. Col. K. Anfilov, "Radar Repairs by Troop Personnel," *Vestnik Protivovozdushnoy Oborony*, no. 1 (1973). T3, 27 June 1973, p. 98.

[22] "The Mass Character of Technical Creativity," p. 8.

Readers of Sidorenko may be interested in another local design modification of this type—a water evacuation system for tanks.[23] "The water that enters the hull of a swimming tank is pumped out by three pumps, two mechanical, and one electrical." The system, however, is not wholly reliable and appears to require specialized maintenance itself.

> There are cases of water not being pumped out, even when the pumps are running .... Only repairmen who are specialists can correct troubles as serious as these.[24]

The range of innovative endeavor, then, is wide. As noted above, the preponderance of local R&D is directed toward maintenance and repair. In this area, the centrally-specified (Ministry of Defense) thematic task, if it occurs at all, is very rare indeed. Innovation proposals are generated within the regiment to meet regimental deficits in state supply. Accordingly, it is regimentally-oriented innovation that will receive primary attention here.

REWARDS

Either because they cannot, or because they have chosen not to, adjust state supply to ensure an adequate flow of up-to-date support equipment, the Soviet military has thrown its weight behind the Socialist Competition to make up the deficit. In its attempt to call forth the technological progress required, a broad and impressive array of rewards are held out to innovative individuals and to units. However, in order that they not be misconstrued as endorsing bourgeois entrepreneurship, the military is quick to point out that the "rights of inventors"—including the receipt of substantial monetary

---

[23] A. A. Sidorenko, *The Offensive* (Moscow, 1970). Translated as no. 1 of the U.S. Air Force series *Soviet Military Thought*. Ch. 7 is devoted to forging water barriers.

[24] "Water Evacuation Equipment," *Tekhnika i Vooruzheniye*, no. 8 (1973), p. 49. T3, 19 February 1974, pp. 142 and 144.

rewards—are direct descendants of the Statute on Inventions signed by Lenin on 30 June 1919. This, rather than they, "stipulated the rights of inventors and established the procedures for paying rewards for inventions recognized to be useful. Among those rewards are the following:

Individuals who have provided the state with valuable proposals have the right to obtain additional living space equal to that of scientists.

Inventors have the right of priority in gaining scientific positions at the relevant scientific research institutions and experimental enterprises.

While few military personnel ever attain these heights, commanders are exhorted to "make full use of the rights afforded them for moral stimulation of innovators." These include "the awarding of valuable gifts and certificates, announcements of gratitude, and the granting of short-term leaves for home to privates, sergeants, and extended service master sergeants."[25]
The prospect of various medals, pennants, honorary titles ("distinguished inventor," "distinguished efficiency expert of the Republic"), and inclusion on numerous honor rolls may further stimulate creative work. While no crisp distinction can be made between moral and material incentives—an academic position (moral incentive) might well carry perquisites such as access to privileged consumer goods outlets (material incentive)—money is the prime motivator. Or, as the Soviets put the ideologically delicate question, "Monetary awards are the basic form of material stimulation." These are paid out of "funds allotted to invention and efficiency work," funds that the Soviets describe as "quite sizeable."[26] Units that are successful in the Socialist Competition "have everything going for them: they get larger salaries and the best material and

[25] Lt. Col. A. Kiselev, "Incentives for Technical Creativity," *Tekhnika i Vooruzheniye*, no. 10 (1971), pp. 36–37. T3, 1972, pp. 119 and 120.
[26] Ibid., p. 120.

personnel," the latter two of which, of course, improve their chances of winning yet further rewards.[27]

At the center of all this creative activity in each unit is the Commission on Invention, approving proposals (pledges), setting bonus levels, establishing criteria for judgment of the competition, adjudicating it, and distributing rewards. It is here that the Communist Party organs play a significant role in the Socialist Competition within units, a role no less significant than that which they play in the Socialist Competition between units. The Party, however, faces a broad array of difficulties in efficiently exercising its titular authority, as we shall see.

Turning specifically to the Soviet Air Force, the reliance on regimental innovation poses a number of problems that are exacerbated by the structure of the competition between separate units.

ADJUSTMENT PROBLEMS AND DEPOT R&D

First, by its very nature, regimental innovation is reactive. A new aircraft system descends upon the maintenance element which then scrambles to catch up to the technology it must accommodate. This in itself represents an adjustment lag. And while in the early 1960s most of the locally constructed equipment in question was *"built by regimental maintenance personnel themselves,"* as aircraft technology has advanced, it has outstripped the capacity of regimental maintenance personnel alone to design and fabricate the required ground support equipment—equipment whose complexity, the Soviets stress, has increased to levels comparable to those of the aircraft themselves.[28] The result has sometimes been that the introduction of new aerospace technology has rendered an existent maintenance base quite obsolete. In such cases (the "infinite

---

[27] Editors' (i.e., Air Force Intelligence Service) footnote to General-Col. Viktor Zakharovich Yakushin, "The Staff in the Struggle for an Effective Training Process," *Krasnaya Zvezda*, 20 April 1977, p. 2. T1, August 1977, p. 201.

[28] Trapans, *Organizational Maintenance*, p. 7. Emphasis added.

k" cases, as defined in Chapter V) this requires virtually the complete re-equipping of the maintenance base.

The following account, written as the first MiG-23 interceptors and the first reconnaissance (Fishbed H) and ground attack (Fishbed J) versions of the MiG-21 were entering the SAF,[29] illustrates the extent to which Soviet maintenance units may fall (indeed, did fall) behind aircraft modernization. It illustrates as well the inadequacy of regimental technology in making up the gap left by short state supply. In exemplifying one of the many RDT&E processes spawned of the necessity to keep pace with aircraft modernization, it should indicate one of the serious adjustment problems the Soviets face.

In the fighter-bomber unit, "outfitting the technical-electrical repair unit [TERU] with more up-to-date technical equipment" was the problem.

> Why did such a need arise? Well . . . industry was supplying equipment for the TERU. But, unfortunately, not enough. Furthermore, some of the equipment had been produced without due regard for the peculiarities of operating aviation equipment under field conditions.

The shortage and maldesign of state supply explains "why the radio repairmen were working to perfect their instruments":

> *With their own hands* they had prepared various visual aids, stands, and working models. However, the specialists of the TERU were not up to creating the more complex devices.

Efforts therefore turned to arranging for depot manufacture of the equipment.

> It would be a good thing to have the equipment which we need produced centrally, . . . in one of the aircraft repair plants. After all, it has much greater resources.

Apparently, the regimental senior officer first convinced higher headquarters (either air division or air army) of the

---

[29] Alexander, *Decision-Making*, pp. 45–51.

practicality of this approach, since the author, the depot's commanding officer, recalls being directed to cooperate with the regimental engineers in the process.

"We are thinking of requesting your aircraft-repair plant to work up and prepare a set of equipment for a TERU," said the general. "Boris Ivanovich Krasusskiy [Senior engineer at the regimental TERU] and his engineers will give you all needed assistance and advice. Work closely with this group."

And, reports the author, "the collective of our enterprise, working closely with TERU specialists," designed and manufactured "a new set of technical equipment." The range of items designed and produced by the depot is, by American standards, astonishing and includes everything from simple dollies and cleanup gear to specialized electronic equipment and heavy machinery:

As is known, the TERU requires not only specialized technical equipment for scheduled maintenance work on the aircraft and its engine, but also power equipment, machine tools, specialized instrumentation and instruments, and finally, general-purpose equipment for the TERU laboratories and services. These were the basic directions around which we did our designing. Actually, each general line was broken down into several groups. In this way there arose a complex of equipment consisting of movable platforms (to enable several specialists to work at the same time on a single item), all sorts of movable stands for final adjustment of the airplane's systems, various laboratory stands, and also shelves and airdrome feed pumps for the open aprons of the TERU. We manufactured collections of instruments for the airplane technicians and for the TERU service groups, as well as specialized instrumentation. Finally, we developed an installation for cleaning dust and metal shavings from aircraft parts, electrical washing machines for the floors, electrographs and many other things. The whole new equipment complex included 49 items. It was laid out and tested on a special model.

That the advancing aircraft technology was fast outstripping the capacities of regimental innovation, and thereby shifting the R&D and fabrication functions up to depot, is clear. Equally clear is it that the Soviets expected depot R&D to become more widespread.

This was our first experience in creating an equipment complex for a TERU. *Obviously, other repair plants will also design and produce such equipment.*[30]

And they have. For example, "a set of instruments for detecting defects in an automatic recording system for aircraft flight parameters" was among the specialized off-aircraft maintenance devices that, in 1978, entered the GSFG by this channel.[31]

While recourse to depot R&D has thus been unavoidable in making up the deficits in state supply, Soviet priorities would seem to lie in the direction of rehabilitating regiments to their former level of self-reliance in aerospace ground support R&D. Evidence that this is a goal would seem to be provided by the fact that some of the technology provided the TERU above was, itself, intended for use in the manufacture of equipment—a transfer of production technology rather than merely of final goods, as it were. This reading seems to agree with many Soviet statements to the following effect:

The equipment needed to service and repair aviation equipment must be constantly perfected because the latter is becoming more and more complex. This is why the technical maintenance *chast'* must constantly work to perfect *production equipment*, and must do everything

---

[30] Col.-Engineer P. Skibinskiy, "The Technical-Electrical Unit Has New Equipment," *Aviatsiya i Kosmonavtika*, no. 10 (1968). T4, 28 May 1969, pp. 96–99. Emphasis added.

[31] Safranov, "Innovators Share," p. 102.

possible to improve *the production process.* This is where the opportunities for inventors and rationalizers are unlimited.[32]

INEFFICIENCIES OF INTER-REGIMENTAL COMPETITION

As mentioned above, the Soviets "organize the competition both between specialists in the groups and between groups on the scale of the TECh." The latter competition is intended to foster a variety of things. The most frequently mentioned goals, however, are "combat readiness and the accident-free nature of flights." "Reducing the time aircraft are in the TECh," and cutting the training time of new maintenance recruits—whose training takes place "in the TECh"—are related goals. Adjudication of the competition is said to "take into account the volume of work, the degree of complexity of technological operations . . . the quality of accomplished work . . . and the times of accomplishment."[33]

Precisely because aircraft have grown so complex, and because their readiness has such high priority, and finally, because the requisite level of complex diagnostic and repair technology has not been forthcoming from the state, there is keen competition between units in the design and manufacture of that technology. However, given the rewards for useful innovation, and the competitive edge afforded by improved maintenance and training through the internal use of those inventions, why should any unit give away its secrets to a competitor? The structure of rewards actually inhibits the dissemination of knowledge and the broad introduction of leading innovations.

---

[32] Skubilin, "In the Interests of Combat Readiness," p. 9. Emphasis added. The technical maintenance *chast'* referred to is the regimental TECh, as opposed to the aviation repair depot (*aviaremontnoe predpriiatie—aviarempred,* for short).

[33] Major-Engineer V. Shatokin, "Periodic Servicing and the Socialist Competition in the Technical-Operating *Chast',*" *Vestnik Protivovozdushnoy Oborony,* no. 5 (1976), pp. 24–28. T3, 1976, pp. 43; 41; 43; 45.

The work of using inventions and rationalization proposals . . . needs to be improved . . . developments that
are undoubtedly valuable for a broad circle of specialists
fail to be distributed and do not leave the boundaries of
the *chast'* where they were used initially; this fact cannot
be looked upon indifferently.[34]

Failure to adhere to the "Leninist principle of publicity" has
led to wasteful duplications of effort.[35] "Inventors devote a
great deal of time and work developing proposals that have
already been known for a long time."[36]

The wasteful duplication of effort pales in significance by
comparison to the other byproducts of the insularity of regimental innovation. The proliferation of nonstandard equipment is one. Although it was clearly evident in 1965, the
problem has only of late received the high-level attention it
has long deserved.[37]

First, nonstandardization poses a number of interoperability problems even within Soviet forces, to say nothing of its
consequences for Warsaw Pact interoperability, at which level
all the Soviet problems reviewed below would be exacerbated
by, if nothing else, language barriers. Within Soviet forces,
since innovations tend to be specific to the unit and not disseminated, personnel from other units (reinforcements, for
example) are not acquainted with the equipment and, consequently, cannot step in and use it. This is true even where, in
their own units, those personnel have been performing the
same *functions*—even on the same type of aircraft—as the
inventors they are to replace. This, indeed, may underlie in
part the high-level stimulus given to the local development of
airmobile maintenance facilities. Simply stated, unless they
bring their own AGS equipment with them, reinforcing support personnel just won't be able to do the work.

[34] "The Mass Character of Technical Creativity," p. 9.
[35] "Publicity, Comparability of Results, and the Possibility of Practical
Repetition of Experience" (unattributed), *Tekhnika i Vooruzheniye*, no. 10
(1973), pp. 1–3. T3, 10 July 1974, p. 7.
[36] "The Mass Character of Technical Creativity," p. 10.
[37] Trapans, *Organizational Maintenance*, p. vii.

This also may help explain certain of the Soviets' tactical and training practices. Echelonment—the attack in waves of complete multi-unit formations—is the only procedure practical where nonstandard equipment renders infeasible the unit replacement of support (maintenance) personnel. Likewise, preinduction maintenance training is reduced in value when the maintenance equipment on which training must take place exists *only* in the unit which built it. Hence, Soviet recruits train in their operational units. Given the Soviets' grave concern with the inadequacy of training time (discussed below), particularly for ground support of new aircraft, it is understandable that they are concerned with nonstandardization as an impediment not only to interoperability, but to modernization as well. For all of these reasons, the problem of "interchangeability of crews and teams" has gained widespread notoriety in the Soviet military press.[38]

While these problems derive from the tendency of innovations to remain within the producing unit, another set of interoperability/modernization problems results from the specificity of local innovations—their very narrow range of applicability. When, by innovation, a maintenance unit succeeds in "catching up" to a technology that has descended upon it, the unit does so by building equipment that is highly specific to the aircraft model with which it has been equipped; so specific, indeed, as to be quite useless in maintaining aircraft of any other type! This, as we have seen, impedes modernization (where the equipment designed to catch up to one aircraft is rendered obsolete by that aircraft's technological successor). It also undermines interoperability (where a plane of type X recovers to a base whose jerry-built AGS equipment is appropriate only to planes of type Y). Or, as the Soviets put it in an article entitled "When Away from Own Air Base," "it will be difficult to prepare aircraft that have landed at another air base after a mission for their return flight." This, they continue, "is why one of the main conditions for increasing the effectiveness with which aviation is used is training engineer-

---

[38] "Publicity, Comparability of Results," p. 3.

ing and technical personnel in the *chast'* to service several
types of aircraft."[39]

These modernization/interoperability problems explain Soviet goals for depot R&D in aerospace ground support
technology.

> What are our views with respect to the technical equip-
> ment of the future? It will be a selection of *standardized*
> units or, if one may say so, "bricks" out of which it will
> be possible to assemble a test stand for *any type* of avia-
> tion technology.

Regarding modernization in particular, only standardization
and interchangeability will, in the Soviet view, ensure "the
possibility of retuning equipment for new types of aviation
technology" rather than the re-equipping of the entire het-
erogeneous maintenance base with each click of the technological ratchet.[40]

The Soviets write, "At the same time, definite standardization and universality of equipment for maintenance purposes
allows qualified technical personnel to [get] . . . different types
of weapons ready for use."[41]

Soviet engineers, it would seem, are calling for precisely the
commonality and standardization that, in the view of some, are
already so characteristic of Soviet weapons design. Whatever
degree of commonality may be present in the latter area it is
surely absent from the ground support environment. Nor has
design inheritance enabled the Soviets to avoid a number of
serious adjustment problems. In fact, the Soviets seem to be
calling for the adoption of just the sort of "weapon system"
approach for which the U.S. is sometimes derided.

Not only is this extent of local innovation absolutely un-
heard of in the U.S., but U.S. air forces have had in place for
some time the sort of standardization that Soviet maintenance

---

[39] Engineers Major General P. Sigov, Lt. Col. M. Vasil'yev, and Lt. Col.
V. Lysov, "When Away from Own Air Base," *Tekhnika i Vooruzheniye*, no. 10
(1974), p. 30. T3, August 20, 1975, p. 82.

[40] Skibinskiy, "The Technical-Electrical Unit," p. 100. Emphasis added.

[41] Sigov et al., "When Away from Own Air Base," p. 82.

engineers propose.[42] The Navy's Versatile Avionics Shop Test (VAST) system is one example. This is "the major avionic system currently in use for off-aircraft maintenance support diagnostics." Here, the "weapon system" approach has, in fact, constrained aircraft design in the interest of ground support adjustability to new technology. In particular,

> NAVAIR [Naval Air] specifications require that all new procurement aircraft avionic subsystems be VAST compatible. This means that all WRAs (principally, avionics and mission equipment) must include circuitry (or interfaces) that permits testing at a VAST station.[43]

---

[42] One can find scattered cases of local innovation among the U.S. services. For example, in the Army,

> A practice round of the TOW anti-tank missile costs $3,000. A gunner is lucky if he gets to fire one a year.
>
> Often, realistic training is simply not possible in peacetime. For instance, the stiffest challenge facing a TOW gunner is to stand up in a hail of enemy bullets and continue to guide his missile during the 16 seconds it takes to reach its target.
>
> With old-fashioned American ingenuity, however, some units have made training remarkably realistic despite the curb on use of live amunition. The case in point is the First Battalion of the Third Brigade. Using an old rotisserie motor and $500 worth of other odds and ends, the battalion has devised its own TOW shooting gallery. The gunner, looking through his sight, sees a number of vehicles zipping around on an irregular track. He must tell friend from foe, select the most threatening enemy, fire and continue to track the target for 16 seconds. If he has done his tracking correctly, a built-in .22-caliber rifle is fired, knocking the enemy tank off the track. ("On the Ground Look at an Ailing Army," *U.S. News and World Report*, 12 May 1980, pp. 31–32.)

In the U.S. case, however, these truly are isolated events. Local innovation is not the chosen instrument in correcting deficiencies in state supply. It is certainly not a matter of national policy, organized and stimulated on a mass scale, as it is in the Soviet Union. Nothing comparable to the socialist pledge exists in the U.S., nor does local innovation even begin to extend into areas like heavy machinery for production of support equipment. On the contrary, it is hardly mentioned and hardly worth mentioning in the U.S. case, while it surely appears to be a central feature of defense production in the Soviet Union.

[43] Blanco et al., *Technology Trends*, p. 18. WRA stands for Weapons Removable Assembly.

VAST, however, has not prevented U.S. maintenance man-hours per flight hour (MMH/FH) from rising dramatically. How, in the absence of anything comparable to VAST, and under such an uncontrolled AGS acquisition system as theirs—one that, moreover, only swings into operation *after* the change in aircraft technology has occurred—are the Soviets avoiding MMH/FH increases at least as dramatic as our own? It is implausible that they are.

All of the Soviets' adjustment and interoperability problems are encountered even in the cases, like those reviewed above, where local innovative activity actually results in the production of useful maintenance equipment, that is, where innovative activity *succeeds*. This, however, is far from the norm.

Time and again one reads complaints like those of General Safranov, director of the MoD's Department of Invention, who writes of innovative undertakings that "suffer from lack of specificity and are out of touch with the real needs and requirements of the *chast'*." Equally aggravating to the general are the superfluous projects that "are regarded as rationalization proposals when they are no such thing."[44] Criticisms of this sort pervade the literature. For example:

> Innovation and rationalization questions are considered apart from the primary tasks confronting military person-nel ... innovators' creative activities are not aimed at re-solving these problems .... Inexact thematic tasks are sometimes drawn up for inventors and rationalizers with-out taking into consideration actual needs.[45]

The inefficiency of duplicated effort is compounded by the waste inherent in this superfluous activity. But, after all, why should someone break his back in the demanding creation of useful equipment when "equal rewards are established for both a valuable technical concept, in search of which the originator spent much time and energy, and a simple proposal of no great

---

[44] Safranov, "Innovators Share," p. 104.
[45] "The Mass Character of Technical Creativity," p. 9.

value?" Overpayment for the useless innovation and under-payment for the useful one "naturally does not stimulate the creative solution of technical problems of great importance to the *chast'*." Delays in payment even for those innovations that merit introduction have further reduced the incentive for meaningful work. "For example, in the communications forces of one of the military districts, only 20 percent of the *introduced* technical innovations were paid off in 1970." And, while the entreprenurial demiurge must not be encouraged in the inventor, "awards for each introduced efficiency proposal must be paid out within established time periods *irrespective of the position the originator occupies*." The Soviets do more than hint at the possibility of corruption, as in cases where

> funds allotted for efficiency work are spent wrongly . . . to pay premiums for proposals that have no relation to technical creativity. For example . . . for the construction of a beach summer house.

Commissions on Invention are admonished by Lenin himself, from whose July 1919 telegram—protecting the inventor Berkalov from excessive taxation—the Soviets quote:

> We risk subverting the trust of inventors in the State and frightening them away from us. The consequences could be very expensive, measured not in tens of thousands, but in tens of millions of rubles.[46]

Compounding the expense in financial savings forgone through the discouragement of truly productive innovation, is the outright waste in payment for empty activity. Add to this the labor and money expended in the unnecessary duplication of effort resulting from regimental insularity and one

---

[46] Kiselev, "Incentives for Technical Creativity," pp. 120–122. Emphasis added. Lenin reportedly interceded on the inventor's behalf, scolding the Porokhovskiy Raion Soviet of Workers' and Peasants' Red Army Deputies for the "intolerability of the excessive tax imposed on a special prize of 50,000 rubles 'awarded to Berkalev by the Council of Peoples' Commissars' for an excellent invention in the field of artillery." (Ibid.)

begins to sense the inefficiency of the Socialist Competition as a method of making up the shortage of state supply.

Two points deserve passing note. First, this may explain the Soviets' poor reputation as suppliers, to the Third World, of weapon-system spare parts and service equipment.[47] If the Soviets are having a hard time meeting their own requirements, then to be sure very little will be left over to satisfy those of their clients. The second, and more important point is that this whole "system" deserves to be considered as a part of the Soviet defense "sector." Although the exact scale of this remarkably decentralized production is uncertain, its inefficiency raises important questions about the assumed efficiency of Soviet defense production overall.

Not only, however, does this bustle of creative activity waste labor and money—it wastes time. If for no other reason than this, it deepens Soviet problems in training personnel to *use* what sophisticated support equipment the state does provide.

INEFFICIENCY IN THE UTILIZATION OF STATE-SUPPLIED SUPPORT EQUIPMENT

In the mid-1960s, "the equipment shortage problems were linked to, and compounded by, a shortage of skilled manpower." Moreover, out of the inadequate labor force, "only a relative handful of officers—engineers and technicians first class—had advanced technical training." A major in the engineering services characterized the situation prevailing at that time:

> The time taken now to train and send out mechanics is extremely unsatisfactory. It is clearly evident that a person who has just come from tending a machine or combine or is just out of school cannot, in the space of 6–8 months, properly learn the construction, functioning, and regulations for servicing the most complicated complex of

[47] On this perennial difficulty of the Soviet Third World arms program, see Roger F. Pajak, "Soviet Arms Transfers as an Instrument of Influence,"*Survival*, July/August 1981, p. 168.

systems in today's aircraft and its power plant . . . . It is impossible to acquire the necessary skills during this or even a somewhat longer period of time.[48]

While in 1976 the Soviets lengthened the academic course for certain maintenance instructors, the time constraint seems to have relaxed little since the mid-1960s.[49] One reads repeated complaints regarding "the low skills of the personnel due to the limited training time given for training the repairmen". This, in the Soviet view, has been exacerbated by "the irrational use of the working time fund of the personnel."[50] In part, this is blamed on a lack of planning: "The absence of a plan or a plan hurriedly compiled reduces . . . the labor productivity of each repairman." Yet "existing instructions" for the management of ground support activities, "do not contain specific recommendations for the engineers—to plan and evaluate the production activities."[51] As though to parody Say's Law, the invisible hand of the Socialist Competition has called forth a spate of rationalization proposals, planning methodologies, scheduling techniques, and "scientific" management tools to correct the problem.[52] Amidst the flurry of activity, however, one finds large-scale planning errors whose wastefulness is exceeded only by the ease with which they could have

[48] Trapans, *Organizational Maintenance*, pp. 14 and 15.

[49] Harriet Fast Scott and William F. Scott, *The Armed Forces of the USSR* (Boulder, Co.: Westview Press, 1979), p. 343. The Scotts write that "all six of the Air Forces' higher military aviation-engineer schools have five-year courses, the only higher schools in the Air Forces of this length. Three of the schools, located at Irkutsk, Tambov, and Khar'Kov, jumped from three-year to five-year courses in 1976." (Ibid.)

[50] Anfilov, "Radar Repairs," pp. 95 and 98. The working time fund is understood simply as total manhours available.

[51] Col.-Engineer R. Tsymbalyuk, "Scientific Organization of Labor and Shops," *Vestnik Protivovozdushnoy Oborony*, no. 11 (1971). T3, 27 April 1972, pp. 128 and 127.

[52] See, for example, Col.-Engineer B. Shlyayfert, "Planning Maintenance on Aviation Equipment," *Vestnik Protivovozdushnoy Oborony*, no. 5 (1976), pp. 61–65. T3, 1976, pp. 105–112. Jean-Baptiste Say (1767–1832): "Supply created its own demand."

been avoided. For example,

> at present, with the two induction periods (spring and autumn), the future specialists must be selected more carefully. Life has shown that the shops must be staffed with the recruits from the autumn induction. Only in this instance, by the beginning of the intensive period of annual overhauls [spring], is it possible to train good specialists who can effectively service the equipment for two seasons. The men of the May induction can independently perform the annual overhauls only in the second year of service, that is, for only one season.

Due to staffing errors of this sort, the units engaged in major overhauls "frequently include specialists who have poor training, and as a result of this, the quality of the annual overhauls is not always high."[53]

Making matters worse, the Soviets face difficulties in getting maintenance personnel to *use* the complex state-supplied support equipment that advanced aviation technology requires. General Skubilin, chief engineer of the Soviet Air Force, explains that

> aircraft are now saturated with various electronic systems. They incorporate tens and hundreds of thousands of parts . . . . The complexity, diversity, and intensity of communications among the separate systems and devices which make up the complex require basically new methods for monitoring and preparing them for use.

In particular, the complexity of new aircraft systems "has led to the requirement that they be readied for flight with the help of *automatic integrated equipment*."[54]

Of this new aerospace ground support equipment, the Soviets repeatedly stress that "its complexity . . . is no less than

[53] Tsymbalyuk, "Scientific Organization," pp. 128 and 134.

[54] General-Lt. Engineer V. Skubilin, "New Equipment—New Demands," *Aviatsiya i Kosmonavtika*, July 1975, pp. 1–3. T2, October 1975, p. 22. Emphasis added.

that of aircraft."[55] Time and again they emphasize that "aviation engineering service (IAS) personnel must be completely acquainted not only with the aviation equipment but also with the equipment for testing and preparing it." Indeed, for technical personnel,

> one of the most important criteria of their qualification is the ability *to use* modern test-analysis monitoring inspection equipment—the means for instrument testing and analyzing of the status of equipment.

Thus, "the search for ways to master the integrated systems" has very high priority, particularly since the old methods— "diagnosis by a simple inspection or the use of various test instruments"—are "proving to be inadequate."[56]

Yet, according to General Pavlovskiy, deputy minister of defense, "Unfortunately, equipment maintenance does not meet timeless requirements everywhere." All too frequently, in his view, "a subunit has received new equipment, but cares for it with the same old methods."[57] Even though units are reminded that "it is mandatory to use data from objective monitoring equipment," high-ranking officers repeatedly complain that the reportage of equipment readiness fails to reflect its use.[58]

Some point to senior engineers who "unjustifiably undervalue the training of technical personnel" as the sources of the problem.[59] Training in the use of new AGS equipment, where it occurs, is neither sufficiently intensive nor sufficiently frequent. What limited skills are acquired are soon lost through lack of repetition. The critics forget, however, that while the mastery of new AGS equipment has high priority, higher priority is given to aircraft readiness, flight safety, and particu-

---

[55] Olenev, "Competently Maintain," p. 112.

[56] Skubilin, "New Equipment," pp. 22; 27; 22; 26. Emphasis added. IAS stands for *Inzhenerno-Aviatsionnaya Sluzhba* (Aviation Engineering Service).

[57] General Ivan Grigor'yevich Pavlovskiy, "An Officer's Technical Culture," *Krasnaya Zvezda*, 5 February 1977, p. 2. T1, May 1977, p. 137.

[58] Skubilin, "New Equipment," p. 24.

[59] Ibid., p. 28.

larly, the pilot training programs they support. Small wonder, therefore, that senior engineers—understaffed, underequipped, short on labor, and under narrow time constraints—are reluctant to jeopardize these higher priority goals by diverting scarce resources into rigorous training activities lacking any immediate and visible return.

The situation reminds one of the classic problem of innovation in Soviet industry: though limited rewards were attached to innovation, plant managers, whose primary bonus was pinned to an output target, were reluctant to jeopardize its fulfillment by diverting productive capacity into the prototyping of risky, long lead-time technologies.[60] The analogy, of course, breaks down where the current output (equipment readiness and flying schedules) itself is jeopardized by a failure to innovate, that is, to *use* the new AGS technology. The Soviets have apparently reached this point.

But along the way, in the scramble to meet daily goals, little experience and even less confidence has been accumulated in the use of new AGS systems. Indeed, insecurities in their operation have deepened to the point where the chief engineer of the Soviet Air Force himself can stress "the search for ways ... to surmount the sort of *psychological dread* of their complexity," a dread that he observes throughout the forces.[61]

Even if state-supply of the new AGS equipment were adequate, moreover, the Soviets would still face a serious trade-off. Modern AGS equipment must be mastered if new aircraft are to be maintained at the readiness levels called for by intensive pilot training and flight safety. If not, just as in the U.S., ground support problems are "passed on" to the detriment of pilot training. Indeed, the Soviets, as we shall see, have the worst of both worlds—inefficient utilization of the inadequate supply of modern AGS equipment, declining equipment readiness, and, in part because of this, routinized and unrealistic pilot training (see following chapter).

---

[60] See Joseph S. Berliner, *The Innovation Decision in Soviet Industry* (Cambridge: MIT Press, 1978).

[61] Skubilin, "New Equipment," p. 22. Emphasis added.

Returning to the matter at hand, training in the use of new AGS equipment, as in a range of other ground support activities, has certainly not been accelerated by the Socialist Competition. Sheer disorganization, for example, has reduced the value of the Socialist Competition between units, as in cases where "soldiers did not know which company they were competing with, who was ahead in a given phase, who was behind, and so on. . . . Results," needless to say, "proved to be low."[62]

The competition within units, however, is more revealing. "Comparability of results" is the phrase widely used to signal a range of failures in the Socialist Competition within units. For example, unfair competitions between experienced, skilled personnel and green recruits appear to be widespread. "It often happens that one has received the 'five' for the first time, while for the other this already is a natural thing."[63]

Party organs and senior officers are scolded for this, but, "in fact, it is no secret," writes an Aviation Engineering Service major, that "in the organization of the Socialist Competition, the result of labor was often poorly comparable." Responsible officials are directed time and again to "take into account the term of service, the level of training and education" of the competitors.[64] Yet they fail to do so in a great many cases. So many, indeed, as to have created a serious training problem, namely, that experienced maintenance personnel avoid teaching new recruits. Given the apparent ease with which biased competitions are arranged, along with the rewards that may be accumulated through victory in such competitions, why should the experienced technician "pass on his experience" to a potential competitor? Just as the innovative *chast'* does not give away its competitive edge, so the expert has little incentive to reveal his "tricks of the trade." The structure of rewards inhibits the dissemination of knowledge both between and within units.

---

[62] Col. A. Shpilevoy, "Competition Indoctrinates," *Voyennyy Vestnik*, no. 9 (1978), pp. 22–25. T3, 1979, p. 37.

[63] Ibid., p. 38. The "five" corresponds to a grade of "A," the "four" to a "B," and so on.

[64] Shatokin, "Periodic Servicing," p. 43.

Soviet literature presents a ceaseless harangue on this topic:

> Competition is inseparable from comradely mutual assistance. It is important that the leaders in the competition, the outstanding specialists, *pass along* their experience to others.[65]

> It is highly important that the best specialists *pass along* their wealth of experience to all personnel during the competition.[66]

Leonid Brezhnev himself sternly wrote that, due to such abuses,

> the very essence of the competition, the actual justification for doing the work, the actual rivalry in doing the work, that is, the factors to which V. I. Lenin attached so much importance, is emasculated.[67]

Both the insularity of regimental innovation and the avoidance of teaching junior personnel violate the "Leninist principle" of guaranteeing "the possibility of practical repetition of experience."[68] Troops are ceaselessly admonished that

> the effectiveness of the competition increases only when the experience of the front-rankers is repeated time and time again, when yesterday's objective of the right-flankers today becomes the norm for all competitors.[69]

But, what are the objectives of the front-rankers? Refusing to face this basic question, and refusing to admit that the problem

---

[65] "Publicity, Comparability of Results," p. 7. Emphasis added.

[66] Skubilin, "In the Interests of Combat Readiness," p. 11. Emphasis added.

[67] "Publicity, Comparability of Results," p. 7. The author quotes from then Secretary Brezhnev's report in honor of the fiftieth anniversary of the founding of the USSR.

[68] Ibid.

[69] Major A. Guk, "A Flight of Excellent Aircraft," *Tekhnika i Vooruzheniye,* no. 8 (1973), pp. 8–9. T3, 19 February 1974, p. 27.

may run deeper—that there may be a systematic pattern in the failures of the Socialist Competition—many high-level officials instead point to the absence of a clear grading system as the source of abuses.

> At present, unfortunately, there is no uniform opinion on what aspects should be checked in inspecting the production operations of the shops or how to evaluate their work.[70]

Again displaying its "self-correcting" powers to their fullest, the Socialist Competition, heeding the call, expands to include new competitions in devising better grading methods for the Competition itself! All sorts of accounting schemes, comparison formulae, coefficients of labor quality, flow charts, aggregation methods, incentive weighting algorithms, norm documentation rules, and a panoply of other indices and control systems have appeared.[71]

As an indication of the high-level concern for the development of a standard and meaningful grading system, the following "request for proposal" appeared at the end of Lieutenant Colonel Yulin's exposition of his proposal.

> The Editorial Board of the journal "Vestnik protivovozdushnoy oborony" considers that Lieutenant Colonel-Engineer V. Yulin raises a pressing question in his article concerning the search for ways of increasing the effectiveness and quality of servicing combat equipment, and of the effectiveness of the Socialist competition of soldiers for [devising] outstanding indicators in the mastery and upkeep of equipment and armament. The Editorial Board requests all readers to send their opinion regarding the methods of solving this problem suggested in the article, to share their methods, to tell how the results of the Socialist competition are tallied-up in the *chast'* and

[70] Tsymbalyuk, "Scientific Organization," p. 132.

[71] See, for example, Lt. Col.-Engineer V. Yulin, "Standardization and Quality Control of the Operation of Equipment and Armament," *Vestnik Protivovozdushnoy Oborony*, no. 2 (1977), pp. 59–64. T3, 1977, pp. 105–114.

podrazdelenniye and how one determines the criteria for the objective evaluation of its winners.[72]

It would appear that the editoral board (read Ministry of Defense), while starkly aware of the need for a useful standard system, is less than fully informed regarding the vast array of systems which are in use.

Not knowing the methods whereby field reportage is generated; knowing, nonetheless, that it embodies distortion and inaccuracy, the "ruling heights" are clearly disturbed by the resultant degree of uncertainty surrounding the actual readiness of personnel and equipment. And rightly so, since, as the "signal-to-noise ratio" approaches zero, obtaining an accurate picture of the current status of forces—to say nothing of planning to meet future requirements—becomes difficult indeed.

These problems of reportage are by no means new to the Soviets. In the early 1960s, in an effort to wring from regimental authorities a standard information base, "air army and air division headquarters regularly subjected him [the senior engineer] to streams of directives dealing with every phase of maintenance work." Not only did this subject the senior engineers—underequipped, undermanned, and lacking a staff—to enormous "paperwork pressure," but, in addition, all of the newly required "*dokumentatsiia*, it was said, were of little use in planning future workloads and establishing patterns of equipment breakdowns."[73]

Yet, under the vigilant eye of the regimental Communist Party organs, the senior engineer was expected to meet each of his performance targets (for accident-free flying schedules, material readiness, etc.). In attempting to meet output norms, however, accurate data and the calculation of useful planning indices were necessary. Under the additional pressure to submit satisfactory *dokumentatsiia*—however irrelevant this may have been to his planning—it is small wonder that the

[72] Ibid., p. 114, *Podrazdelenniye* are subordinate units of a *chast'*; work centers and squadrons would be examples.

[73] Trapans, *Organizational Maintenance*, pp. 18, 19, and 20. The meaning of *dokumentatsiia* is documentation.

senior engineer kept two sets of books—one for official consumption and one for actual planning.

> It is no secret, [wrote a Soviet line officer] that in the units each engineer, besides a standard logbook, has, as a rule, a logbook worked out by himself, which contains data on aircraft and engine performance, periodic [scheduled maintenance] work, and so forth.[74]

When planned results were not forthcoming, the same higher authorities whose interference and centralized direction had shackled performance, instituted ill-conceived corrective reforms. For example, in 1962, they attempted to institute a sort of "automatic quality control" system. "In short, the personnel of a given work center were required to inspect the work performed by another." Under the tight equipment and labor situation, however, training had been narrowly specialized and it was hard in the time available to generate the skill required to satisfy requirements at any particular work center, much less to familiarize "specialists" with the responsibilities of other work centers. Lacking the training required to accurately evaluate the activities of others, each work group adopted a "you scratch my back, and I'll scratch yours" attitude, the result being that work quality declined. In those instances where one group actually had the audacity to criticize another, the result was "prolonged bickering, and aircraft occasionally flew with known defects."[75] This system of cross inspection is still in use today, when all the constraints that undermined its effectiveness in 1962 are even tighter.[76] And, as noted earlier, today's central instructions are apparently no more useful to the regimental senior engineer than the *dokumentatsiia* referred to above. Small wonder, then, that regimental planners have devised their own nonstandard methods, and that field reportage is looked upon with suspicion by higher authorities.

---

[74] Ibid., p. 20.
[75] Ibid., pp. 19 and 18.
[76] Guk, "A Flight of Excellent Aircraft," p. 28.

The Soviets have invested very heavily in the modernization of the Air Forces, and in Frontal Aviation especially. In
fact, excluding the National Air Defense Forces,

> between 1967 and 1977, spending for the Air Forces in-
> creased more rapidly than spending for any other mili-
> tary service . . . by far the largest increase in Air Forces
> spending between 1967 and 1977 was for Frontal Avia-
> tion, [whose] share of Air Forces spending rose from less
> than 60 percent in 1967 to over 70 percent in 1977.

In ruble terms, then, total spending in 1977 on Frontal
Aviation alone amounted to roughly 16 percent of total defense spending, or *twice* the 8 percent absorbed by the nuclear
Strategic Rocket Forces in that year.[77] It is only natural,
therefore, that top political and military authorities, as we
have seen, are very concerned that modernization not be
undermined by the tangle of problems reviewed thus far.
Enormous pressure has been brought to bear on the Party
organs within the military to reverse the trends, solve the
problems, and untangle all of this—in short, to make the
Socialist Competition work and put the maintenance base on
an up-to-date and even keel once and for all. Party *appa-
ratchiki* (operatives) who are found to be involved in abuses
of the Socialist Competition are visited with harsh penalties
indeed. Widely publicized expulsions from the Communist
Party, for example, are among them.[78]

But, as the entire history of the problem should have made
clear to authorities, Party operatives are not trained to solve
technical problems of planning, management, and resource

[77] *Estimated Soviet Defense Spending*, pp. 3–4. The estimate is in rubles. In
1977, the most recent year for which specific data are available, the Air Forces,
excluding the National Air Defense Forces, accounted for 22 percent of total
expenditures. Seventy percent of this alone would yield 15.4 percent for
Frontal Air.

[78] Major R. Chekmarev, "Work Rhythmically, with No Surges," *Tyl i
Snabzheniye Sovetskikh Vooruzhennykh Sil*, no. 12 (1978), pp. 41–43. T3, 1979,
p. 62.

allocation, problems whose complexity has increased dramatically in the wake of military modernization. Indeed, the remoteness of Party personnel from such matters, perhaps more than any overt complicity, has certainly contributed to the ease with which the Socialist Competition has continually been abused.

Under pressure, then, to untie the knot of problems, but lacking any real expertise in the operational management of affairs, and tacitly having ruled out the delegation of authority to those who might use it efficiently, the Communist Party organs turn to the only method remaining—rigidity.

While recourse to strictly defined and highly detailed procedures has failed to contain the "widening gyre" of indiscipline, the presence of such procedures has lent to the Soviet ground support environment its peculiar mixed character in which a wide sphere of uncontrolled, wasteful, and yet "rewarding" activity exists side by side with a sphere unique in the *Modern Times* images it conjures—images of droning regularity, of the Henry Ford era, and of its hallmark, the assembly line.

"WORK RHYTHMICALLY, WITH NO SURGES"

The routinization of maintenance work began in earnest with the first experiments in the "Flow-Line Method" (*Potochnyi Metod*) in the early 1960s.[79] Today, the Party and higher military push for efficiency in maintenance consists primarily in the drive for that method's uniform adoption and for the strictest possible adherence to its principles. Written in 1965, the following description requires little revision today:

> Essentially "flow-line" requires strict sequences of operations, specialist dispatch, and detailed time standards ("norms") for each operation and process. The problem then consists of positioning personnel and equipment and

---

[79] The section title is from ibid., p. 60; see also Trapans, *Organizational Maintenance*, p. 29.

of assuring a rapid and rhythmic flow of aircraft (or, if the aircraft is stationary, of personnel and equipment) between such positions.[80]

Attesting to the uninterrupted high-level backing for the process, General Skubilin, chief engineer of the Soviet Air Forces, writes, in 1973, that

> the productivity of labor has increased significantly in those technical maintenance *chasti* that have ... introduced the flow-stand method; that is, they have broken the entire production process down into a series of operations. Each operation is performed at a definite stand equipped with special monitoring and checking installations and control consoles. The aircraft being serviced, as well as its equipment and units, moves through the whole gamut of operations, moving from stand to stand at *rigidly fixed times*. This gives continuity to the technological process and, even more important, maintains the rhythm required by the process. The result is that when all of the work for which time limits have been set is completed, the aircraft are returned to the squadrons *at identical time intervals*.[81]

"Of course," the general continues, "not all technical maintenance *chasti* are able to use this organization of the production process at this time, but it is absolutely essential that they attempt to do so."[82] Hence, a prime goal of depot R&D has since 1968 been that it make possible the performance of maintenance work "on an assembly-line basis."[83] In use both in flightline and scheduled regimental maintenance, the flow-line method turns on its detailed time norms for personnel. These

---

[80] Ibid.

[81] Skubilin, "In the Interests of Combat Readiness," pp. 4–6. Emphasis added. See also Lt. Col.-Engineer M. Shishkin, "For Outstanding TECh," *Tekhnika i Vooruzheniye*, no. 5 (1975). T3, 10 December 1973, p. 14.

[82] Skubilin, "In the Interests of Combat Readiness," p. 6.

[83] Skibinskiy, "The Technical-Electrical Unit," p. 99.

are derived from the so-called "sequence diagram" determining the order in which the discrete maintenance tasks are accomplished. From a 1973 account, we read:

> In the process of maintenance operations on aircraft, each specialist must, *in strictly determined sequence*, carry out operations.[84]

Although high-level support has grown dramatically, the rigidity has been preserved intact since 1963, at which time

> every specialist, when working according to the plan chart, always carries out the same operations in the same strictly defined and always identical sequence, this having been *predetermined*. Also, when working on the aircraft he always uses the same devices and tools in a strictly *predetermined* and always identical manner.[85]

Once the sequence of operations has been fixed, the so-called "technological schedule" (the time norms for each specialist) is arrived at by the use of data obtained from time and motion studies. The perfection of these time and motion data is the goal of the "comparatively young science—ergonomics," whose name provides a thin veil indeed for the undiluted Taylorism it in fact denotes.[86] In any event, "it is the sequence diagram, and the technological schedule that is drawn up using the sequence diagram as its reference, that provide continuity."[87]

An example of the sequence diagram and technological schedule from the mid-1960s is provided in Figure 3.1. Note the strict sequence of operations and the time standards for each in minutes and seconds. All accounts would indicate that

[84] Shishkin, "For Outstanding TECh," p. 14. Emphasis added.

[85] Trapans, *Organizational Maintenance*, p. 34. Emphasis added.

[86] Colonel-Engineer P. Shlayen, Lt. Col.-Engineer A. Karasev, and Lt. Col. of the Medical Service V. Romanov, "Military Education and Psychology: Ergonomics Recommends ...," *Vestnik Protivovozdushnoy Oborony*, no. 2 (1977), pp. 55–58. T3, 1977, p. 97.

[87] Skubilin, "In the Interests of Combat Readiness," p. 6.

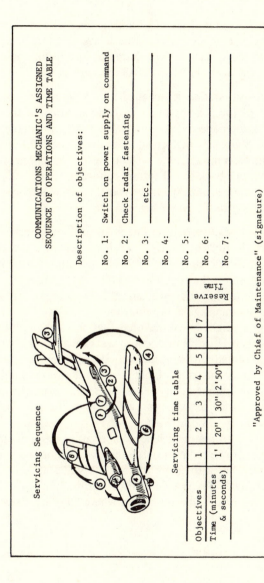

COMMUNICATIONS MECHANIC'S ASSIGNED
SEQUENCE OF OPERATIONS AND TIME TABLE

Description of objectives:

No. 1: Switch on power supply on command

No. 2: Check radar fastening

No. 3: _____ etc. _____

No. 4: _____

No. 5: _____

No. 6: _____

No. 7: _____

"Approved by Chief of Maintenance" (signature)

Servicing Sequence

Servicing time table

Objectives	1	2	3	4	5	6	7	Reserve Time
Time (minutes & seconds)	1'	20"	30"	2'50"				

FIGURE 3.1 The Flow-Line Method: "Plan-Chart" Used by Mechanic in Preflight Inspections
SOURCE: Trapans, *Organizational Maintenance*, p. 38.

contemporary versions differ from this only in their level of detail.

Finally, at the center of activity is a dispatcher who monitors the flow of work, eliminating whatever delays may threaten its conformity to the strict sequence diagrams and technological schedules that govern the process. As to facilities,

> the dispatcher's station is installed in a building with a good view of the parking areas and the territory of the technical maintenance *chast'* on which a major part of the maintenance work is performed. The dispatcher station has an intercommunication system, telephone connections, and a call-back signal system connecting it with all the maintenance groups, with the *chast'* engineer's office, and with many of the *podrazdelenniye*.[88]

The overriding directive that, in one form or another crowds the literature, is to "constantly and rigidly execute the requirements of the documents."[89] "Each operation" is to be "carried out without the slightest deviation from the requirements of the control documents," and the Party organs are to see to it that the message is brought home.[90]

In passing, it might be conjectured that this enhances the ease with which Third World countries can absorb Soviet weaponry; presented with a sufficiently detailed maintenance "cookbook," their unskilled labor may still accommodate quite advanced equipment. Of course, the Soviets' rigidities are thereby transplanted as well, as evident in numerous Arab performances in the Middle East.

Before turning to the inefficiencies inherent in the flow-line method, it is important to notice that this extraordinary degree of rigidity conflicts with goals the Soviets value at least as highly as the strict observance of time norms. For example, Socialist Competitions are applauded where "*the most impor-*

---

[88] Ibid.

[89] M. Vanyushkin, "Each Flight Is Supported Effectively," *Vestnik Protivo-vozdushnoy Oborony*, no. 10 (1978), pp. 42–45. T3, 1979, p. 97.

[90] Skubilin, "New Equipment," p. 83.

tant thing was achieved—the independence of young technicians." Similarly, "increasing the *personal* responsibility of all
specialists of the TECh" is referred to as a "patriotic duty."[91]
In general, the capacity for initiative, leadership, and flexibility in the face of uncertainty are recongnized by the Soviets as
very important traits to be instilled in all personnel. Personnel
are exhorted to show creativity and initiative at least as often
as they are sternly warned to conform to the norms. Given
these conflicting goals, to quote an unattributed Soviet article
of April, 1978:

> One might well ask what kind of creativeness can be in-
> volved in servicing weapons and equipment where every-
> thing is described in pertinent documentation dealing
> with technical standards and where the engineer may not
> deviate from a single point.[92]

One certainly might. In a sense, however, the rigidity of the
flow-line is defensible. The extreme complexity of new AGS
equipment, when combined with the inadequate training of
personnel in its use (a problem aggravated by the time-
consuming Socialist Competition), has left the Soviets little
alternative but to prescribe everything down to the last detail.
If training were better, the Soviets might prefer to loosen up
a little and decrease the rigidity that, under current constraints,
is an unavoidable concomitant of modernization. The open
questions remain, however. Although we will not address
them, they are certainly worth asking. Why have the Soviets
not adjusted training programs in order to obviate the necessity of such rigidity? Why have they not ensured an adequate
supply of AGS equipment, relying instead on a process that
not only fails to meet supply requirements, but wastes precious
training time in addition?

---

[91] Shatokin, "Periodic Servicing," pp. 45 and 46. Emphasis added.

[92] "Military Engineer and Equipment: Efficiency—A Demand of the Times"
(unattributed), *Vestnik Protivovozdushnoy Oborony*, no. 4 (1978), pp. 68–71.
T3, 1979, p. 101.

The flow-line method—its rigid sequences of operations, exact positioning of personnel and equipment, and its narrow time norms—may seem in some sense rational, *given* all the questionable programs that have made rigidity unavoidable. But this in no way redeems it as an operating procedure. While it may be practicable under conditions of certainty, "much of maintenance is characterized by randomness of defects."[93] And, in adjusting to uncertainty, the flow-line is of low efficiency indeed.

It is very hard to see how, even in peacetime, one goes about "predetermining" the sequence of repair operations that will be required *after* a sortie during which unforeseen breakdowns may occur. Pursue for a moment the possibilities in the event that unforeseen malfunctions occur. There are two: (1) The predetermined control documentation is adhered to. Since it is out of phase with the aircraft's *postflight* mechanical status, it *automatically* misallocates resources, and the quality of work is compromised. (2) The predetermined documentation is dispensed with and the aircraft is removed from the utilization cycle to be reevaluated. Then, after "cumbersome recalculations," new sequence and time norms are generated for its service preparatory to a second takeoff.[94]

In neither case would turnaround operations be conducted efficiently. However impractical the system may be in peacetime, it could easily prove to be far less practical under combat conditions. Here, defects are far more unpredictable since combat flying places a far greater strain on the aircraft and of course, there is an enemy (i.e., unpredictable battle damage) as well. Under these circumstances, the second, or "recalculation," approach is out of the question if any kind of sortie rate is to be generated and sustained. If, on the other hand, the predetermined control documents are rigidly applied, the plane will simply drift farther out of phase with each sortie, and random defects and automatic maintenance deferrals will accumulate. Failure to address them out of a mindless

---

[93] Trapans, *Organizational Maintenance*, p. 31.
[94] Ibid.

adherence to the quickly irrelevant documents will soon produce all sorts of performance degradations or ultimately, virtual attrition.

Moreover, the familiar "fixed positions" of the flow-line may not be available in war. Dispatchers and senior engineers may not be available either. Are lower level personnel prepared to show initiative and take command? Has there been any delegation of authority that would allow them to experience the leadership they may be called upon to exercise? The answer to each question would certainly appear to be "no."

Of course, as has undoubtedly occurred to the reader, under combat conditions, neither of the two possibilities worked through above would be literally applied. Perhaps not. Certainly neither is suitable for combat. Nevertheless, logically speaking, they are the only possibilities formally within the flow-line framework. Given their impracticality, as illustrated by the admittedly literal scenarios above, it is natural to expect that the flow-line would be dispensed with in war. Fine. Where, however, do Soviet ground support personnel receive training in other, more flexible methods—methods, for example, like America's POMO and POST, in which authority is regularly delegated; in which the chain of command is more fluid ("any specialist can become top man on the flight line"); in which a higher degree of decentralization was introduced precisely to avoid such overdependence on a dispatcher; in which "surges" are "a way of life" rather than anathema? Again, the answer would appear to be "nowhere." POMO and POST were designed specifically to ensure a flexible and efficient response to unexpected aircraft defects, and thereby to minimize their adverse effects on sortie rates. The flow-line method is terribly inflexible by comparison and is ill-equipped to handle uncertainty without severe effects on either performance (sortie effectiveness), sortie rates, or both. POMO and POST, moreover, were designed to simulate wartime deployment and to afford maximum flexibility is basing. The flow-line, brittle, cumbersome, and inefficient even at a home base, becomes a virtual shackle when transplanted to an austere and rudimentary field base. As the Soviets are very well aware, operation from such fields would subject sophisticated aircraft to particularly severe strains, necessitating more maintenance precisely where less could be provided![95]

SUMMARY AND CONCLUSIONS

In light of all that has been presented above, it is implausible that the Soviets, in their Frontal Air modernization program, have avoided problems at least as severe as those encountered by the U.S. in its own tactical air force modernization. Nowhere, in Soviet "design philosophy," in the R&D and acquisition process(es) for AGS equipment, in the organization, planning, or management of ground support activities, or in the Soviet training base, is there the slightest evidence of an advantage in (a) the avoidance of severe problems in adjusting to new aircraft technology or in (b) efficiently conducting day-to-day ground support activities.

The purportedly unique features of Soviet weapons design—features widely assumed to mitigate problems of the sort America has encountered—are of dubious uniqueness in the first place, and are, per se, of little relevance to the questions at hand. Second, many of the *successful* measures the U.S. has taken to minimize its, still serious, problems have not been instituted by the Soviets, even though the Soviets *themselves* have called for their adoption. The standardization inherent in the VAST system is one, while the flexibility and decentralization of POMO/POST is another.

Not only have the Soviets failed to adopt measures that have been successful in mitigating modernization problems, but the Soviets are vigorously pursuing courses of action that

[95] Two revealing discussions of the topic are: N. Artemov, "At a Field Air Base," *Znamenosets*, no. 8 (August 1978), p. 12. T1, January 1979, pp. 36–38, and Col. B. Vorob'yev, "At an Alternate Airfield," *Tyl i Snabzheniye Sovetskikh Vooruzhennykh Sil*, no. 8 (August 1977), pp. 74–76. T1, April 1978, pp. 117–119. Problems encountered by the Luftwaffe in operating from dispersed, rugged fields are discussed in Charles Hunt, *Airfield Survivability and Post-Attack Sortie Generation*, Concept Issue Paper 80-2, Doctrine and Concepts Division, Directorate of Plans, HQ USAF, February 1980.

they recognize are exacerbating those problems. They have failed to ensure an adequate flow of modern, state-produced AGS equipment and, instead have chosen to throw a great deal of high-level support behind the Socialist Competition to make up the deficit. Not only does the approach *build in* an adjustment problem (since local R&D reacts after the fact), but it provides strong incentives for insularity and the concealment of *successful* innovation. These combine with the specificity of each insular innovation to ensure a proliferation of nonstandard and narrowly applicable AGS equipment. This process, totally foreign to the U.S. experience, creates yet further problems of adjustment and interoperability. The insufficient supply of state-produced equipment, moreover, is utilized inefficiently: nonuniformities and distortions in reportage, lack of planning methods, misallocations of labor, incentives *against* teaching new recruits, and wasted time (duplicated or simply empty innovative activity) have all contributed to the difficulties the Soviets report in utilizing what quantities of advanced AGS equipment are supplied by the state. As all of the problems in adjusting to new aircraft technology multiply, the efficiency of day-to-day operations declines. Lacking either the skilled labor force on which flexibility must rest or the skills to manage it even if it did exist, the Party has focused its energies on the petrification of maintenance—on the flowline method and its rigid sequences, fixed positions, and strict time norms.

Add to all of this the facts that U.S. maintenance personnel receive roughly twice the training time as their Soviet counterparts (and that none of it is detracted from by either Socialist Competition or formal political indoctrination); that on a per-plane basis, the U.S. spends far more than the Soviets do on maintenance equipment and spares for aircraft (and produces standard equipment centrally); and that the better-equipped, more experienced labor force is itself roughly 40 percent larger (per plane) than its Soviet counterpart. Considering all of this as a backdrop to the rest, if the Soviets do not have modernization problems at least as severe as our own, then something quite remarkable is going on. As the next chapter makes clear, the rigidity of the maintenance base has contributed to the routinized quality of Soviet pilot training. In turn, pilot capacity for little beyond the routine precludes the training of ground support personnel in generating and sustaining realistic wartime activity levels—activity levels that the U.S. (TAC pilots *and* ground support) approximates twice a week. Despite these apparently serious Soviet constraints, in framing our analysis in Chapter V, the Soviets are generally credited with ground support efficiencies and air combat prowess greater than would be plausible in the U.S. case. This review of the Soviets' relative deficiencies therefore functions as a check on the conservatism of the assessment in Chapter VI.

CHAPTER IV

SOVIET EFFECTIVENESS IN THE AIR

The same conflicting goals and contradictory system of incentives at work in the ground support process are present in the training of Soviet combat personnel.

The capacity to respond quickly and effectively to unforeseen developments, to show flexibility and initiative in a dynamic and uncertain combat environment, are regarded by the Soviets as primary goals of training. In turn, the extent to which an exercise confronts commanders and troops with the unexpected is seen as the foremost index of its realism.

Yet the Soviets' incentive system, by the excessive concern with high grades that it produces, has stymied the very creativity it was meant to foster. The problem prevails not only in the Soviet Air Forces, but in the Ground Forces as well. As is discussed, this has been exacerbated in each case by the introduction of new technology and has deepened Soviet problems in coordinating the operations of air and ground forces.

PILOT SKILL

Perhaps the least complicated method the Soviets have adopted in attempting to ensure a modicum of realism in training is to conduct unit exercises in unfamiliar terrain. Yet, General-Colonel Yakushin, chief of the main staff of the Ground Forces writes that the intended effect is nullified by "commanders and staffs [who] seek—by all means possible—to familiarize their personnel with the new terrain in advance." According to Yakushin, "Their ambition to get a good grade explains this," but he admonishes that "a grade acquired due to simplification and indulgence does not reflect the personnel's true level of preparedness and therefore cannot satisfy anyone." By way of contrast, and reflecting the high priority accorded flexibility, the general writes,

> It is another matter entirely when a subunit operates in unfamiliar territory, using a variant that they are not familiar with ahead of time. Then, both commanders and soldiers have to fully use the knowledge and skills acquired during daily training; they must show initiative, quick thinking, creativity, decisiveness and other moral-combat qualities in a training battle. It is possible that someone will get a fairly low grade in such exercises. Yet the grade will mean much more than a good grade received under simplified conditions."[1]

The same concerns are shared by General-Lieutenant of Aviation Pavlov. "Hero of the Soviet Union" and "Honored Pilot of the USSR," the "old master" asks if the new technology has outmoded his time-honored skills.[2] "Is it possible that I am fighting for the past? Has the development of new equipment and weapons made frontline soldiers' mastery of combat, tactical findings, and creative approaches obsolete, stripping them of their instructiveness and educational value?" The general finds that "simplification and indulgence" underlie his sense of being "behind the times." In training, he writes, "the pilots imitating the target fly only in a straight line, without changing altitude or speed."[3] General of Aviation Konstantinov derides the same "oversimplified approach."

> The officers in training were placed in a situation where they did not have to concern themselves with which tar-

---

[1] General-Col. Viktor Zakharovich Yakushin, "The Staff in the Struggle for an Effective Training Process," *Krasnaya Zvezda*, 20 April 1977, p. 2. T1, August 1977, pp. 197 and 198.

[2] These are honorary titles recognizing the individual's outstanding contribution to the defense of the Motherland in the Great Patriotic War (World War II).

[3] General-Lt. G. Pavlov, "Inexhaustible Reserve," *Krasnaya Zvezda*, 4 August 1976, p. 2. T1, April 1977, pp. 100 and 102. "Simplification and indulgence" is the formula used to denote cases in which training missions are altered in order to allow easy fulfillment. The "letter" of the prescribed mission is followed, but the intended mission is stripped of its challenging features in order that personnel may receive high ratings.

gets to fire at first, what rate of fire to use, etc. They knew all this beforehand, including the "enemy's" action, the target's flight profile, their routes and other data.[4]

Predictably enough, when "every action is planned in advance," commanders are at a loss when confronted with the unexpected.[5] Konstantinov recounts an exemplary exercise in which "the 'enemy' unexpectedly changed the axis of attack" (in accordance with a scenario "known beforehand only to the higher headquarters"). At this point, "it was obvious to everyone that the unexpected maneuver of the 'enemy' aircraft had caught the [commanding] officer by surprise."[6]

While the Soviets are well aware that "in modern combat the most unexpected situations are possible," their simulations of enemy tactics are, according to Konstantinov, "just too simplified and rigid."[7] Precisely because of the need for flexibility, he adds, "this type of training is hardly beneficial."[8] Or, as the hard-nosed Pavlov puts it, "without mincing words, these comrades would have a hard time under combat conditions."[9] The same judgment is reached by American analysts, who note that "Soviet operational practices are surprisingly 'pro forma' with little continuing effort to enhance their skills under realistic conditions. Many of their 'sorties' appear to be rather canned 'once around the flagpole and back.' In short, they appear to maintain their flying skills, but not their combat proficiency."[10]

---

[4] General-Col. Anatoliy Ustinovich Konstantinov, "Thorough Knowledge of Affairs," *Krasnaya Zvezda*, 13 March 1977, p. 2. T1, June 1977, p. 140.

[5] Directorate of Soviet Affairs, Air Force Intelligence Service, *Soviet Press Selected Translations*, June 1977, p. 139.

[6] Konstantinov, "Thorough Knowledge," p. 141.

[7] Col. V. A. Uryzhnikov, "In a Complex Situation," *Krasnaya Zvezda*, 7 January 1977, p. 1. T1, April 1977, p. 97; and Konstantinov, "Thorough Knowledge," p. 142.

[8] Konstantinov, "Thorough Knowledge," p. 142.

[9] Pavlov, "Inexhaustible Reserve," p. 102.

[10] Edward T. Timperlake and Steven Leveen, "A Methodology for Estimating Comparative Aircrew Proficiency," a report prepared for the Theater Forces Division, Office of Strategic Research, Central Intelligence Agency (Arlington, Va.: The Analytic Sciences Corp., 1981), pp. 7–25.

Air-to-ground training appears to be shackled by the same sort of routinized unrealism. "Pilots fly the same patterns over the same ranges year after year and then perform poorly when conditions are varied ever so slightly."[11] Pilots ordered to deviate from the routine mission have required a greater number of target approaches than planned (increasing their exposure to air defenses) and have experienced degradations in accuracy.[12] High ranking officers note, in particular, training deficiencies in the acquisition and destruction of "small mobile targets." General of Aviation L. Nosov, in diagnosing the problem, points to cases in which "the tactical training range was idle." "Seldom," he writes, "were exercises in tactics carried out in the subunits."[13] Similar cases lead General Pavlov to concur in this view. He writes that

> changes in the bombing conditions caused the poor results. The pilots had been flying the same routes for a long time and had only worked out the combat action problems for their own range under normal target conditions. They did not work out the tactical background.

Yet, much to the frustration of General Pavlov, in evaluating just such unrealistic exercises, "people are assuming that the simulated enemy air defense system has been destroyed, but they have simply not thought the situation through. How can someone go into combat without the necessary skills?" Apparently, officials accountable for the simplification of combat training often seek refuge in the argument that it is "justified by flight safety requirements." The argument carries little weight with the likes of General Pavlov, in whose view, "the whole point was to make it easier to obtain outstanding ratings on a basic mission."[14]

Nor is it clear that the "outstanding ratings"—even those achieved under simplified conditions—are themselves deserved.

---

[11] Directorate of Soviet Affairs, Air Force Intelligence Service, *Soviet Press Selected Translations*, April 1977, p. 86.

[12] Pavlov, "Inexhaustible Reserve," p. 102.

[13] General-Major L. Nosov, "Sudden Combat Task," *Krasnaya Zvezda*, 27 May 1976, p. 2. T1, April 1977, p. 105.

[14] Pavlov, "Inexhaustible Reserve," p. 102.

It is particularly disturbing to some that higher unit headquarters (divisional or air army) allow the flow of misinformation to proceed unimpeded up the chain of command, all the way to the highest levels, which (assuming they are made aware of the misreportage at all) are then forced to intervene. For example, one reads that

> fighter aviation regiment "X" has a reputation among the troops in the air defense district as being one of the most advanced. But the time came for a comprehensive inspection and its former achievements were noticeably dimmed. It became clear that indulgence in fulfilling combat training missions was permitted, evaluations of individual pilots and aviation specialists were exaggerated. . . .
>
> Naturally, we severely questioned the commander and other unit officers. But another fact emerged. Representatives from higher headquarters had often visited the unit. After every trip, they had reported that affairs in the regiment were all right and that missions were being executed successfully. What do these inspectors lack? Thorough knowledge, competence, high principles, and high standards? It turned out that their supposedly helpful work in the unit was of low quality.
>
> The district Military Council and Political Directorate had to take pertinent and effective measures to correct the unit's affairs.

"Intolerant" of such cases of "complacency" and "deterioration of responsibility," General Konstantinov finds it especially unsatisfactory when personnel failures are sloughed off on equipment. Recounting deficiencies in a unit's operation of radar equipment, the general quotes the unit's commander as saying, upon examination of the problem, "Now it is clear, the equipment let us down." Further investigation revealed that "the problem was nevertheless not in the equipment, but in the people—in their insufficient knowledge of their apparatus, and of the rules for operating it correctly."[15]

---

[15] Konstantinov, "Thorough Knowledge," pp. 143 and 142.

All of these are among the many reported cases in which, to quote the general, "the possibilities of socialist competition were weakly exploited."[16] But, on the contrary, these are precisely the sorts of cases in which the Socialist Competition *is* exploited—literally exploited. Consider the "socialist pledges made during the year of the 60th anniversary of the USSR Armed Forces." We are told that "one of the main points" is: "Do not allow flight accidents because of *human* errors."[17] How does one ensure that the socialist pledge is fulfilled? By blaming what are actually human errors, on the equipment! There is every incentive to do so.

Flight safety is, of course, an important issue. In fact, "the Soviet Air Force has a flight safety service . . . composed of senior pilots who make periodic inspection trips to units."[18] Not only is it important for obvious reasons of morale, but it bears on material readiness. Particularly where, as in the Soviet case, maintenance skills lag behind aircraft technology, even minor accidents can result in weapons being out of action for a long time. General Skubilin, chief engineer of the Soviet Air Force underlines the problem:

> New equipment from the standpoint of its recovery to operation is causing a number of rather complex problems to be moved up to first priority. While damage previously was limited most often to the skin of the aircraft or to one or two of its systems, now, with the multiple increase in density of saturation of the structure's volume with parts, assemblies, and functional components, practically any damage is complicated."

While, as we have seen, the Soviets face difficulties in training technicians in the use of automatic monitoring equipment, the alternatives—"diagnosis by a simple inspection or the use of

[16] Ibid., p. 143.

[17] Warrant Officer L. Dubovsky, "Attention: Technical Monitoring Post," *Znamenosets*, no. 8 (August 1978), p. 13. T1, January 1979, p. 39. Emphasis added.

[18] Directorate of Soviet Affairs, Air Force Intelligence Service, *Soviet Press Selected Translations*, April 1977, p. 85.

various test instruments"—are, the general stresses, "proving to be inadequate."[19] Thus, even "minor" accidents can have a serious impact on equipment readiness, which is a high priority goal. The problem is that equipment readiness conflicts with a goal of equal priority when, to avoid accidents, complex aerial maneuvering is prohibited. Equipment damage may thereby be minimized, but so will pilot skill, a critical factor in air combat. General Aleksandr Babayev, commander of the 16th Air Army in East Germany, exemplifies the ambivalence produced by the conflict of goals. He boldly asserts that "in hothouse conditions, it is impossible to prepare real air warriors." Some degree of complexity in aerobatic training ought to be allowed, he emphasizes, and "not just one a month, as some commanders seem to think."[20]

Not only do young pilots receive little practice themselves, it would appear that they seldom even witness the execution of advanced aerial maneuvers. Babayev certainly suggests as much in venturing, further, that "it would be useful for the aviator who is most experienced in complex flying and combat maneuvers to periodically practice *demonstration* flights." Beyond this, however, and stopping far short of recommending anything like "dogfighting," the general calls merely for the relaxation of restrictions on aerobatics upon return from practice sorties. He proposes that "a pilot returning to the airdrome after intercepting his target, with the permission of the chief flight controller," be authorized to "carry out two or three figures of complex pilotry in a specially designated airspace area." Even this modest proposal, however, is qualified. "Naturally, these exercises are planned in advance." Even where such limited maneuvers are allowed, the unit commander, taking into account the pilot's training, may "authorize him to carry out only parts of the exercise, and not the whole complex of aircraft maneuvers." But, wanting not to qualify his proposed reform out of existence, Babayev swings the other way,

[19] Skubilin, "New Equipment," p. 26.

[20] General-Col. Aleksandr Ivanovich Babayev, "Flight and the Combat Maneuver," *Krasnaya Zvezda*, 23 December 1976, p. 2. T1, April 1977, p. 109 and 108.

warning that "when this is done in order to be overcautious, then willingly or not there are losses in military preparedness."[21] The net result is an unfocused proposal giving the maximum discretion to precisely the commanders Babayev is criticizing.

There are those, moreover, who question whether such "overcaution" in fact reduces the number of accidents. From the Odessa Military District, the chief of the Aviation Pilot Safety Service writes that "pilots' achievement of high quality flying skill is inseparable from the struggle for accident-free flying operation."[22] The argument is obvious. Accidents are never planned; the avoidance of accidents thus hinges on the pilot's capacity to react to the unexpected. However, it is precisely the rigidity of pilot training that prevents the acquisition of that ability. As Babayev puts it, "because of his lack of resolute training, some young pilot may be lost in a flight situation that is the least bit complex."[23]

The Soviets, it would seem, have failed to arrive at a consensus on the compromise to be struck between controlled flying, comparatively safe, and realistic combat flight training with its inherent dangers. At the higher levels there is debate and ambivalence. The vacuum left in the absence of any firm resolution of the problem is certainly not filled by the Socialist Competition.

As we have seen, while the actual goals of safety and realism conflict, this in no way prevents the attainment of high *grades* in both flight safety and pilot training. The Soviet solution? Prohibit complex aerial maneuvering (this minimizes accidents, ensuring high grades in flight safety) and simplify the simulated enemy to the point where no aerobatics are required to achieve high scores in air-to-air interception. While high grades in both safety and interception are thereby assured, the net result is routinized and unrealistic training, low combat

---

[21] Ibid., pp. 108–110. Emphasis added.

[22] Col. Aleksandr Grigor'yevich Yarchuk, "Even Though the Accident Did Not Occur," *Krasnaya Zvezda*, 26 January 1977, p. 2. T1, April 1977, p. 92.

[23] Babayev, "Flight," p. 109.

skill, and operational rigidity. Routinization has a self-per-petuating side as well.

In the U.S., when new aircraft are introduced into the inventory, pilots are converted from less sophisticated systems to the newer ones. F-15 pilots, for example, are converted from the F-4, and it takes between twelve and eighteen months to accomplish the conversion. There is some evidence that the Soviets do not convert experienced pilots, say, from the MiG-21, to new aircraft like the MiG-23 Flogger or SU-24 Fencer. The commander of aviation in the Red Banner Far Eastern Military District shares the widespread view that "it is easier to train an unskilled person than to retrain someone who is skilled. Retraining, as is well-known, requires breaking an established stereotype and complex psychological restructuring."[24] This must be particularly so when already experienced pilots "fly the same patterns over the same ranges year after year and then perform poorly when conditions are varied ever so slightly," as discussed above. To the extent that the Soviets are converting experienced pilots to the new systems, perhaps the rigidity we see is a "counter-routinization program" designed to break the "established stereotype," as the commander puts it.

The observed rigidity of pilot training, however, is also consistent with the training of green Soviet recruits directly for the new systems. Though DOSAAF (The Voluntary Society for Assistance to the Army, Air Force, and Navy) administers a number of preinduction training programs, these appear to involve few flying hours—very few, if any, of which would be spent in combat aircraft in any event.[25] While this training

[24] General-Lt. V. Pan'kin, "Lieutenants' Flights," *Krasnaya Zvezda*, 11 August 1976, p. 2. T1, April 1977, p. 87.

[25] DOSAAF is discussed in Scott and Scott, *The Armed Forces of the USSR*, pp. 307–315. The Scotts mention the possibility that new (post-1970) DOSAAF schools have provided some flying on the MiG-17, introduced in 1953. While the Scotts do not provide their evidence for this, the Air Force merely states that, in DOSAAF's flying program, "participants learn to fly gliders, sports aircraft and, in some cases, even jet aircraft." Department of the Air Force, *Soviet Aerospace Handbook* Pamphlet 200-21 (Washington, D.C.: Government Printing Office, May 1978), p. 139.

may perform an acclimatizing function, for all intents and purposes, Soviet pilots train in their operational units. Roughly "one squadron per regiment is mainly responsible for training."[26] Soviet pilots, according to the Joint Chiefs of Staff, fly approximately one-hundred hours per year while NATO pilots "must fly twenty hours each month."[27] In addition, as a result of their maintenance shortfalls, Soviet pilots, unlike their U.S. counterparts, spend a significant portion of their non-flying time in cross-training for maintenance activities and in practicing those activities, to say nothing of the non-flying time consumed by their political indoctrination. In addition to flying over twice as much as their Soviet counterparts, NATO pilots have the benefit of simulators far more sophisticated than those reported to be in use by the Soviets. Indeed, while simulators are an industry in the U.S., few, if any, Soviet simulators are reported in Western compendia, and those discussed in the Soviet military literature are locally jerry-built. Even assuming that major depots are involved in simulator manufacture, it is highly unlikely that these would provide representations of advanced air engagements of the sort simulated in the U.S. (very advanced American computing and display technology, for example, is involved).

These constraints alone would make it difficult to prepare raw recruits for anything but routine flying in the limited time available, and the constraints gain immeasurably in significance as the sophistication of Soviet aircraft increases. In either case, then, with pilot conversion or without, the Soviets will find it difficult to counter the inertia of routine. The problem would persist even if high level agreement were reached, high-level directives were implemented, and field results were accurately reported regarding the balance between flight safety and combat realism in training.

---

[26] Berman, *Soviet Air Power in Transition*, p. 38.

[27] Department of Defense, Joint Chiefs of Staff, *United States Military Posture for Fiscal Year 1979* (Washington, D.C.: Government Printing Office, January 1978), p. 112. The NATO figure is from Berman, *Soviet Air Power in Transition*, p. 57.

Moreover, it deserves mention that while a few reformers like Babayev are tentatively proposing modest allowances in the way of narrowly constrained aerobatics, the U.S. is conducting high intensity dissimilar air combat training under the Navy's Topgun program and in Air Force exercises like Red Flag.[28] Not only that, but the U.S. *can* at least simulate Soviet aircraft by "sovietizing" F-5Es. Even if the Soviets tried to develop "aggressor squadrons" like America's, how could they simulate an F-15? Where is the technology? Have they ever captured an F-15? American experts scrutinized Belenko's MiG-25 rather closely. Indeed, the U.S. Air Force is reported to possess outright a dozen MiG-21s and four MiG-23s.[29]

Finally, while the likes of General Pavlov lament the lack of study given to military history and the apparent disinterest in combat experience, U.S. pilots have logged a great deal more combat experience since World War II than their Soviet counterparts, Korea and Vietnam being the prime examples. Not only does American training incorporate that experience, but the U.S. has learned a great deal from the winners in Middle Eastern air combat, while the Soviets must glean their insights from the losers.

In the face of all these differences, and of all the serious constraints under which the Soviets are operating, what is one to make of such characteristically ominous reports as the following:

For the last six years the USSR has produced an average of three new fighter aircraft a day, 365 days a year. During this period the Soviets have averaged more than 1,000 aircraft per year while the U.S. production rate has been

---

[28] Dissimilar air combat training includes engagements between aircraft of different types or models (e.g., F-5s vs. F-15s as against F-5s vs. F-5s).

[29] *The Military Balance 1981-1982* (London: The International Institute for Strategic Studies, 1981), p. 9. Soviet Air Force lieutenant Viktor I. Belenko defected in 1976, landing a MiG-25 in Japan. Western experts were amazed to find vacuum tubes rather than transistors in its avionics, among other technological shortcomings. See John Barron, *MiG Pilot* (New York: Reader's Digest Press, 1980).

about half that. . . . over the next six years, U.S. analysts believe that Soviet growth in aircraft production will provide an increase from today's 4,200 baseline to more than 10,000 units. They expect the equivalent of 36 U.S. fighter wings to be earmarked for Soviet frontal aviation. . . . over the next five years the USSR will produce as many MiG-23s as there are aircraft in the entire U.S./NATO (including France) inventory in the Central Region.[30]

America has the benefits of over twice the flying time, sophisticated simulators, far more realistic training, and the planned conversion of experienced pilots. Yet, its modernization program—which is dwarfed by the reported Soviet production rate—has witnessed serious shortfalls in personnel readiness.

With less than half of America's flying time, with a greater portion of non-flight time expended not on pilotry but on maintenance and indoctrination, lacking anything comparable in the way of simulators, under routinized and far less realistic training, and apparently hampered by misreportage and the evasion of responsibility, the Soviets are nonetheless reported to be incorporating sophisticated new combat aircraft at a rate equivalent to thirty-six U.S. wings over the next six years; this is six wings per year! With all of America's advantages, the U.S. has difficulty merely converting one wing per year, to say nothing of the additional time required to attain the highest levels of personnel readiness. If the Soviets succeed in this program without extremely severe reductions in readiness—reductions far more dramatic than America's—then it will surely be remarkable.

It cannot be overemphasized that, historically, superior pilot skill (technological superiority aside) has proven to be more than the equivalent of numbers. The favorable exchange rate of approximately ten Japanese planes downed for each American was sustained by U.S. pilots in the Pacific throughout the years 1943–1944. "Certainly a very considerable factor" was

[30] "Eastern Bloc Augments Attack Force," *Aviation Week and Space Technology*, February 6, 1978, pp. 57 and 58.

"the longer training which the U.S. pilots underwent compared to the Japanese pilots."[31] Data sets from Korea and Vietnam, Rand researchers conclude, "strongly support the proposition that pilot skill is perhaps the critical element in air-to-air combat."

> In the 1950 Korean conflict, American F-86 Sabre jets were often matched against Soviet MiG-15 aircraft flown by Chinese Communist pilots. Both jets were considered to have similar performance packages and both sides rotated pilots through combat tours. The outcomes were grossly dissimilar: 484 MiG-15s were shot down while only 48 Sabres were lost, an exchange ratio of 10:1. A difference of this magnitude, especially given the tactical advantages of the MiGs, can best be attributed to the superior skills of the Sabre pilots.[32]

U.S. Navy data have confirmed that the Topgun dissimilar air combat program mentioned above, which continues today, had a significant impact on U.S.–Vietnamese exchange ratios.

> The vital importance of *pilot skill* is illustrated by the experience of U.S. Navy pilots who during the first phase of the air war in Indochina (1965–68) achieved kill ratios in air combat of F-4s against MiG-21s of 2.3:1. This was considered unacceptably low by Navy officials, who sought to correct it by instituting the so-called Topgun (Dissimilar Air Combat) pilot retraining program during the bombing pause of 1968–70. When intensive air combat was resumed in the 1970–73 period, Topgun pilots flying

[31] Phillip M. Morse and George E. Kimball, "How to Hunt a Submarine" in *The World of Mathematics*, ed. James R. Newman, vol. 4 (New York: Simon and Schuster, 1956), p. 2172.

[32] Peter deLeon, *The Peacetime Evaluation of the Pilot Skill Factor in Air-to-Air Combat* R-2070-PR (Santa Monica, Calif.: The Rand Corporation, January 1977), p. 22. This study provides an excellent introduction to the primary problems of measurement and historical interpretation of pilot skill as a factor in aerial combat. The author provides a valuable overview of the literature in this area and introduces a number of quantitative indices and formal relationships useful in modeling air-to-air combat.

essentially the same planes against the same adversaries improved their kill ratios to 12.5:1—a 400% improvement based primarily on improved human performance.[33]

While aircraft performance differences surely play a role in exchange ratios, the Middle Eastern experience is hard to explain without recourse to the vastly superior skills of Israeli pilots in 1967, 1973, and 1982. The Israelis, "who had achieved an incredible 20:1 dogfight kill ratio in 1967, actually *improved* upon this and achieved 40:1 in 1973."[34] In the summer of 1982 over Lebanon, the Israelis reportedly shot down eighty-six Soviet-made Syrian fighters without losing a single one of their own.[35] While the measurement of pilot skill and the analysis of its contribution to such high ratios is the subject of much research, it is hard to dismiss the claim that even "differences in equipment and hardware technology are swamped by differences in pilot skill under all but the most unfavorable force ratios."[36]

And how much more unfavorable those ratios would have to be in order for the Soviets to erode, along with NATO's superior pilot skill, NATO's continuing technological edge.

EFFECTIVENESS OF RECONNAISSANCE

Routinized training, while it adversely affects pilot skill and the capacity for initiative, creates problems in many areas of the command and control system. Reconnaissance is such an area.

The Soviets do not yet possess a system equivalent to the U.S. AWACS, for example. And, while AWACS is merely one element of NATO's tactical reconnaissance system, few would

---

[33] Steven J. Rosen, *What a Fifth Arab-Israeli War Might Look Like: An Exercise in Crisis Forecasting*, Center for Arms Control and International Security Working Paper no. 8 (Los Angeles: University of California, November 1977), p. 22.

[34] Ibid., p. 23.

[35] Herzog, *The Arab-Israeli Wars*, p. 348.

[36] Rosen, *What a Fifth Arab-Israeli War Might Look Like*, p. 23.

dispute the superiority of Western technology in the area of reconnaissance. The Soviets are clearly committed to improving their theater reconnaissance capabilities, and it is reasonable to assume that such systems as the MiG-25 and the Soviets' AWACS, MOSS, have enhanced their capability to collect and transmit reconnaissance data. Still, it is reported that "while MOSS can under optimum conditions detect low-altitude targets over water, it has no such capability over land; and lacking a height-finding radar, it has only limited capabilities for airborne control and vectoring of interceptors." Until the control problem is solved, even the new MiG-25M Foxbat E, which is reported to possess "a true downward-looking target search and tracking system," will face the serious problem "of having to locate the area in which to look for the low-altitude target."[37]

Even where the most sophisticated reconnaissance technology is available, however, it cannot be effective if the critical information it yields is not used. In the Soviet case, because of their routine pilot training, the problem of use may prove to be far more intractable than that of technology.

For example, where a deviation from the predetermined flight plan is commanded on the basis of reconnaissance data, Soviet pilots, once airborne, apparently find it difficult to make the shift. General Nosov of the Soviet Air Force cites a characteristic case in which, after the formation had taken off, new aerial reconnaissance information was received at command. On the basis of that information, the ground-based commanders decided that an in-flight targeting change was called for. Yet, when the pilots "were commanded to switch targets while in flight, they could not make an accurate bombing approach on the designated targets; part of the force had to be wasted on an alternate target." Again, the problem lay not in any failure of reconnaissance technology, but in the flyers' capacity to utilize it. While the reconnaissance information was available, "the flyers did not make use of this knowledge,

[37] Petersen, *Soviet Air Power*, p. 36. Information is sparse, however, concerning the system's capabilities under various levels of ground clutter.

apparently relying on their past training." That is, General Nosov continues, they had been "systematically trained to carry out attacks on targets which were *predetermined* at the airfield." Why do commanders permit the sort of "simplification and indulgence" that breeds this rigidity? General Nosov reports, "the stress, they say, is on raising the class rating of flight personnel.... Therefore, tactics are neglected."[38]

In addition to the cases in which pilot rigidity hampers the use of available reconnaissance, the Soviets record many cases in which tactical reconnaissance is simply not available. Both types of reconnaissance failure have proven to be of particular detriment to the coordination of ground operations with air strikes. For example, the Soviets can support ground forces with artillery, as well as with helicopters and planes. The Soviets have modernization programs under way in each area. In cases where artillery and aircraft are combined in the support of ground forces, poor reconnaissance has reduced efficiency. Soviet officers regularly bemoan cases in which "the results of air strikes against the enemy were of no consequence to the gunners. Their rounds often struck the same areas that had just previously been worked from the air." Tellingly, they add, "the duplication did not stem from any desire to achieve the maximum possible suppression of the 'enemy,' but from uncoordinated decisions.... Was this fire required? With what density? It's difficult to say. We had no bomb damage assessment data available."[39]

FLEXIBILITY AND THE PLAN

If war were perfectly predictable, reconaissance and, in turn, flexibility would not be necessary. While some sort of war plan is obviously essential, an ability to adjust the plan is no less important. The Soviets are the first to recognize this. "Coordination between the ground forces and aviation requires exceptional precision and diligent agreement on targets, time,

[38] Nosov, "Sudden Combat Task," pp. 105 and 106. Emphasis added.

[39] Lt. Col. A. Zakharenko, "The Lessons of Coordination," *Krasnaya Zvezda*, 5 August 1977, p. 1. T1, November 1977, p. 301.

and lines. Here the significance of regulatory documents—the schedule of operations of ground based subunits and flight plans—cannot be overemphasized." At the same time, the Soviets realize that "coordination devoid of flexibility cannot be sufficiently effective." Yet one reads accounts like these:

> The subunit was late with its approach to the assigned line. The defenders immediately took advantage of this, committing their tank reserve to the resultant breach. How vital it was to receive support from combat helicopters during these decisive minutes! However, neither the combined-arms commander nor the representative from supporting aviation called for the rotary-wing aircraft. *The plan did not call for this.*

> During the exercise...*no thought was given to making any corrections to the plans.* The combined-arms commander never called for an air strike unless it had been envisioned beforehand.

> On-call resources are usually employed to accomplish unforeseen missions which arise suddenly. The aviators had a group of fighter-bombers and a flight of combat helicopters on alert for takeoff at any moment. However, this was *not reflected in the plan*, and they never left the ground.[40]

The Soviets' system of command and control may underlie these deficiencies in flexibility and initiative, as former Secretary of Defense Harold Brown suggests. "Owing to certain aspects of Soviet heritage, their combat operations tend to be governed by specific rules. Proper application of these rules requires centralized authority and detailed control over subordinate units, and it results in rigidity and stifling of initiative in the Western sense." Pointedly, he adds, "the inflexibility inherent in such a system, coupled with the tendency of seniors to distrust subordinates and to provide them with only minimum essential information on the evolving tactical situation,

---

[40] Ibid., pp. 299–301. Emphasis added.

could have adverse consequences in the face of rapidly changing, often unpredictable battlefield situations, particularly if their means of control are disrupted by U.S. forces."[41]

Just how little information is provided lower-level Soviet officers is suggested by their complaints:

> The planning documents upon which our coordination is built seemed to me to be incomplete. They only reflected the time that aviation approaches the forward edge. But we need to know its location and condition at any moment, its readiness to commit reserves, types of air strikes, and concomitant results. In other words, the plans must be more detailed and supplemented by new data as the battle develops.[42]

Another officer urges that "in determining the basic time indices for supporting aviation it is important to take the most *insignificant features* of the ground battle into consideration." Remarkably, these "insignificant features" include: "the size of the offensive front, depth of the defensive zone, duration and formation of the artillery support for the attack, the sequence of movement, deployment, and commitment of the second echelons and the reserves into battle, and many, many more items."[43]

Denied such data, should Soviet subunits be cut off from higher authorities, their effectiveness will hinge on precisely the lower-level creativity and initiative that, by all accounts, they so sorely lack. The problem cuts across all the Soviet services. Concerning the Soviet navy, a study for the U.S. Defense Nuclear Agency concludes that "despite the exhortations for initiative at the lower operational levels, the impression is gained that the whole system depends on everything going just as prescribed, that the loss of a communication link or com-

---

[41] Department of Defense, *Annual Report of the Secretary of Defense for Fiscal Year* 1982 (Washington, D.C.: Government Printing Office, 1981), pp. 74–75.

[42] Zakharenko, "The Lessons of Coordination," p. 301.

[43] Major I. Gerasimenko, cited in ibid., p. 302. Emphasis added.

mand echelon would be more than disruptive, perhaps even catastrophic."[44]

OTHER COMMAND AND CONTROL PROBLEMS

It has been pointed out that unavailability of reconnaissance data and difficulties in the flexible use of available reconnaissance have led to inefficiencies. To some extent these may derive from inefficiencies within the Soviets' system of processing and distributing reconnaissance information. General Grinkevich, the chief of staff of the Group of Soviet Forces, Germany, suggests as much in stressing that "the struggle to gain time in the process of organizing combat operations has become a primary task." "In particular," he notes, "we must change the purpose and content of warning orders and fragmentary orders, firstly to give commanders a more complete orientation on forthcoming operations, and secondly, to *keep from repeating data which is already known.*"[45]

How often have we been told of the Soviets' capacity for high armored rates of advance and of their capacity to use these to achieve "breakthroughs"? Very often. Yet the chief of staff observes that high rates of advance may become a liability and that they alone do *not* ensure the *exploitation* of whatever breakthroughs might be achieved by mass and velocity. Here, decision time becomes the key.

One who is blind or who otherwise lacks the sensory apparatus required to avoid obstacles would be ill-advised to get into a car and drive it at the highest possible speed. Ideally, a staff is a type of sensory apparatus for a commander. It receives information, cuts away the unimportant or peripheral, and processes the essential, presenting it to the commander in

[44] R. O. Welander, J. J. Herzog, and F. D. Kennedy, Jr., *The Soviet Navy Declaratory Doctrine for Theater Nuclear Warfare*, report prepared for the director of the Defense Nuclear Agency (McLean, Va.: The BDM Corp., 1977), pp. 38–39.

[45] General–Col. D. Grinkevich, "Command and Control in Response to Contemporary Requirements," *Voyennyy Vestnik*, no. 4 (April 1976), pp. 47–51. T1, November 1977, p. 296. Emphasis added.

a format allowing him to make a timely and informed choice from among his alternatives. But, the general points out that precisely "the increase in mobility and maneuverability of troops, their increased firepower, and the dynamic nature of combat operations have changed the nature of staff control activities." He is concerned that these not be "organized clumsily, without considering the capabilities of modern means of armed struggle and the nature of combat."[46]

Apparently, however, the Soviet staff has not kept up with the technology, either figuratively or literally. Literally, General Grinkevich emphasizes that the "modern means of armed struggle," their increased mobility and speed, have created new logistical problems for command and control. He reports that "often, mistakes in control are manifested as a result of lack of knowledge of the capabilities of the logistics base of the control facilities." But staff skills have failed to keep up with the increased tempo of modern combat in another, far more important sense. The Soviets themselves focus directly on command and control weaknesses as the principle impediments to the *exploitation* of breakthroughs achieved by mass and surprise. The general recounts his exemplar as follows:

> The initial attack was sudden and powerful, and this dumbfounded the "enemy." The attacking subunits broke through the defense and went over to pursuit of the "enemy."

However, the enemy, "soon began to offer resistance," and finally, "the enemy's large grouping broke into the rear of our attacking troops."

In response to this development, and in order to exploit the breakthrough that mass and surprise had afforded, the commander:

> was assigned the mission of turning the subunits by almost 90 degrees and striking the "enemy" in the flank in an hour and a half, in coordination with adjacent units and avia-

---

[46] Ibid., pp. 295 and 291.

tion. The distance to the line of probable encounter with the enemy was about 30 km.

Here is where the troubles begin. First, "instead of quickly changing the direction of movement," the subunits were "halted." Then, "after spending almost 40 minutes on "consideration," he still did not assign the mission for setting up reconnaissance or for coordinating among the subunits in a timely manner." In particular, they "were not coordinated either by place, or time, nor by target." "Fifty minutes were left for the 30-kilometer march, for deployment, and for delivering the strike." And, the general reports, "it should be no surprise to learn that the subunits arrived late at the advantageous position." His diagnosis focuses on the "inadequate training of the commander and his staff." But the key is "*the inability to appreciate time.*" Specifically,

the collection of situation data and their evaluation are accomplished slowly, decisions are often made in the old way, and the same can be said for the sequence of work. In particular, it still happens at times that, having halted the subunits, the commander clarifies the mission he has received, estimates the situation for a long time, makes his decision slowly, and only then assigns the mission to subordinates. The latter in turn perform their work in the very same order. All of this takes a lot of time, and as a result, even a decision thought out in detail may turn out to be unrealized.[47]

The very dynamics of the "breakthrough" under modern conditions exacerbate the problems since (a) high tempo produces "frequent and abrupt *changes in* the situation," and (b) high numbers—particularly high numbers *of divisions*—"increases the number *of information sources*" and thereby, "the volume of work" with which higher staffs must contend, overloading them and increasing the sluggishness of the entire process. (In this respect, the Soviets' numerical predominance may be a decidedly mixed blessing.) Yet in the Soviet view, the

[47] Ibid., pp. 291–292 and 295. Emphasis added.

very same factors that exacerbate decision problems make ever more stringent the demand for "*immediate* reaction on the part of commanders and staffs."[48]

Under these demanding new conditions, moreover, commanders are constantly reminded that "modern combat is combined-arms combat," calling for swift and efficient allocations of combined resources.[49] All the more bitter, therefore, are Soviet complaints that ground force "combined-arms commanders don't have an in-depth knowledge of aviation subunits and, in turn, aviators can only judge the development of the ground battle in the most general terms." Predictably, after exercises, the Soviets find officers reporting that coordination was lacking: "The aviators fought according to their rules . . . and the ground-based subunits followed theirs." Soviet ground force commanders openly complain that their "knowledge of the capabilities of aviation remains insufficient." Ground commanders' intelligent suggestions for raising efficiency in combined arms operations would indicate that their contact with aviators has indeed been slight. "We need to get together with aviators more often, and not just at exercises. Joint technical conferences, tactical briefings, and discussion of results in accomplishing ordinary missions *would be* of use."[50]

In speaking of the commander's technical culture (*kul'tura*), General Pavlovskiy, deputy minister of defense and commander in chief of the Soviet ground forces, writes that it centers on "his ability to competently . . . combine the resources of all weapon types, and to use them with maximum effectiveness." In particular, he stresses that "the commander must primarily learn to use his combat equipment in the dynamics of battle, in swiftly changing situations." In combined arms, this quickly leads us back into a familiar problem. According to the general, "sometimes, in a relatively calm and static situation, an officer is prudent and correctly assesses all factors when giving a subunit its task. But as soon as the troops begin moving, his

[48] Ibid., p. 290. Emphasis added.

[49] Ibid., p. 292.

[50] Zakharenko, "The Lessons of Coordination," pp. 300, 301, and 302. Emphasis added.

former tactical-technical culture is not apparent in his decisions; he is incapable of using his knowledge with the speed demanded by battle." His stern admonitions seem to apply particularly to troops whose equipment is new. "It cannot be tolerated that sometimes subunits with new and better combat equipment and weapons act in their old way, within their former limits, and do not strive to make exhaustive use of their advantages."[51]

Yet the very performance advantages to which the general alludes, have exacerbated combined-arms command and control problems. Professor of Military Sciences Uryzhnikov writes that "the successful interaction of crews and groups of planes can only be provided by clear and uninterrupted command and control during the dynamics of combat." Increased aircraft speed and range, as well as newly acquired capabilities to operate at lower altitudes, have made this more difficult for the Soviets, particularly given the high degree of pilot-reliance upon ground controllers.

> The command and control process for fighters may be conditionally divided into two stages. The first stage runs from take off to detection of the air enemy; the second is from the moment the target is detected until it is destroyed. In the first stage the crews of the [ground—Ed.] command posts which are vectoring the aircraft have a large responsibility. However, no matter how great the potential of command and control from the ground, the success of a group in an air battle depends in the first place on the commander/flight leader.[52]

Target "acquisition"—sighting, or "pre-acquisition" might be better terms—in air interception would seem to remain largely the responsibility of ground-based controllers.[53] Many

---

[51] Pavlovskiy, "An Officer's Technical Culture," pp. 134–136.

[52] Uryzhnikov, "In a Complex Situation," pp. 98 and 97.

[53] According to the U.S. Air Force, Soviet "air intercept training retains its traditional emphasis on strict ground control intercept, with little attention to free air combat outside the ground control intercept system." Dept. of the Air Force, *Soviet Aerospace Handbook*, p. 45.

examples support this. Aviators are time and again commended as "masters of air combat" who have "performed all the actions transmitted by the flight controller." As recited in the Soviet literature, such transmissions might convey the rough location of the enemy, action orders, and would provide headings. ("One more target in your area. Attack! Your course and altitude are . . ." would be characteristic among the obviously colloquial renderings in their literature.)[54]

The increased range of Soviet tactical aircraft and their capacity to operate at lower altitudes than previously have complicated the problems inherent in the ground control of interception and, particularly, of ground attack (interdiction) operations. "The demands for continuous and stable control have especially grown now that the range of air operations has greatly expanded."[55]

Specifically, in the course of certain missions, increased range combined with lower flight altitude have created pressures to streamline the transfer of control from one ground station to the next. Higher speeds have made this even more imperative since obviously positional errors will cumulate more rapidly at higher speeds. Professor Uryzhnikov analyzes a case in which, "at first, communications from the ground were clear. Then the 'enemy' began 'jamming.' The flight leader did not receive one of the [ground-to-air—Ed.] commands. Then a supporting pilot transmitted by radio: 'I see a group of planes.'" Given only "such a vague report," the flight leader was "perplexed" and "demanded a more detailed description of the target, indicating its direction and distance." And, "finally, more exact information came in." But, in the meantime, the tactical advantage was sacrificed and "the battle was essentially lost." The problem, finally, arose from "the fact that the commander who directed battle from the command post, was indecisive. He did not transfer command and control of the group of fighters to a different post, although of course he knew that radio communications deteriorated at a certain dis-

---

[54] Major A. Koshchavko, "Master of Air Combat," *Vestnik Protivovozdushnoy Oborony*, no. 4 (1978), p. 45. T3, No. 4, April 1978, p. 67.

[55] Uryzhnikov, "In a Complex Situation," p. 97.

tance from the ground radio station, especially in a flight at low altitudes."[56]

It would seem that, under this sort of breakdown in communications, pilot "initiative" would have been called for. Yet Uryzhnikov points out that, aside from being in violation of the plan, it could also negate the low altitude capabilities in which the Soviets have invested so heavily. As he puts it, "What could the flight leader have done to reestablish communications? Increase altitude on his own initiative? This would have been a violation of task's conditions." In this situation, "moreover, had he deviated from the plan, 'the enemy's' ground radar would have immediately detected the fighters." Obviously, Frontal Aviation's low-altitude capabilities decline in value where command and control deficiencies require formations to either increase altitude (and hence, vulnerability) or sacrifice targeting data in the face of communications gaps. Well aware of the implications, Uryzhnikov admonishes, "the situation itself dictated the need to transmit command and control of the fighters to another point in good time." Only this, he continues, "would have guaranteed the reliability and continuity of communications." Linking the problem to the Soviets' advancing aircraft technology, he emphasizes that "the role of this factor, as is well known, grows more and more as a flight increases speed and decreases altitude."[57] Beyond the obvious problem of jamming, the transfer of control may run amok in many ways.

Major Milyakhovskiiy, a ground controller, recalls an incident illustrative of the curious problems that can arise in the transfer of control. Milyahkovskiiy was to assume control of two pairs of fighters in flight, vector them "to targets in turn, after which they were supposed to land at an alternate airfield." After the formation was airborne, he recalls,

> The tactical controller informed me of the interceptors' azimuth and range and briefed me on the target coordinates. I detected them on the scope and immediately

[56] Ibid., pp. 95 and 96.
[57] Ibid., p. 96.

reported:

"I observe the targets!"

The vectoring generally was successful and the first pair's leader announced that he had made a "launch." The other intercept also took place without disruption. Fighters of the second pair moved precisely into the rear hemisphere of the "enemy" aircraft and "hit" him at the given line. Now it remained to vector the aircraft to the alternate airfield.

I immediately gave them all a new course. But what was this? Only three blips on the screen changed flight direction, although all four pilots reported execution of the order. I again repeated the prescribed course to the "unheeding" pilot. He confirmed:

"Roger. I am following the course you gave."

But he continued to fly off away from the group. And here I finally realized that I was tracking a completely different aircraft on the scope. Now it became clear why the "stranger" was not following my orders. But then where was the one I was controlling . . . ?

It was only with great difficulty and with the help of a senior comrade that I succeeded in finding my ward among the multitude of "fireflies" on the IKO [plan position indicator] scope. Of course, the error could have led to very serious consequences. And it all happened because I was imprecise in assuming control of fighters from the duty controller.[58]

It seems reasonable to assume that in the severely crowded airspace of a central European war, such problems could be multiplied and, although wrongly considered a "fine point," they could exacerbate the sorts of IFF (Identification Friend

[58] Major V. Milyakhovskiiy, "The CP Controller and the Flight Crew," *Vestnik Protivovozdushnoy Oborony*, no. 12 (1978), pp. 36–39. T3, December 1979, pp. 57–58.

or Foe) problems encountered by the Soviets even in peace-time exercises.

> For example, an experienced controller, Capt. R. Volkov, vectored a pair of fighters against a radio-controlled air-craft target on the range. The leader confidently entered battle and, after launching a simulated missile, he "hit" the target. Later Volkov authorized him to disengage. But the wingman already was on the approach. Without having checked to see whether or not the first interceptor had emerged from the onboard radar's angular field of view behind the aircraft, the controller gave the wingman the command to search for the target.
>
> The pilot naturally performed everything on order from the ground. In a little while he had lock-on . . . of his own leader.[59]

The classic IFF problem, however, is the case in which ground-based antiaircraft defense batteries shoot down their own aircraft because they are unable to distinguish incoming enemy aircraft from friendly aircraft where the latter are tailed by, are tailing, or share the flight profile of the enemy. The problems are deepened where the friend and foe are each exe-cuting maneuvers for purposes of "lock-on" or evasion, all within an airspace covered by the battery. If the battery is further subjected to the foe's jamming, the IFF problem is even worse. And when one considers the very high density of the deployed Soviet surface-to-air missile (SAM) system, the likely electronic (jamming) environment, and the high intensity of aerial combat the Soviets envision, it is not hard to under-stand why the Soviets are concerned with improving their IFF capability.

The purely technical side of the IFF problem is extremely complicated and little research is available concerning either the state of Soviet IFF technology or Soviet R&D in this po-tentially very important area. The more interesting question,

---

[59] Ibid., p. 59.

in any case, is the extent to which the routinization of pilot training may detract from the IFF training of ground (i.e., SAM) batteries.

From the Soviets' point of view, the ground battery's problem in the simplest one friend/one foe case is "to detect both targets in good time, identify our aircraft, immediately open up aimed fire against the enemy and destroy it—and all of this under conditions where, in addition to everything else, the air enemy is maneuvering and jamming the operation of the radar." The Soviets seem to be chiefly concerned with "identifying and tracking the aircraft to be destroyed, *no matter what kind of maneuvers it performs.*" In training batteries to track maneuvering aircraft, the Soviets stress that "they must be able to skillfully operate the manual mode of target range tracking."[60]

Second, the Soviets stress that in IFF training, "it is necessary to use at least two aircraft simultaneously so as to work out all problems which involve firing in a complex situation, when friendly and enemy aircraft are operating in the air."[61] Given, then, that the Soviets are chiefly concerned with training batteries to perform IFF when the aircraft involved are executing complex maneuvers, the question—and we can do little more than ask it—is this: where do Soviet ground batteries get their training? As noted earlier, aerobatics of the sort IFF training is said to require is all but absent from most Soviet pilot training. And dogfighting—the real IFF test—is virtually prohibited. Who provides ground batteries with the realistic dogfights and other aerial engagements and maneuvers that the Soviets cite as the keys to IFF training? The size of the Soviet surface-to-air missile system would certainly dictate a very high number of such engagements if adequate IFF training were to be provided to all batteries. While, in all likeli-

---

[60] Lt. Col. S. Nekhoroshev, "When Friendly and Enemy Aircraft Are Airborne," *Voyennyy Vestnik*, no. 5 (May 1976), pp. 88–89. T1, November 1977, p. 297. Emphasis added.

[61] Ibid.

hood, some aerial maneuvering takes place in the course of advanced pilot training, one cannot but doubt that this alone is furnishing Soviet air defense batteries with a supply of aerial engagements—not to mention dogfights—adequate to meet their IFF training requirements.

It hardly needs to be added that, in foul weather, not only IFF, but many of the other command, control, and communications problems mentioned above become even more severe. But, in all-weather pilot training the familiar incentives for a high class rating have lead to "simplification and indulgence." In this case, it would appear "that negligent commanders are filling squares by simply sending pilots up in bad weather and then down again, with no substantive mission to perform."[62]

Finally, it should be recognized that this entire complex of command and control problems is itself occurring in the course of a C^3 modernization program—the automation of command and control. The U.S. Joint Chiefs of Staff write that the "automation of Soviet command and control is evolving slowly."[63] To be sure, longer-term goals of that program would involve the elimination of a number of the problems reviewed above, the ground control switching problems and certain inefficiencies in the use of reconnaissance among them. While there is debate within the Soviet military concerning the feasibility and potential effectiveness of the "computer at the command post," the program undoubtedly has the support of

[62] Directorate of Soviet Affairs, Air Force Intelligence Service, *Soviet Press Selected Translations*, p. 106. The point, here as elsewhere, is not that the Soviets' problems are necessarily unique. Every air force, for example, faces the tradeoff between flight safety and realism in training. While the Soviet Union may address such universal problems in a particularly inefficient way, the concern for flight safety is a constraint on the realism of U.S. adverse weather training as well. For instance, "safety considerations preclude training with the complex F-111 in Central Europe in the bad weather for which it was specifically designed; the crews have to deploy to the Mediterranean where they simulate all-weather operations in clear weather." Schemmer, "Pentagon, White House, and Congress Concerned," p. 29.

[63] Dept. of Defense, Joint Chiefs of Staff, *United States Military Posture for Fiscal Year 1979*, p. 115.

the highest levels.[64] Marshal Grechko himself urged that

> the task of mastering scientific methods for command and
> control on the basis of new technical facilities becomes
> quite urgent. Command and control must improve along
> with achievements in scientific-technical progress.[65]

In fact, the Soviets probably hope that automation will secure
military benefits normally associated with decentralization
(e.g., flexibility, greater efficiency) while avoiding the *political*
cost of decentralization itself—without, that is, any sacrifice
in the centralization of command.

While it is hard to judge the exact scale of the automation under way, it is clear that the familiar incentive system,
pressure for grades, and attendant training problems are
complicating the process—challenging in its own right—of
introducing troops to computer technology. The editors of the

---

[64] See David Holloway, *Technology, Management and the Soviet Military
Establishment*, Adelphi Paper No. 67 (London: The International Institute for
Strategic Studies, April 1971). A somewhat more contemporary, though less
detailed account that addresses the connection of automated C^3 to other areas
of Soviet military operations research may be found in John Ericson, "Soviet
Military Operational Research: Objectives and Methods," *Strategic Review*
(Spring 1978), pp. 63-73. By far the most useful contemporary accounts are
provided by the Soviets themselves. For background, see: A. N. Romanov and
G. A. Frolov, *Avtomatizatsii Sistemy Upravleniya* (Principles of automating
control systems) (Moscow: Military Publishing House, 1971), T4, January
1973; and P. N. Tkachenko et al., *Matematicheskie Metody Modelirovaniya
Boevykh Deystviy Takticheskikh Podrazdeleniy pri Pomoshchi Elektronnykh
Vychislitel'nykh Mashin* (Mathematical models of combat operations. Mathematical methods for modeling combat operations in tactical units with the
aid of electronic computers) (Moscow: Soviet Radio, 1969), T3, April 1973.
The classic Soviet work on military operations research, their "Morse and
Kimball," as it were, is I. Anureyev and A. Tatarchenko, *Primeneniye Mate-
maticheskikh Metodov v Voyennom Dele* (Application of mathematical methods in military affairs) (Moscow, 1967), T3, January 1973. All of these, as well
as many similar works containing numerous mathematical problems and
solutions in tactics and force allocation are available in English translation through the National Technical Information Service, Department of
Commerce.

[65] Grinkevich, "Command and Control," p. 295.

Antiaircraft Defense Herald have deemed the training issue to be of sufficient importance to merit commentary from the Lenin Archive. The prescient Ilyich divined the overall problem. "V. I. Lenin wrote that in the absence of people capable of knowledgeably using the latest improvements of military technology, expenditures on this technology are fruitless."[66]

The Soviets repeatedly mention the unique psychological dread evoked in troops by the computer. "Psychological hardening of automated control system specialists" is demanded often. "Ways of improving the psychological stability of personnel operating the automated systems of control" are sought. "Psychological training of soldiers" is discussed.[67]

In addition to this "lack of confidence in the use of automatic equipment," all of the "contradictions of the Socialist Competition" seem to be in bloom here, just as they are in the acquisition of ground support equipment and in the training of pilots. "The socialist competition is formally organized.... all sorts of falsifications, excessively high grades in determining outstanding soldiers and competition winners are permitted. ...[Commanders] do not react to the systematically repeated, so-called 'trivial,' deficiencies in operating and maintaining computers, which occur at the fault of individual specialists" (i.e., *not* the equipment); "comparability of results" is not ensured; "stereotyping and simplification at classes" is condemned; leading specialists do not pass on their experience, etc. All of these familiar things and more one reads. "Unjustifiably little attention is paid to perfecting the modern training-material base.... What a broad field of activity exists here for the ... efficiency experts and innovators." A broad field, indeed. And, in order to make sure that the Socialist Competition is exploited only in the intended sense, the Party is exhorted to "deeply penetrate into questions of combat training," and to increase its vigilance in seeing that "the socialist competition

[66] Lt. Col. G. Gryakvin, "In Order Skillfully to Master Automated Systems of Control," *Vestnik Protivovozdushnoy Oborony*, no. 7 (1977), pp. 63–67. T3, 1978, p. 108.

[67] Ibid., p. 109.

actively facilitates the skillful mastery of the automated control system apparatus by officers."[68]

Still, the Soviets have every reason to be concerned that the latest round of socialist pledges will be fulfilled by the same general method—by denuding the intended missions of all but their formal specifications, by devoting one's real creative energies not to the performance of assigned duties, but to the distortion of those duties, their reduction to the least demanding level consistent with the collection of those rewards held out precisely to ensure the robust and conscientious fulfillment of duties. So characteristic is this of Soviet behavior that Chief Air Marshal Kutakhov's poignant remark—so apt in the military sphere—might well be taken as a critique of the Soviet system at large:

> You see, our every good beginning at some time takes a turn, somehow the rational substance evaporates from it, and only the formal shell remains. This results from the fact that we make a living and creative task to fit a kind of procrustean bed and regulate everything without exception.[69]

The problems of military effectiveness finally derive from this far deeper problem, a political problem whose solution would call for nothing short of fundamental changes in the Soviet system itself. There are a few who, like Kutakhov, recognize this fact, but who also see the Soviet Union flanked by enemies, her sovereignty and influence resting principally on her military capabilities; to them it must seem particularly problematic that the Soviet state—by its very rigidity and all-pervasiveness—should operate to the detriment of its own defensive might; that its militarism should detract from its military capability. And yet, it does.

---

[68] Ibid., pp. 109, 111, and 113–115.

[69] Lt. General P. Kutakhov and L. Fil'chenko, *Aviatsiya i Kosmonavtika*, no. 11 (1962), p. 56; as cited in Trapans, *Organizational Maintenance*, p. 28.

CHAPTER V

THE ART OF WAR AND THE CRAFT OF THREAT ASSESSMENT

RECALLING THE PROBLEM

However revealing the preceding chapters may be on Soviet political, cultural, or other questions, they support the military point made earlier; namely, that a mere enumeration of peacetime inventories—"bean counting"—does *not* constitute an analysis of military capabilities. Although they must be accounted in any such analysis, static peacetime inputs alone are very poor indicators of dynamic wartime output (performance in the execution of missions).

The latter, the wartime *effectiveness* of a force, will vary dramatically depending upon precisely such operational factors as those we have been discussing: combat skill, efficiency in support functions, tactical decisionmaking, coordination, and other "arts of war." These cannot be captured by any static accounting of inert implements of battle (e.g., planes). Until such operational factors are better appreciated, our assessments of the Soviet threat can only be distorted and incomplete. Still, not even their appreciation will suffice to assess any specific threat; just like the bean count itself, a merely qualitative appreciation of operational matters falls short of the mark.

After all, *so what* if the Soviets have combat flexibility problems (Chapter IV)? So what if they face difficulties in maintaining and supporting their most advanced weaponry (Chapter III)? Even if, in light of the previous chapters, we knew (and we do not) that the Soviets' problems in each area were worse than those of the United States, again, so what? Would any of that show the Soviets to be incapable of executing the attacks of concern to NATO? No.

How much flexibility or sustainability do the Soviets *require* to execute those attacks? To execute *any specific threat*? To execute the tactical air (Frontal Aviation) threat elaborated in the Introduction of this book? There, fairly concrete Soviet objectives were set forth, and their achievement was posited as Frontal Aviation's new offensive conventional mission, one whose importance to NATO was stressed. Having progressed beyond bean counting to an appreciation of dynamic and operational "art of war" factors, are we now in a position to address that question of Soviet capability?

Is it plausible that Frontal Aviation could execute that two-phased conventional attack? What level of destruction *is* plausible? More than that attack? Less? How much more? How much less? How quickly? With what force remaining to do other things?

No. Clearly, we are not in a position to make a reasoned judgment—not even a ballpark estimate—on any such concrete questions of capability. Yet, a thousand and one judgments of precisely this nature are made whenever it is asserted that "the Soviets are superior" or, for that matter, when such assertions are denied by the heretical. Neither the believers nor the heretics generally offer much beyond the bean count or the "counter-bean count," as the case may be, to support their conflicting orthodoxies. Even when such bean counting "contests" end in a draw, the only thing they've really demonstrated is the essential inconclusiveness of that entire level of debate. That result, of course, is still preferable to the usual conclusion that, *because of* some bean asymmetry, the Soviets are "superior." But ultimately, counter-bean counting, while it may be useful in discrediting extravagant claims, is no more powerful an analytic approach than bean counting itself; "a rose by any other name," as it were.

Rather, to get a grip on questions of actual capability, one has to posit concrete military objectives and take a cold hard look at what would actually, physically, be involved in achieving them. Inputs are not enough; one has to *relate inputs to outputs*. The ease with which that may be done will, of course, vary from case to case. In this case, it is possible to do it, and having done so, to arrive at a reasoned judgment on the plausibility of Soviet success, and on a variety of other questions as well.

The purpose of the present chapter is to suggest one way in which to bridge the gap between inputs and outputs, and in particular, to show how the *qualitative* operational insights accumulated in the preceding chapters can be applied in *quantitatively* assessing the Frontal Air threat; that application, as described in the Preface, is the analytical purpose of those chapters.

The threat assessment proper is presented in the final chapter (with sensitivity analyses in Appendix C). Not all the steps in setting up that analysis will be presented here; only those that reveal its logical structure and the quantitative *function* of the above qualitative ("art of war") insights will be presented. But for those who wish to reconstruct and duplicate, expand on, or challenge the assessment, all the steps that—for reasons of technicality—are not presented in this chapter are available in full in Appendices A and B.

SPECIFYING A CRITERION OF SOVIET SUCCESS

The first step, however, is to be even more specific about the threat itself. As was discussed in the Introduction, the prevalent Western assessments of Frontal Aviation—the offensive arm of the Soviet tactical air forces—envision a two-phased attack. For the moment, let us focus on Phase I, the so-called "independent air operation."

This is a conventional interdiction (ground attack) campaign against selected NATO air defenses (to create a "corridor"); key NATO command, control, and communications assets; land-based theater nuclear missile launchers; theater nuclear weapon storage sites; and NATO tactical air bases (including nuclear-capable and nuclear-armed aircraft on quick reaction alert). Phase I is a preemptive non-nuclear

Soviet attack to degrade NATO's nuclear response capability.[1] Frontal Aviation is assumed capable of executing the attack within a very narrow time frame, perhaps on the opening day of the war.

Unfortunately, even this level of military specificity is wholly inadequate for purposes of threat assessment. What is really, physically, involved in executing this attack, in destroying these targets? What *measure* of output, and what *level* of output can serve as a criterion of Soviet success? For example, would total sorties flown be a good measure of output? Not especially. Sorties, per se, don't destroy targets. To destroy targets, one has to deliver munitions. So, a better approach would be to count the targets, estimate how many (appropriate) munitions would, if accurately delivered, be required to destroy each, and add up for *the total number of Soviet conventional air-to-ground munitions that would have to be accurately delivered to suppress the target set.*

Here, then, is the type of Soviet *output* with which we, as planners, are concerned. Output is expressed in units which (a) reflect the reality of the Soviets' military problem (i.e., to destroy targets) and (b) provide a single, succinct criterion against which to compare Soviet performance (expressed in the same units, accurately delivered munitions).

Now, counting targets and estimating how many munitions would be required to suppress each is a very arduous business. It is also an uncertain business. For example, while the phrase "NATO's C^3" seems clear enough at first blush, depending upon what one means by it, "NATO's C^3" could encompass everything from the West German Postal Service to the British Parliament. The physical objects that might reasonably be included in NATO's C^3 are terribly wide-ranging. Divisional, corps, army group, and theater command headquarters would be natural candidates. The inclusion of thousands upon thousands of NATO electronic telecommunications, warning, target acquisition, and data processing systems would be no less reasonable. A vast number of these are small, highly mobile,

---

[1] Conventional air superiority would also be achieved by its successful execution.

and easily camouflaged. Which, from among the enormous array of components, is one to choose? To what set of targetable objects does the analyst think he is referring when he says "NATO's C³"—much less when he confidently asserts that Soviet Frontal Air has acquired the capacity to destroy "it"?

Assumptions and judgments on our part are unavoidable. But as in every other step in setting up this analysis, the attempt is made to be *conservative*. Where error seems likely, try to err on the side of favorability to the adversary. If his success appears implausible on assumptions which (however inaccurate) err on his behalf, then, on more accurate assumptions, his success ought to appear even less plausible. Perfect realism is not essential to bound a threat, to answer the question stressed above—is it plausible?—but conservatism is. The qualitative discussion above functions as a check on the conservatism of those assumptions, as we shall see.

In line with that requirement, the Phase I target set developed in Appendix A is as narrowly circumscribed and delimited as seemed consistent with prevailing concerns and assessments. For example, essentially all moving targets were excluded, thus placing an absolute minimum demand on a technology that even the U.S., which leads, has not perfected: "look-down" target acquisition. The Soviets, moreover, suggest training laxity in the type of evasive, spontaneous, long-range, searching for ground targets that would be involved. But no such capabilities are called for to hit our Phase I targets (summarized in Table 5.1), whose coordinates are assumed to be known in advance, tailored to the sort of routine training of which the Soviets themselves complain. Unrealistic? Probably. Unfavorable to the Soviets? Not in my judgment.

But a judgment it nonetheless is. Admitting that, like every judgment, it could be wrong, four even less demanding Phase I target sets (discussed in Appendix A) are provided in Chapter VI, where the threat assessment proper is presented.

Having executed the Phase I attack, Frontal Aviation's operation would enter its second phase. Its operational objective would be to consolidate the gains, and facilitate the tactical maneuver, of the ground forces. There are two respects in

TABLE 5.1

Phase I Target Data Inventory

Target Class	Number	DGZs/Target[a]	DGZs
C^3	234	5	1,170
TNW	320	8	2,560
TNW Storage	100	12	1,200
DGZ Subtotal			4,930
Air Defense Corridor	909	2	1,818
Tactical Air Bases	50	222	11,100
Total DGZs			17,848

SOURCES: See Appendix A.

[a] A specified munition delivery point is referred to as a designated ground zero, or DGZ. Thus, the total DGZs the Phase I target set represents is the criterion of success, that is, the total number of accurately delivered munitions required to destroy it.

which Phase II should be a great deal tougher for the Soviets than Phase I. By contrast to those of the independent air operation, Phase II's objectives demand extremely close coordination with the Red Army. Second, they drive Soviet targeting toward NATO assets of greater mobility: engaged NATO ground forces, and NATO elements moving in (or into) the theater of battle.

The Phase I attack—at least as idealized here—can, to some extent, be preplanned, "machined in" by rote. The Phase II operation, designed to exploit fleeting tactical opportunities, cannot be preplanned. In turn, aerial reconnaissance and up-to-the-minute ("real time") damage assessment, timely and accurate staff work, fluidity and decisiveness in combined arms (air-ground) target allocation—teamwork—and a secure, continuous, and flexible system of ground control are factors of greater criticality to the second phase than to Phase I.

The shifting positions and greater mobility of Phase II targets, moreover, place a greater premium on target acquisition (and "look-down" discrimination from ground clutter) than would the larger fixed-site targets of Phase I. Finally, depending on the success of Phase I's attack on NATO's airbases (which would determine the permissiveness of the Phase II air defense environment), Phase II operations could demand much higher levels of counterair pilot skill and evasive initiative than would a truly preemptive attack, as contemplated in Phase I.

Each phase is demanding, but the latter is characterized by greater uncertainty and, of the two, would call for a correspondingly higher level of Soviet flexibility in a wider spectrum of missions, from aerial reconnaissance to ground-based command and control. But flexibility is a commodity in which, for all their defense spending, the Soviets appear to be in short supply. No one is more well aware of that fact than the Soviet high command itself, as the preceding chapters suggest.

If the first commandment of threat assessment is "be conservative," then the second is "limit the analysis to the necessities of the problem." If it proves implausible that the Soviets could complete Phase I, then, clearly, it is even less plausible that they could execute Phase I and *then* execute the more demanding Phase II. Indeed, Frontal Aviation would have to emerge from the independent air operation with a substantial force intact if it were to prosecute its subsequent operations. So, to address the question, "is the *two*-phased mission plausible?" it may be sufficient to examine the first phase alone. In fact, it will prove more than sufficient, as demonstrated below.

THE BEANS

Having established a useful measure of output and a criterion of Soviet success, the next critical step is to identify the Soviet force that might actually be available to execute the attack, were deterrence to fail. This is bean counting, but it's a good deal trickier than one might suspect. What are the relevant beans, the direct producers of *output*, as we've defined it?

For example, Soviet Frontal Aviation, the service of interest, includes a great many helicopters and tactical cargo planes. Should they be counted? Among the tactical fighters, some are trainer versions of limited combat capability; others are configured for electronic warfare or reconnaissance. Should they be counted as direct attackers? How many of the Soviets' multipurpose (i.e., capable of either ground attack or air-to-air combat) planes would be used, not as fighter-bombers, but as fighter escorts, to protect the actual attack force? The advanced fighter-bomber force is largely dual-capable (i.e., nuclear or conventional); what portion would be withheld for nuclear options? And how many planes would be allocated to Long-Range Aviation (a separate Soviet service) for its attacks on the periphery of the European theater, notably the U.K., now that Frontal Air's own forces have acquired the requisite range and payload capacities? Simply to work with a total inventory (all the beans) would be very misleading.

Since we are gauging Soviet success by the total ground attack munitions that must be delivered, the relevant (i.e., commensurable) beans are the Soviet planes that are actually designed and allocated to deliver ground attack munitions against the target set of interest (i.e., the Phase I set above).

Just as the target set is developed conservatively (as small as is plausible), so the relevant beans should be counted conservatively (as high as is plausible). The bean count is available in Appendix A. Out of all Soviet Frontal Air Forces deployed in Eastern Europe and in the Western Military Districts of the Soviet Union, and on assumptions that, if anything, inflate the force, the relevant beans number 1,682 (see Table A.4). This is the force of *pure* attackers, and, at over twenty-three U.S. wings' worth (72 per wing), it is comparable in size to the entire U.S. Tactical Air Command—that is, big.

READINESS

Not all these Soviet beans would be ripe, however. There remains the question of material readiness (we assume perfect pilot readiness below).

Peacetime "mission capability" and "deployability" were distinguished in Chapter I. The reader may recall that the former index bears information concerning the wartime sustainability of forces. As such, it embodies considerations of wartime logistics and the wartime management of ground support activities. It is a more demanding measure of readiness than "deployability," which makes no implicit judgment regarding sustainability or wartime ground support. This index presents the aircraft in essential isolation from the rest of the "weapon system" and registers the fraction of inventory that, for better or worse, could be brought to bear initially.

Commentary on the Soviet Air Force is rather insensitive to this distinction and, in turn, to its wartime implications. Thus, it is difficult to assess reports that "as more sophisticated aircraft such as the MiG-23 and SU-19 entered the inventory, the proportion available for assignment is reported to have declined to perhaps 70%."[2] While some such tradeoff between complexity and readiness is all too familiar to Americans, the questions remain: "Available for assignment" to do what? For how long? In what environment? Given what support infrastructure? When one recalls that mission capability rates for the American F-111 run in the 35 percent range, 70 percent sounds remarkably high, particularly if, as many claim, the Soviets' advanced ground attack plane (the SU-24 Fencer) may be thought of as "a slightly scaled down version of the F-111."[3]

The Soviets, as noted in Chapter III, indulge in peacetime cannibalization and face serious logistical constraints as well. Indeed, leaving wartime transportation issues aside, the Socialist Competition itself has encouraged the local manufacture of maintenance equipment and weapon system spare

[2] Berman, *Soviet Air Power in Transition*, p. 38.

[3] Colin Gray, "Soviet Tactical Airpower," *Soviet Aerospace Almanac, Air Force Magazine*, March 1977, p. 63. The Fully Mission Capable rate is 34.35% for the average month of fiscal year 1978 over all F-111 series aircraft including Air Force Reserve and National Guard. Computed in Epstein, *Political Impediments*, p. 55 from data presented in *USAF Summary*, Department of the Air Force (Washington, D.C.: Directorate of Cost and Management Analysis, Comptroller of the Air Force, March 1979), p. FOR.14. A peacetime Fully Mission Capable rate of 34% for the F-111D in particular is given in U.S. Congress, Senate, Committee on Armed Services, *Department of Defense Authorization for Appropriations for Fiscal Year 1982, Part 5—Preparedness: Hearings before the Senate Committee on Armed Services on S.815*, 97th Cong., 1st sess., 1981, p. 2451.

parts in order to make up deficits in state supply. But peace-time reliance upon cannibalization and projected wartime logistical shortages are among the factors underlying the low mission capability rates assigned to U.S. systems. It seems implausible, given the indications that the Soviets share the same problems, that their mission capability rate should be *twice* as high.

The 70 percent figure, then, while its exact meaning is some-what obscure, seems best interpreted as a measure of Soviet initial deployability. That is the general sense in which the term "readiness" will be employed in the technical analysis below. The wartime sustainability of Soviet operations—the other half of preparedness—will be handled separately under the topic of virtual attrition, taken up shortly.

Detailed assumptions are presented and discussed in Appendix A. But in summary, the ready, specifically ground attack force, from all Soviet Frontal Air Forces deployed in Eastern Europe and the USSR's Western Military Districts, will be assumed to number 1,109 frontline aircraft, a very significant force. Each of these, moreover, is assumed to carry four (appropriately tailored) air-to-ground munitions (see Appendix A). The initial loading of the attack force, then, is 4,436 munitions.

So, as a very crude preliminary gauge of the Soviets' problem, that initial loading, if accurately delivered, alone would erase a full quarter of the Phase I criterion (17,848 accurately delivered munitions). When one considers that the "average" Soviet aircraft might fly many missions in a single day, their problem doesn't seem that challenging—or does it?

RELATING INPUTS TO OUTPUTS

That, of course, depends on everything in between the relevant beans (the inputs) and the military goal they would achieve (the requisite output).

The number of such intervening factors (e.g., NATO's defenses, the Soviets' own operational shortcomings and "frictions") is, of course, immense; the true complexity of their interaction, equally so. But that has never prevented anyone from passing judgment on the Soviet threat, and it will not prevent us from attempting to do so more systematically.

The set of equations developed in Appendix B relates inputs to outputs. Like every other application of mathematics to the physical world, that system of equations is an *idealization.* Those stocks in trade of classical physics—frictionless surfaces, perfect vacuums, isolated systems, and elliptical planetary orbits—are, likewise, idealizations. Just as in physics, there are sharply increasing costs, in mathematical complexity and unwieldiness, to increasing "realism." So, before barging ahead to incur them (or to scold approaches that avoid them by design), it is worth recalling that, to construct a plausible *bound,* it is not necessary to attain *depictive precision.* Rather it is necessary to capture what—to the best of our knowledge —would be the dominant factors, and to do so conservatively; that is, without "building in" any assumptions biased against the Soviets.

Admitting the complexity of the "real" Soviet air campaign, those dominant factors are nonetheless discernible through the deafening "fury of war." Although the "conductor" (i.e., the high command) can choose the tempo, the underlying meter of all such operations is the same; the basic "beats" are these:

1. Some number of Soviet planes (the relevant and ready beans) launch the attack. Of those attackers,
2. a certain number elude attrition and make it to their targets, where they
3. launch their munitions (*n* per plane). Some of those munitions prove accurate; others miss their specified aim points (designated ground zeros, or DGZs). Having spent their payloads,
4. the Soviet planes head home. Along the way, some, again, suffer attrition.
5. Those that survive are rearmed at their bases, and receive as much maintenance as the tempo of war (and the enemy, NATO) allows before
6. taking off for the next sortie; and so on, until the music stops.

Each of these cycles is a sortie, and by definition, the number of cycles the Soviets complete per day is their sortie *rate*, the tempo.

Taking into account the latter's own limits and consequences (discussed below), the equations of Appendix B essentially formalize the above steps so that, over time, Soviet force attrition and the cumulative delivery of munitions can be tracked conservatively. When attrition finally consumes the simulated Soviet force, the total number of munitions that (in expected terms) have been accurately delivered on their DGZs is directly compared to the Phase I criterion of Soviet success—the target set, expressed in the same units (DGZs) of output (Table 5.1, above).

Since the simulation, albeit very crude, is *conservative* in its crudeness, it will suffice for purposes of bounding.

CENTRAL ASSUMPTIONS

Some of those conservative assumptions are completely formal, and have to do not with the specific numerical values employed, but with the purely algebraic, or logical, structure of the analytic procedure itself. One of these is rather subtle, and should be brought out explicitly.

The Phase I success criterion, recall, is expressed in designated ground zeroes or specified munition delivery points. It decomposes the Phase I target set into 17,848 separate "slots," if you will, for accurate munitions. Thinking of each accurate delivery as a marble, the success criterion presents a Chinese checkerboard of slots, one for each marble.

The equations developed in Appendix B, however, simply compute the *total* number of Soviet air-to-ground munitions which, in expected value, are delivered accurately over the course of the air campaign. The equations, that is, simply produce a bag of marbles (accurate deliveries). The Soviets "succeed" if the number of marbles in the bag is greater than (or equal to) the number of slots on the Chinese checkerboard.

Hidden in that aggregate comparison, however, is an "invisible hand" that deftly draws each marble from the bag and neatly places it in the *next open slot* on the board. Thus, by simply comparing *total* accurate deliveries (the bag) to the *total* DGZs of the target set (slots on the board) the analytic procedure inherently imputes a type of perfect efficiency to the Soviets: no munitions are delivered redundantly. Or, to put it differently, perfect damage assessment and efficiency in co-operative cross-targeting are assumed. A simple example will illustrate why this is so. (See Figure 5.1.)

Employing our "comparison of totals" approach, one would conclude that two Soviet planes, each carrying three muni-tions, would suffice (*ceteris paribus*) to cover three targets, at two DGZs apiece. The equations plop six marbles (accurate deliveries) into the bag and the "invisible hand" *distributes* these over the six slots in the board (two DGZs per target). Each plane hits its primary target (targets one and three) and then they combine their remaining munitions to suppress a third target (target two).

But, this fluid, cooperative shift to a third target requires, aside from greater range (unlimited in our simulations), a great deal of pilot flexibility and efficiency in command and control. Did targets one and three get their required dose of two muni-tions? This is the question of damage assessment. Though the real Soviets express concern about it, the simulated Soviets do it perfectly.

However, damage assessment would be only the first step in a reconnaissance/command-and-control process at whose every turn the Soviets report peacetime deficiencies. Sluggish

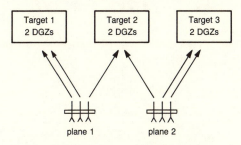

FIGURE 5.1 Perfect Cross-Targeting

staff work, overloads of information, the repetition of data that is already known, difficulties in using automated, computerized information processing systems; these are all problems of open concern to the Soviets. But they are all solved, instantaneously and without a hitch, by our simulated Soviet battle managers.

To assume, as the analytic framework does, irrespective of the specific numbers that are plugged into it, that such perfectly efficient teamwork and cooperative cross-targeting is executed everywhere, in a hostile environment, over a target set numbering in the thousands of DGZs, seems favorable to the Soviets. Certainly, U.S. Air Force planners would not generally assume their own forces to be capable of it when sizing up an air campaign, even though American reconnaissance, pilot training, and notably, information processing, remain in advance of the Soviets. The consequences of this simplifying assumption, moreover, are significant.

Returning to the illustrative example above, had more *realistic* assumptions been made, and perfect efficiency in the above sense ruled out, a third Soviet plane—a 33 percent increase in the force—would be required to do the same job, and in doing it, that force would waste munitions in the same proportion. (See Figure 5.2.) So, while the Soviet attack force is

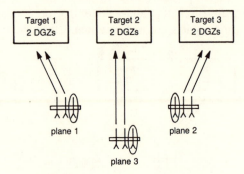

FIGURE 5.2 No Cross-Targeting. (Circled munitions are either wasted or delivered redundantly.)

accounted conservatively (i.e., large) to begin with, this implicit efficiency assumption artificially inflates it, by crediting the Soviets with a capacity to do with two planes what would otherwise require three. That particular ratio is, of course, illustrative. But the artificial force "boost" is there.

Is the analytic framework unrealistic? Decidedly. But is it unfavorable to the Soviets on that account? Not in my judgment. That is a *quantitative* judgment of analytical conservatism. But the purely *qualitative* appreciation of Soviet operational, "art of war," problems was necessary to make it. The craft of threat assessment is to simplify conservatively, but an appreciation of the "arts of war" is critical in judging whether one's simplifying assumptions are, in fact, *conservative*.

Two other types of purely formal simplifying assumptions are the exclusion of various factors from consideration, and the treatment of factors that would tend to vary *as if* they were constants. Many such assumptions will be encountered below, and in the Appendices. As in the above case, as long as they do not bias the analysis against the Soviets, such assumptions (unrealistic though they may be) will not endanger the construction of a plausible bound. In that sense, bounding and "modeling" (understood to be the attempt at mathematical depiction) are profoundly different enterprises. The former is necessary to assess threats, the latter—while it would be nice—is not. In turn, to criticize the first for the sins of the second is beside the point.

IVAN AND SAM REVISITED

Beyond such issues of "formal conservatism" is the more familiar question of what numbers to plug into one's idealizing equations, particularly on the Soviet side. A more extended discussion of this problem was presented in the Preface; it might profitably be reviewed at this point. Briefly, where trustworthy data are available, they are used. Where, as is frequently the case, they are not available, two options present themselves.

First, one can stop, "throw in the towel," and regress to bean counting. Or, one can try to proceed like a rational animal:

by fighting off the conditioned response that perfect measurements are necessary to make a reasoned judgment on bounds; by drawing the most intelligent inferences one can from the data that *are* available; and by varying one's assumptions so that the *consequences* of irreducible uncertainty may be gauged (sensitivity analysis). At the very least, the procedure will *identify* the critical areas of uncertainty, perhaps inspiring the collection of more useful data. At most, it will *reduce* uncertainty itself. But it will eliminate neither uncertainty nor the need for judgment.

Paradoxically, as long as *thousands* of numerical judgments are made simultaneously and *implicitly*—as in all higher discussions of the "global correlation of forces"—methodological calm prevails. But, somehow, judgments rendered *explicitly* on a *particular* number will provoke, from the same strategic gallery, a storm of affronted protest—"How do you know?!"

But I do not claim to "know." Nor should anyone be cowed out of analysis by pseudoscientific demands that an inherently illusory certitude be demonstrated. What degree of numerical precision is really required to do the job? The job is to establish a plausible *bound* on Soviet capabilities. To do that, it is sufficient to use numbers the Soviets are *unlikely to exceed;* once again, conservatism as against realism. Those may be the "wrong" numbers, in an engineering sense, but they will err on the side of favorability to the Soviets. If, on those assumptions, Soviet success proves implausible, then the "right" numbers would only render it less plausible. As stressed in the Preface, even the determination of numbers the Soviets are unlikely to exceed involves judgment. Some of those judgments, and the bases for them, are offered below.

Assumed Soviet Sortie Rate

Although other, even higher, values are entertained in the sensitivity analyses of Appendix C (see under Sortie Rate Demanded), we begin by assuming a Soviet sortie rate of six per day.

Even a cursory review of Chapter III should suggest how generous an assumption this is: the rigidity of the "flow-line"; an undersupply (and maldesign) of state-produced aerospace ground support equipment; difficulties in enforcing the use of what limited quantities of advanced AGS equipment is supplied; absorption of tight maintenance training time in the wasteful duplication of insular and nonpublicized innovation (features that tighten time constraints by reducing the value of predeployment training); misallocations of labor, all added to the myriad and time-consuming dissimulations that plague the Socialist Competition—these and more Soviet problems were described. Each of them would detract from the wartime efficiency of ground support activities, which, as discussed in Chapter I, is a critical determinant of the sortie rate.

Soviet dissatisfaction with the rigid flow-line system and all of its adverse effects, in turn, is evident in the priority accorded the inculcation of flexibility, independence, and personal initiative among technicians—capabilities, again, that have formed the basis for the U.S. Tactical Air Command's decentralized POMO system, also described in Chapter I, and designed to maximize American sortie rates under combat conditions. Moreover, by contrast to Soviet practice, the U.S. simulates those wartime sortie surges twice a week under POST.

Even so, the Soviets—with roughly half the support manpower per plane (see Appendix A)—are assumed here to generate a sortie rate fully *twice* as high as the U.S. Tactical Air Command's *goal* of three sorties per day. Unrealistic? Probably. Unfavorable to the Soviets? Not in my judgment.

Assumed Soviet Accuracy

Even if the Soviets had two pilots for each plane (higher than the highest American wartime crew ratio of 1.77 for the A-10), this sortie rate would require three combat sorties per crew per day.[4] Experts are emphatic regarding the enormous

[4] The A-10 crew ratio is given in Kolcum, "Difficulty of Challenge Determines Credit in Grey Flag," p. 195.

physical and psychological strain this pace would entail. We will assume not only that Soviet crews can take it, but can deliver with a mean accuracy of 0.75 throughout (i.e., that every munition launched has a 75 percent probability of hitting its designated ground zero).

In peacetime, under optimal daylight conditions, free of any harassment of any kind (electronic or other ground- or air-to-air), firing on a stationary target set out with crystal clarity against its background, the most highly skilled U.S. pilots using the most advanced air-to-surface munitions guidance systems known are reported to have scored 92 percent direct hits.[5]

U.S. officials, however, would be very ill-advised to plan on the assumption that such peacetime "laboratory" hit probabilities would be duplicated in war. While peacetime scores are generally reduced for wartime planning purposes, some, like former Secretary of Defense Brown, have warned that the wartime reduction factors in use may not be conservative enough. The difference between peacetime and wartime lethality has been disturbingly great. "For instance," Brown writes, "we assume that the kill reliability of the AIM-7E will be 0.5. Yet in Vietnam, the AIM-7E demonstrated a kill probability of only 0.11"—off by a factor of over four.[6]

Of course, the AIM-7E is an air-to-air missile, and would have a different "lab" score and wartime deflater than air-to-ground missiles. But, in the latter case, what little data is available indicates that precision-guided (laser and electro-optical) munitions (PGMs) achieved hit frequencies of between 0.41 and 0.55 when used in 1973 against bridges in Vietnam (Operation Linebacker), despite computer simulations by Texas Instruments a year earlier projecting accuracies close to

[5] "Variety of Air-Surface Weapons Studied," *Aviation Week and Space Technology*, 6 February 1978, opp. 165. The 92 percent figure refers to a test sequence of "about 178 firings" of the TV-guided Maverick (AGM-65A/B).

[6] Quoted in Schemmer, "Pentagon, White House, and Congress Concerned," p. 34.

100 percent for laser-guided bombs; again off, by a factor of roughly two.[7]

The Soviets' attack would not enjoy conditions even remotely resembling the U.S. peacetime "lab" environment described above. Especially were it to proceed around the clock as is generally assumed, the Frontal Air attack would not have optimal bombing conditions. At all times, Soviet pilots would be subjected to every manner of harassment (electronic and otherwise). Targets would not be set out with crystal clarity. They would have to be distinguished from background clutter. The discrimination, moreover, would have to be made flying at high velocities and low altitudes. This is particularly difficult, and it would still be so even if Soviet target acquisition systems were as sophisticated as the most sophisticated U.S. systems. This problem, that is to say, is one that the U.S. is far from having solved.[8]

Thus, even assuming that Soviet peacetime laboratory hit probabilities were in the 90 percent range, environmental and technological factors would surely reduce them in war. Beyond these important factors, moreover, there remain questions of Soviet wartime pilot skill. As discussed at length in Chapter IV, peacetime pilot skills in the Soviet case do not likely exceed U.S. pilot skills in this area. The more important point by far, however, is that the same factors constraining the development of Soviet pilot skills in peacetime would immeasurably increase their susceptibility to degradation in war.

---

[7] The figures 0.41 and 0.55 are computed from data given in *The Tale of Two Bridges and The Battle for the Skies Over North Vietnam*, USAF Southeast Asia Monograph Series, Volume 1, Monographs 1 and 2, ed. Major A.J.C. Lavalle (Washington, D.C.: Government Printing Office, 1976), p. 90. The lower figure counts only confirmed hits, the higher figure counts probable hits as well. The Texas Instruments projections are from "Smart Bombs" in *Commission on the Organization of the Government for the Conduct of Foreign Policy, Volume 4*, Appendix K, eds. Graham T. Allison et al. (Washington, D.C.: Government Printing Office, June 1975), p. 195.

[8] See Natalie W. Crawford, *Low Level Attack of Armored Targets*, P-5982 (Santa Monica, Calif.: The Rand Corporation, August 1977).

In particular, the less one is challenged by uncertainty in peacetime, the more one will be caught off guard by it in combat. "Simplification and indulgence," routinized and unrealistic exercises—these aspects of Soviet peacetime training, to recall the concerns of General Babayev, increase the likelihood that Soviet pilots will be "lost in a flight situation that is the least bit complex." War in Central Europe could be complex beyond all imagining. Deviations from the routinized mission would be unavoidable. Even in peacetime, however, the Soviets report accuracy degradations when missions are disturbed from their rote profiles.

The actual delivery of munitions, moreover, would be only the last step in the process of mission alteration, and would be preceded by a number of critical links; delivery might not be the weakest one.

Imagining that the relevant aerial reconnaissance is collected, that it is successfully transmitted *to* the command and that, upon its (instant?) analysis, ground controllers are instructed to order deviations from the Frontal Air plan, will the Soviet pilot *receive* the ground controller's order to deviate? Enhanced capacities for low-altitude flight and increased range and velocity are aspects of Soviet advancement that have multiplied problems of continuity in communications between an aircraft and any given ground controller. In addition, the same new capabilities appear to have deepened Soviet problems in preserving the integrity of ground control data links when the transfer of control is required.

Even assuming that all (and there are many more) such steps in the mission alteration process are successfully executed, and assuming that the pilot responds with the specified mission change, target acquisition still must occur before any weapons delivery. But, as reviewed above, Soviet military leaders report laxity in training for low-altitude target acquisition, as reflected in the peacetime necessity for repeated unplanned passes at the newly designated target. Only after all of this would a munition be delivered, and if Soviet reports are true, with degraded accuracy at that.

The point is that a great many things have to "go right" in order to change targets and destroy them—that is, to actually run an air campaign. The Soviets record peacetime problems at every step, from the reconnaissance phase through weapons delivery. In wartime, when, as the Soviets repeatedly stress, change is unavoidable, the severity of those problems could be far greater.

In what this analyst feels to be an estimate favorable to the Soviets, we will assume Soviet "lab" scores of 90 percent. Although military experience cautions that war may degrade accuracy by factors of two or more, we will derate the Soviets' "lab" hit probability by a mere 15 percent for *wartime* environmental, technological, pilot skill, and command, control, and communications problems.

The result is an assumed wartime hit probability of 0.75, higher than U.S. planners would generally assume in working back to their own force requirements. Considering in addition the absence in the Soviet case of either (a) munitions guidance systems as advanced as America's, or (b) such U.S. ground attack aids as forward-looking infra-red (FLIR) systems, the assumed wartime hit probability of 0.75 can only be regarded as favorable to the Soviets.

Assumptions Concerning NATO's Air Defense:
Soviet Actual Attrition

While the Soviets' offensive lethality is assumed to be as high as is plausible (if not higher), NATO's defensive lethality is, if anything, assumed to be just the reverse.

Single-shot kill probabilities for ground-based air defenses are, again, functions of many variables. While they are difficult to estimate, on average, they are agreed to be low. The Soviet value has been estimated at 0.05 (or, speaking very loosely, a kill for every 20 shots).[9] We will assume a NATO value of 0.05

---

[9] Major Tyrus W. Cobb, "Tactical Air Defense: Soviet-U.S. Net Assessment," *Air University Review*, March-April 1979, p. 28.

as well, both for ground-to-air and air-to-air missiles, in spite of the fact that, in the latter case, the AIM-7E's Vietnam score, although less than a quarter of projections, was over twice this high.

This numerical assumption—the assignment of a low Soviet estimate to NATO—basically denies the West any technological advantage in ground-based target acquisition, tracking, illumination, or accuracy. The assumption that the term is constant over time, moreover, frees the Soviets from any of the increases in aircraft vulnerability that may result from sustained maintenance deferrals (discussed below); for example, reductions in maneuverability through structural or hydraulic (swing-wing) failures, engine malfunctions, or avionic (jamming and other electronic countermeasures) degradation.

Finally, in estimating the *number* of shots to which each Soviet attacker would be exposed per sortie (see Appendix A), all those shots that the Soviets might take at their own planes were omitted. That is, perfect Soviet IFF is assumed throughout, though it is doubtful whether Soviet training provides the basis for such infallibility.

As a closing example, there is a second type of attrition that should be recognized beyond the direct form accounted for above; "warfare's greatest losses are not to the sudden and violent carnage of battle, but to the day-to-day losses brought on by wear and tear."[10]

Assumptions Concerning Virtual Attrition

As discussed in Chapter I, certain peacetime criteria of mission capability are often dispensed with in war. Military history includes many cases in which aircraft performed missions of which, by such peacetime criteria, they would not have been judged capable. But, while things are pushed to the limit in war, limits still exist. Sustained maintenance deferrals, par-

[10] James F. Dunnigan, *How to Make War* (New York: William Morrow and Co., 1982), p. 323.

ticularly in punishing wartime environments, can override even the most selfless willingness for combat. Aircraft defects can cumulate and ramify to the point of effective inoperability —the point at which direct maintenance personnel are simply incapable of returning the system to service, even under the vastly relaxed definitions of combat worthiness that have prevailed in war. Either the system receives more sophisticated attention or it will not perform; in certain cases, its restoration may prove infeasible regardless. Formally, such instances are straightforward reductions in the force; this is virtual attrition.

The term, however, is used to cover a wide variety of phenomena. In its most general usage, any mission failure that is not the result of direct enemy countermeasures is virtual attrition. It may be of longer or shorter duration. It may be a direct consequence of maintenance deferrals, and it may occur for reasons only indirectly related to maintenance. We shall use the term in a restricted sense, as denoting only maintenance deferral-related events that effectively remove the aircraft from participation in air operations.

The most subtle aspect of the phenomenon is its intimate relation to the sortie *rate* itself. As noted in Chapter I, to get at that relation, the basic idea is this:

First, we develop an estimate of the full (regimental plus depot) peacetime maintenance manhours per flight hour (M) for advanced Soviet Frontal Air deep interdiction planes: the full load, with *no deferrals*, and expressed in *Soviet* manhours. This might be thought of as the aircraft's *demand* for maintenance.

Second, having estimated (conservatively) that value, it is easy, by methods of Appendix B, to compute the fraction of that total peacetime maintenance (M) that must be deferred in order to surge up to any specified *wartime* sortie rate (e.g., six, as assumed above).

Finally, with each sortie flown at that surged rate—equivalently, at its requisite level of deferral—the probability of virtual attrition grows, and in expected value, so does the attrition itself.

The first problem, then, is to arrive at a reasonable estimate for the average Soviet total (regimental plus depot) maintenance manhours per flight hour (M) for frontline ground attack aircraft: the SU-24 Fencer, SU-17 Fitter, and MiG-27 Flogger D. While in the American case modernization has been attended by a dramatic increase in the value of this index (see Chapter I), no estimate of its Soviet value seems to have been attempted.

Chapter II argued that the Soviet value hinges on the *relative* adjustability of their ground support environment to changes in aircraft technology. What we require, therefore, is some measure of that adaptability. In particular, we need to measure (to bound) the change in total maintenance manhours per flight hour (M), induced by a decline in intersystem commonality (i.e., technological change).

Consider two systems, *system zero* and *system one*. Let $C(1, 0)$ denote the percentage of system one's subsystems that are also subsystems of system zero.[11] Let us imagine that system one is some follow-on to system zero, and that it "inherits," or incorporates, some of system zero's subsystems and has some new ones of its own.

By definition, the divergence of system one from complete commonality with system zero is: $1 - C(1, 0)$. This, in other words, is the fraction of system one's subsystems that are, in some sense, "new." Expressed as a multiple of $C(1, 0)$, the divergence of system one from complete commonality with system zero is given by:

$$\frac{1 - C(1, 0)}{C(1, 0)}.$$

Similarly, suppose system one's total maintenance manhour per flight hour (MMH/FH) requirement is M_1 and system zero's is M_0. Then the change in required MMH/FH

---

[11] $C(1, 0) \neq C(0, 1)$ in general. Obviously, if systems one and zero are identical, then $C(1, 0) = 1$ (or, for any system a, $C(a, a) = 1$). If systems zero and one share no subsystems whatever, then $C(1, 0) = 0$. Throughout, we assume that $0 < C(1, 0) < 1$.

is $M_1 - M_0$, and, expressed as a multiple of M_0, the change in MMH/FH is given by:

$$\frac{M_1 - M_0}{M_0}.$$

Define k to be the ratio of these two indices. That is:

$$k = \frac{\dfrac{M_1 - M_0}{M_0}}{\dfrac{1 - C(1, 0)}{C(1, 0)}}. \tag{1}$$

This ratio, k, gives us a crude measure of the adaptability of the ground support environment to a change in technology, as the latter is reflected in the denominator. If $k = 0$, then the ground support environment is perfectly adaptable; the introduction of new subsystems (denominator > 0) does not increase M. This would require that new skills, equipment, and manpower levels had been perfectly anticipated as the new technology is introduced. The higher k is, the less adaptable is the ground support environment to technological change. The limiting case, "$k = \infty$," would indicate a ground support environment so absolutely rigid that the introduction into that environment of a new system incorporating even a single new subsystem (extreme design incrementalism) would render completely obsolete the skills, equipment, and personnel available for the new system's maintenance; even the slightest technological advance would shoot M up to "infinity."

All of this may be clearer if we rewrite Eq. (1) as

$$\frac{M_1 - M_0}{M_0} = k\left(\frac{1 - C(1, 0)}{C(1, 0)}\right) \tag{2}$$

and graph it as a function of $C(1, 0)$ for various k values increasing from k_1 to k_3. (See Figure 5.3.)

As is evident, the higher k is, the greater is the increase in maintenance manhour requirements induced by a divergence from complete commonality, i.e., by the introduction of a new system (system one) incorporating new subsystems. At $k = k_1$,

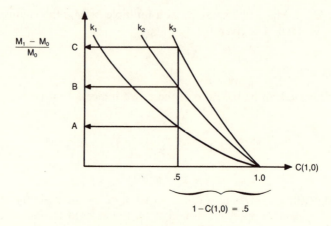

FIGURE 5.3 Dependence on k

the maintenance manhour ratio rises to A with the introduction of a system incorporating 50 percent new subsystems. At $k_2 > k_1$, the same divergence from commonality induces an increase in the maintenance index of B, and so forth for $k_3 > k_2$. Thus, if the Soviets' k is higher than America's, a *smaller* rate of technological change would still induce an equally (or more) dramatic increase in required maintenance manhours per flight hour. The graph in Figure 5.4 illustrates this "principle of relativity."

Even granting the Soviets more technological commonality and incrementalism than in the U.S. case—that is, assuming that each new generation of aircraft represents a smaller value of $1 - C(1, 0)$—this does *not* mean that Soviet maintenance manhours per flight hour haven't risen as much as America's have. Indeed, if the Soviets' k value is sufficiently greater than America's, a far *less* dramatic change in technology can produce a far *greater* increase in maintenance manhour requirements than the U.S. has experienced. This is illustrated in Figure 5.5, where the Soviet divergence from commonality is $1 - C(1, 0) = 1 - .75 = .25$ while the U.S. value is $1 - C(1, 0) = 1 - .5 = .5$. Nevertheless, the Soviets' higher k value

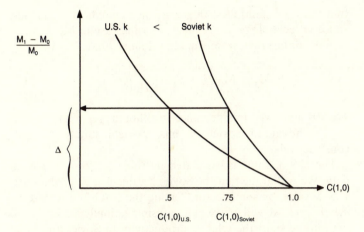

FIGURE 5.4 Principle of Relativity. (Δ is a standard mathematical symbol used to denote the change in some variable, in this case $(M_1 - M_0)/M_0$.)

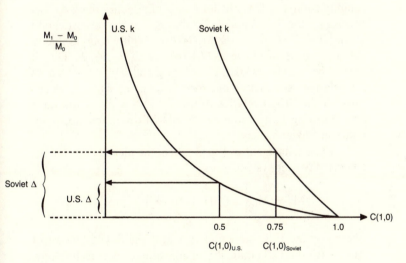

FIGURE 5.5 k as Multiplier

translates, or multiplies, this twice as "incremental" an advance in technology into a far greater increase in M.

Now, notice that, from Eq. (2), it follows that

$$M_1 = M_0 \left\{ 1 + k \left(\frac{1 - C(1, 0)}{C(1, 0)} \right) \right\}. \qquad (3)$$

To estimate M_1 (maintenance manhours per flight hour) for the advanced Soviet systems, we will simply proceed constructively.

The U.S. k value is calculated in Table 5.2 from available data. We will argue that the Soviet k value is greater than the U.S. k value by some factor. Taking the MiG-21 Fishbed as *system zero*, we will arrive at a plausible estimate for M_0 (taking into account the relative productivity of Soviet and U.S. maintenance manpower and the U.S. M for the U.S. system most closely related to the MiG-21 technologically). For an advanced Soviet *system one* then, all that remains is to estimate its commonality with the MiG-21. One might assume, for example, that the SU-24's commonality with the MiG-21 is roughly comparable to the level of commonality observed between, say, the F-14A and A-7E; that is, that the sophistication of the *SU-24 relative to the MiG-21* is roughly comparable to the sophistication of the *F-14A relative to the A-7E*. This, it should be noted, avoids the confusing and irrelevant issue of the relative "simplicity" of Soviet aircraft as against American—of the SU-24 relative to the F-14A—while at the same time allowing us to estimate the SU-24's maintenance manhours in Soviet terms.

As a last refinement of Eq. (3), then, the idea is that, for the advanced Soviet system,

$$M_1 = M_0 \left\{ 1 + k(1 + \delta) \left(\frac{1 - C(1, 0)}{C(1, 0)} \right) \right\} \qquad (4)$$

where k is the U.S. value and $(1 + \delta)$ is the Soviets' factor of relative (to the U.S.) difficulty in adjusting to new technology. (Again, system zero is the MiG-21.) All factors other than k are, of course, Soviet. Now, let's just fill in the blanks.

To begin, M_0 denotes the Soviet M value for the baseline system zero, the MiG-21 Fishbed D, the Soviets' first "all-weather" interceptor (entered service 1965). The U.S. aircraft now used by the American "aggressor" squadrons designed to simulate current Soviet air-to-air combat forces is the F-5E. The U.S. M value for this aircraft is 20.[12] Robert Berman cites the F-4 as being the system most similar to the MiG-21.[13] The lowest M value over all F-4 models is 34 maintenance man-hours per flight hour.[14] We will assume, very favorably to the Soviets that, in Soviet manhours, the benchmark MiG-21 is even lower than the F-5E. We will assume that it is midway between the F-5E (M = 20) and the F-5A/B. The latter absorb fewer maintenance manhours per flight hour than any other planes in the U.S. inventory. Their M value is 16.[15] Therefore, we will assume that $M_0 = \frac{1}{2}(20 + 16) = 18$ Soviet maintenance manhours per flight hour.

If, indeed, American technicians would find the MiG-21 Fishbed D most similar to the F-4 in its maintenance requirements, then, since in U.S. terms, the F-4's M is 34 (minimum), our Soviet ($M_0 = 18$) value in fact assumes the Soviet ground support environment to be a good deal *more* efficient than is the American, on a day-to-day basis. For all the reasons given in connection with sortie generation above (and many more below), this seems favorable to the Soviets.

Proceeding to the next factor, $k(1 + \delta)$, in Eq. (4), the U.S. k value (over all aircraft for which complete data was available) is computed in Table 5.2 to be 0.95.

In order to estimate M_1 for the Soviets, the factor $(1 + \delta)$ was appended to the U.S. k value above. This factor registers the Soviets' relative (to the U.S.) rigidity and inadjustability to technological change. A $\delta < 0$ would imply that the Soviet

[12] This figure was provided by the U.S. Air Force Doctrine and Concepts Division, Deputy Directorate for Long-Range Planning, Directorate of Plans in 1979.

[13] Berman, *Soviet Air Power in Transition*, p. 52.

[14] Blanco et al., Technology Trends, p. 26.

[15] Figure on F-5A/B courtesy of the USAF Doctrine and Concepts Division, 1979.

TABLE 5.2
The U.S. Average k Value

Aircraft Pair	$\dfrac{M_1 - M_0}{M_0}$	$\dfrac{1 - C(1,0)}{C(1,0)}$	k
F-4J = 1 F-4N = 0	$\dfrac{5.04}{35.52} = 0.14$	$\dfrac{0.09}{0.91} = 0.10$	1.40
A-7E = 1 A-7B = 0	$\dfrac{4.05}{19.96} = 0.20$	$\dfrac{0.31}{0.69} = 0.45$	0.44
F-4J = 1 A-7E = 0	$\dfrac{16.55}{24.01} = 0.69$	$\dfrac{0.38}{0.62} = 0.61$	1.13
F-4N = 1 A-7E = 0	$\dfrac{11.51}{24.01} = 0.48$	$\dfrac{0.33}{0.67} = 0.49$	0.98
F-14A = 1 A-7E = 0	$\dfrac{35.96}{24.01} = 1.50$	$\dfrac{0.54}{0.46} = 1.17$	1.28
F-4J = 1 A-7B = 0	$\dfrac{20.60}{19.96} = 1.03$	$\dfrac{0.45}{0.55} = 0.82$	1.26
F-14A = 1 F-4J = 0	$\dfrac{19.41}{40.56} = 0.48$	$\dfrac{0.58}{0.42} = 1.38$	0.35
F-4N = 1 A-7B = 0	$\dfrac{15.56}{19.96} = 0.78$	$\dfrac{0.44}{0.56} = 0.79$	0.99
F-14A = 1 F-4N = 0	$\dfrac{24.25}{35.52} = 0.68$	$\dfrac{0.58}{0.42} = 1.38$	0.49
F-14A = 1 A-7B = 0	$\dfrac{40.01}{19.96} = 2.0$	$\dfrac{0.63}{0.37} = 1.70$	1.18 $\Sigma = 9.50$

U.S. average k value $= \dfrac{\Sigma}{10} = 0.95$

SOURCE: Computed from data presented in Blanco et al., *Technology Trends.*

ground support environment has been *more* adjustable than that of the U.S. Positive δ's impute *less* adjustability to the Soviets (equal divergences from complete commonality more dramatically raise the Soviet M), while a δ of zero would set Soviet adjustability equal to that of the U.S.

As was documented in Chapter III, it is hard to believe that the Soviets have avoided adjustment problems at least as severe as those encountered by the U.S. The Soviets have failed to supply adequate quantities of advanced aerospace ground support equipment, relying on the Socialist Competition to make up the deficit. But the inherently reactive and "after the fact" nature of local innovation builds in an adjustment lag even where it succeeds. The extreme specificity of locally generated AGS equipment, moreover, renders it unadaptable to follow-on aircraft technologies. Indeed, aircraft technology has advanced to the point where regiments find themselves incapable of designing and fabricating equipment of the requisite sophistication. Thus, an increasing reliance on depot R&D has emerged. This process, the evidence suggests, only *begins* when—after much time and, presumably, effort—the regiment can demonstrate its inability to produce the technology, regimental production being the apparently preferred course (judging from the flow of *manufacturing* technology from the depot to the regiment). Then an interval of preliminary depot assessment ensues, followed by a collaborative R&D endeavor, culminating in virtual re-equipping of the obsolete regimental facility. Presumably, this would be followed by a training period *in* the regiment on the new depot-supplied equipment, subject to all the serious constraints on the efficiency of Soviet training generally.

Although standardization is an apparent *goal* of depot R&D, nonstandard equipment continues to proliferate. Its nonstandardization, high specificity, and limited production runs (due either to limited depot responsibilities or to the insularity of regimental innovation) have reduced the effective training time of recruits since, as noted above, predeployment training is useless if the actual equipment exists only in the producing units (or in a limited number of depot-supplied units) that possess it.

Many of those factors that reduce the day-to-day efficiency of ground support activities also reduce adjustability to new technology. For example, the fixed positions, detailed time norms, and sequence diagrams of a given flow-line become obsolete with the introduction of new aircraft technology and new maintenance requirements. How long must it take the Soviets, following depot production (and training on depot-produced equipment) to identify and then implement the "new" appropriate flow-line? Notwithstanding all the systemic inefficiencies of the method per se, it could take quite a while, particularly since depot R&D itself begins *after* the built-in lag of regimental innovation is fully played out on the stage of the Socialist Competition.

It might be noted that variations in equipment will likely generate an equally colorful variety of flow-lines and implementation times. Where is a centralized authority to begin in standardizing procedures so that "the" impact of a new technology could be predicted in any meaningful sense?

Misreportage of equipment status and labor productivity, nonuniformities in their local assessment (no uniform grading scheme), and lack of Party expertise in managing the technological transition all combine with the familiar abuses of the Socialist Competition not only in deepening the Soviets' adjustment problems, but in militating against their orderly and planned correction.

That the problem is of deep concern to high Soviet military authorities is evidenced by their advocacy of greater standardization, now a prime goal of depot R&D; advocacy, that is, of precisely such approaches as the U.S. Navy's VAST system (see Chapter III) and the analogous U.S. Air Force Standard Hardware Module Program.

In short, while advocating them, the Soviets have failed to adopt measures like VAST and POMO that have been successful in minimizing the serious adjustment problems the U.S. has encountered. Not only have the Soviets failed to adopt successful U.S. measures, but to make matters worse, they are vigorously pursuing demonstrably unsuccessful courses quite foreign to the U.S. experience. Soviet "design philosophy," moreover, provides not the slightest promise of relief from their adverse effects since, as established in Chapter II, and formalized above, the whole question turns not on the technology per se, but rather on the ground support environment's adjustability to a *change* in technology.

The assumption that the Soviets have enjoyed *greater* success than the U.S. in adjusting to new technology simply runs counter to this fund of evidence. While the extent of the Soviets' relative disadvantage in this area is open to question, there is no basis for assuming that they enjoy any advantage whatsoever.

Mathematically, this is to say that negative δ values are implausible. To this analyst, $\delta = 0$ (Soviets and U.S. equally adjustable) is not plausible either. While it is hard to imagine any particular upper bound on the index, in what this author judges to be an estimate favorable to the Soviets, we will assume that $\delta = 0.15$, or that the Soviet ground support environment is 15 percent less adjustable (in the strict sense defined above) than is the American. Recognizing, however, that reasonable and equally informed people may disagree on judgments of conservatism, a range of alternative δ values and their consequences is provided in the sensitivity analyses of Appendix C.

Incorporating this estimate, Eq. (4) now reads:

$$M_1 = 18 \left\{ 1 + (0.95)(1 + 0.15) \left(\frac{1 - C(1, 0)}{C(1, 0)} \right) \right\}.$$

All that remains, therefore, is a reasonable estimate for the extent of Soviet frontline ground attack technology, which is not present in the 1965 vintage MiG-21.

Internal consistency has never been a hallmark of the American defense debate, but one of its more glaring anomalies deserves note in this connection. On the one hand, we are regularly admonished that the Soviets are fast eroding the West's once clear technological edge in the air. Well, clearly, the West has not been standing still technologically. So if, starting from behind, the Soviets are gaining, then they must be going *faster* than the West in some sense. Yet the common wisdom on Soviet "design philosophy" holds that the Soviets are more cautious, restrained, technologically conservative than we; in short, that they go *slower* in some sense.

But, if they're going slower, how can they be going faster, eroding the West's edge? The point is that you can't have it both ways. As usual, the truth probably lies somewhere in between. Certainly, a legitimate concern with Soviet technological progress would lead one to believe that Soviet frontline attack aircraft have *less* in common with the old MiG-21 than the American F-4J has in common with the F-4N.

Otherwise, they could hardly have progressed beyond the MiG-21 to the point of comparability with anything as advanced as the American F-111. For the F-4J and F-4N,

$$\frac{1 - C(\text{F-4J, F-4N})}{C(\text{F-4J, F-4N})} = 0.10.$$

The divergence from complete commonality is slight.

Attributing to the Soviets greater conservatism than the U.S. has demonstrated, we will assume that their frontline aircraft have *more* in common with the elder MiG-21 than the F-14A has with the A-7B. The same statistic, computed for these two aircraft, is 1.70 (see Table 5.2).

We will assume this to be the Soviets' bracket and will assign their side of the "technological arms race" the average of these two values. Completing the right-hand side of Eq. (4), then, we will assume

$$\frac{1 - C(1, 0)}{C(1, 0)} = (1.70 + 0.10)\frac{1}{2} = 0.9.$$

Finally, then, our best estimate of the average frontline M value is, recovering all of Eq. (4):

$$M_1 = 18\{1 + (0.95)(1 + 0.15)(0.9)\},$$

or

$$M_1 = 35.70.$$

This, it might be noted, compares very favorably with the F-111's value of $M = 54$ and attributes to the Soviets a remarkable degree of ingenuity in design, wringing major advances in performance (see assumed Soviet accuracy above) from minimal introductions of new technology.[16]

The methodological point bears repeating. Here was a case (perhaps the best one) in which *no* Soviet value was available. We therefore asked "What would the value depend on; what are its basic constituents?" With a little thought (the relativity argument) these proved to be identifiable, and American data was available on them. Then, by applying purely *qualitative* arguments, it was possible to draw a reasonable *quantitative* inference, allowing analysis to proceed.

Using this value and a few others developed in Appendix A (e.g., direct Soviet maintenance personnel per plane), the equations of Appendix B allow calculation of the Soviet sortie rate that is feasible with absolutely *no deferrals* of maintenance. From there, the same equations allow one to calculate the fraction of the above Soviet peacetime M value (35.7) that would have to be deferred in order to surge up to the assumed Soviet sortie rate of six per day. In the case of advanced Soviet systems, that sortie rate would dictate truly precipitous deferrals of maintenance, on the order of 80 percent deferred.[17] This would increase their susceptibility to virtual attrition (our original topic) considerably. In judging that susceptibility, recourse to the American experience will again prove useful.

Relative U.S. and Soviet Susceptibility to Virtual Attrition

Highly sophisticated weapon systems may suffer virtual attrition due to technological failures that are not even possible in less sophisticated systems. On the other hand, virtual attrition may occur for reasons of peacetime training or wartime

---

[16] Figure on F-111 courtesy of the USAF Doctrine and Concepts Division, 1979.

[17] Maintenance deferral rates for most of the runs presented in Chapter VI and Appendix C are given in the Annex of Epstein, *Political Impediments*. The exact figure to which I allude above is 0.84, the Simulation I (see next chapter) value. See dissertation Annex, p. 427.

labor efficiency that have very little to do with system durability. If one had to generalize, the U.S. would appear to be—relative to the Soviets—more susceptible to the former sources of virtual attrition, while the Soviets would appear to be more susceptible to the latter.

An extreme example of virtual attrition on the U.S. side is provided by the Air Force's Pave Tack FLIR attack aid program. Presence of the Pave Tack pod affects, among other things, the weight and drag of aircraft, such as the F-4E and F-111F, on which it is mounted. The flight control computers found on these aircraft are programmed to take into account the aerodynamic effects of the Pave Tack pod in solving their flight control problems. The trouble is that without constant attention (i.e., even at minuscule deferrals), the computers provide the "with pod" flight control solution even when no pod is present. Weapons delivery accuracy, in such cases, is virtually zero and, although the aircraft have not been shot down (actually attrited), they might as well have been, given their near-zero effectiveness.[18] This is virtual attrition by what, finally, is a software failure, but it is an affliction reserved only for the technologically advanced—a "rich man's disease," as it were.

Although it is generally agreed that Soviet systems are in some respects "simpler" than U.S. systems, this alone does not warrant the assumption that their susceptibility to virtual attrition would be lower. For example, vacuum tubes, though simpler, are far less resistant to vibrational fatigue than are integrated circuits, and the low-altitude profiles assumed for new Frontal Air interdiction forces would subject avionics to an especially rough ride. There is reason to doubt, moreover, that Soviet "design philosophy" has maximized the wartime reliability of ground attack avionics. In particular, the design principle of simplicity, when applied to *both* the avionics *and* the airframe, may result in far lower avionics field reliability than greater complexity might have afforded.

---

[18] I am grateful to the Rand Corporation's Engineering and Applied Sciences Department for this example. Interview, Summer, 1980.

As was discussed in Chapter II, the Soviets' simpler variable geometry wing scheme (hinging the armament close to the fuselage on an immovable portion of the wing) circumvents the U.S. requirement for servomechanisms compensating the armament for variations in the wing's changing angle to the line of flight. The Soviet avionics suite is simpler in that such servomechanisms are absent. But, in adhering to the simplicity principle in design, some performance is traded away in the unavoidable, or nonreducible, lift imparted by the fixed portion of the wing—a portion larger than in the U.S. case.

By comparison to the U.S., then, the avionics are simpler, both component-wise (vacuum tube versus integrated circuit) and in the subsystem count (no servos), the latter as afforded by the simpler sweptwing scheme. Does the coincidence of all these "simplicities" enhance the reliability of the avionics? The simpler wing, since it has greater lift, will subject *each* simpler (vacuum tube) component of the simpler (fewer components— no servos) avionics suite to far greater vibrational fatigue. Intuitively speaking, the greater the lift, the more violent will be the effects of a turbulent, dense, low-altitude medium. Second, the "fixed-portion" swing-wing scheme leaves a greater length of leading edge perpendicular to the incident air stream, adding to the air resistance and, hence, the shock. In addition, Dr. Alexander has noted a "lack of detailed finishing" as characteristic of Soviet simplicity.[19] This increases further the air resistance encountered at low altitude, adding a third order of shock to Soviet systems.

Overall, while the particular simplicity of Soviet avionics appears to increase their vulnerability to such fatigue, the simplicity of the Soviet airframe appears to leave them highly exposed to vibration. Is a "simple" avionics suite more reliable if a "simple" airframe exposes each of its (fewer) components to greater stress? Would greater reliability be achieved by a more complex (with servos) avionics suite mounted on an airframe subjecting each of its (more numerous) components to less fatigue? "Laboratory" avionics reliability, in the latter

[19] Alexander, *Weapons Acquisition*, p. 8.

case, might be lower, but its resistance to wartime environmental degradation could be significantly higher! Its *wartime* durability, in turn, might be higher, and thus, its capacity to operate under sustained deferrals of maintenance could be greater. The performance of nonelectrical components of Soviet avionics, under sustained deferrals, may be equally delicate. Robert Lucas Fischer, correctly noting that "simple technology is not necessarily more reliable," writes, "it is reported that the MiG-21's gyro gunsight has to be realigned after any turn of more than 2.7 g."[20] Failure to provide such maintenance, it would appear, could produce systematic errors perfectly analogous to the Pave Tack case mentioned above.

The unrealistic and routine features of Soviet peacetime flying leave such questions more open still since, due to "simplification and indulgence," as it were, Soviet avionics in peacetime may never be exposed to wartime environmental stressing—and certainly not for days in succession at high sortie rates and, as noted above, exceedingly high deferral rates.

On the purely technological side of the virtual attrition coin, then, the extent of any Soviet wartime advantage is unclear. However, nontechnological factors loom even larger as likely sources of Soviet virtual attrition in any case.

By all accounts, the Soviets do less "gold-plated" maintenance in peacetime than the U.S. Thus, they would appear to have less "slack" maintenance to begin with. An equal percentage of total M deferred would thus be likely to cut deeper into the truly necessary manhours than in the U.S. case.

Second, the Soviets seem to lack any intermediate (ML_2) cushion to fall back on in war. Soviet depots appear to be remote facilities and shipment of aircraft for depot repair would require use of transport, which in war would likely be strained (or at least allocated) to reinforce the ground battle.

---

[20] Robert Lucas Fischer, *Defending the Central Front: The Balance of Forces*, Adelphi Paper no. 127 (London: The International Institute for Strategic Studies, Autumn 1976), p. 3ln.

Even assuming depot repair of aircraft would be given priority over the ground campaign, shipment would be time-consuming and aircraft could remain virtually attrited for a long time. For example, F-4 depot repair times of two years became the norm during the Vietnam war.[21]

Among the main issues, therefore, is the likelihood that depot repair would be necessary in war—the likelihood that Soviet regimental cadres alone would prove unprepared to meet wartime supportability requirements. The routinized and unrealistic features of Soviet peacetime training make this an extremely difficult estimate (and not only for us). But a number of things seem clear.

Since, by all accounts, Soviet peacetime flying does not expose aircraft to wartime stress, one can easily imagine Soviet direct maintenance personnel confronted in wartime with aircraft defects they have literally never seen in peace. Even in peacetime, the Soviets report that fault isolation (finding what went wrong) now absorbs 80 percent of maintenance time.[22] These are faults induced by simplified and unrealistic flying. Would the Soviets, in war, divert personnel from the turnaround of functioning aircraft first to fault isolation and then to the repair of unfamiliar aircraft dysfunctions? This does not seem likely. Virtual attrition seems far more likely.

If, as this analyst suspects, the "design philosophy" of the regimental innovator is to produce as simple a device as will allow the satisfaction of peacetime (simplified) maintenance duties, then an interesting possibility presents itself: no equipment may even exist, either to diagnose or to repair dysfunctions not called forth by peacetime flying. Even given the wartime "will," the wartime "way" may not be open.

While the strictly reliability-related aspects of virtual attrition *may* loom larger for sophisticated U.S. systems, the difference may be more than offset by the deficiencies of Soviet

[21] Schemmer, "Pentagon, White House, and Congress Concerned," p. 30.
[22] Yulin, "The Use of Precision Charts," p. 113. The centrality of fault isolation as a U.S. maintenance problem and its connection to "black-boxing" are discussed in Epstein, *Political Impediments*, p. 95.

peacetime training and the rigidity of wartime operational management. All things considered, there is little reason to assume any particular Soviet *advantage* in regard to virtual attrition.

If it is implausible that the Soviets would do any *better* in this area than the U.S., then we will not be biasing the analysis against the Soviets by assigning them the American virtual attrition probability. The obvious question, then, is "how badly would the U.S. do on the virtual attrition front?" In this analyst's judgment, quite badly.

The American estimate involves both formal and numerical judgments. Each is presented in Appendix B. But to take one example—a point from the assumed virtual attrition probability curve—those judgments imply that, for sophisticated American systems (e.g., the F-15) operating in the type of punishing wartime environment the Soviets would face, a maintenance deferral rate of 30 percent, sustained for fifteen combat sorties, would result in a probability of virtual attrition slightly greater than 80 percent (see Appendix B). The same function by which that point is generated is applied, fairly in my view, to the Soviets.

Now, this may seem tough on the Soviets, but it's tough on them because (a) they're no better than the U.S., and (b) the U.S. is bad. Moreover, anyone who feels this to be unduly harsh should bear in mind that the definition of virtual attrition has been less than fully general and, if anything, unduly lenient.

Limited, as it has been, to maintenance deferral-related events, many other sources of virtual attrition have been stayed from the Soviets' path. The defense, for example, does not attack a single airbase. Thus, virtual attrition of aircraft through actual attrition of ground support personnel, while a phenomenon to which the Soviets appear particularly vulnerable, is one to which they are not exposed in our simulations. Ivan has "his" station on the flow-line, and "his" specialized function—perhaps he uses essential equipment of his own devising on which others lack training or experience. Who takes over for Ivan? "Interchangeability of personnel" is a problem of open concern to the Soviets, one they record little success is redressing. Such flow-line breakdowns could be sources of virtual attrition, even where aircraft operate from their home bases. Beyond this, however, the insularity and system-specificity of local innovation have combined with the same highly specialized (one aircraft type) training of Soviet ground support personnel to produce a serious interoperability problem. Bases other than an aircraft's home base may be thoroughly unfamiliar with its technology and are unlikely to possess ground support equipment adaptable to the system's repair. Spare parts, where they were "home-base fabricated," are likely to be in equally short supply, as would be the skills necessary to fix "foreign" (and especially battle-damaged) aircraft in any event.

Recovery to alternate bases, therefore, could easily result in virtual attrition. But, while the Soviets would face serious interoperability problems, no interoperability is called for in our simulations. Nor are sortie rates penalized for the time that would be spent rerouting aircraft under even the most efficient response to airbase attack.

NATO's destruction of Soviet bases, moreover, would be only the most obvious and inelegant—though surely the most decisive—exploitation of Soviet problems. Even in peacetime, the Soviets report difficulties in the reassertion of ground control once data links are broken. NATO attacks on the ground control system, or jamming of that system, even the forcing of Soviet aircraft outside their data links—any one of these and more could easily lead to serious pilot disorientation and the uncoordinated search for alternate recovery areas—and to virtual attrition. The same tactics could induce mission aborts, failures of target acquisition, bombing redundancies, multiple target passes (and greater exposure to defenses), and other losses in sortie effectiveness. None of these tactical opportunities is exploited; no attrition of Soviet maintenance personnel takes place; no Soviet airbases are destroyed.

In failing to attack Soviet airbases, moreover, the simulated defense forgoes a classical avenue to air superiority—destruction of aircraft on the ground. Not only, then, have important sources of *virtual* attrition been ignored, but the Soviets have not been subjected to this basic type of *actual* attrition either.

In short, NATO's entire defense is represented as a totally static and unresponsive entity, at no point challenging the Soviets with anything unexpected or requiring that they diverge one whit from the implicit "fire plan" played out below. The Soviet pilot is never challenged to diverge from the routine, to maneuver, or to show initiative or creativity. Neither does the simulated defense challenge the Soviet ground support or ground control systems with any unexpected counters.

Moreover, as icing on this cake of conservatism, the Soviets are even awarded a "free" (i.e., attritionless) first sortie; perfect surprise is, in that sense, assumed. As for deception—the great equalizer between the Soviets' conflicting doctrinal precepts of mass and surprise—the Soviets are assumed to be perfectly deceptive in replacing their deployed force of trainer aircraft with exclusively frontline ground attack systems.

If our assumptions are biased, then surely overall they are biased in favor of the Soviets. In fact, to many, all of this may seem an exercise in "worst case" analysis. But as stressed in the Preface, "worst *plausible* case" is different from "worst *possible* case." Indeed, no analysis of any kind is needed to arrive at the latter—just imagine the worst! But when the former is conducted in a balanced and thorough way, many of the more alarming estimates of Soviet capability are seen to be unwarranted.

CHAPTER VI

SOVIET CAPABILITIES AND SOVIET DOCTRINE

Against the Phase I target set (i.e., the criterion of Soviet success), and four even less demanding alternates, listed in Table 6.1 below, two main simulations are conducted.

Simulation I is a furious attack in which Soviet forces deployed in Eastern Europe are joined by those of the USSR's Western Military Districts to maximize the initial mass of the Frontal Air assault. Together, those combined forces operate at an exceedingly high intensity (a sortie rate of six per day) with the intent of completing the Phase I (conventional counternuclear) operation in the shortest possible time, and going on to Phase II (coordinated with, and in support of, the ground forces).

Simulation II addresses the question of whether Soviet results improve if, instead of that furious, high intensity attack from maximum initial mass, Frontal Aviation operates at a more measured pace (three sorties per day), sustaining echeloned operations (Soviet forces in Eastern Europe launch the attack alone, followed two days later by those of the Western Military Districts) over a longer period of time. The comparison is revealing on the question of Soviet doctrine, taken up below.

In each simulation, numerical assumptions discussed in the previous chapter, and others given fully in Appendices A and B are simply applied in the equations developed in Appendix B. The results are tables of Soviet force attrition and cumulative target destruction (in designated ground zeroes) over time. Those tables are presented in Appendix C. Plotted as curves, Simulations I and II are graphed in Figure 6.1, below the Phase I criteria to which they are compared in the discussion that follows. The corresponding tables in Appendix C

TABLE 6.1
Phase I Target Data Inventory with Alternates

Target Class	Number	DGZs/ Target	DGZs
FULL PHASE I			
C^3	234	5	1,170
TNW	320	8	2,560
TNW Storage	100	12	1,200
Subtotal			4,930
Hawk/Hercules[a]	909	2	1,818
Tactical Air Bases	50	222	11,100
Total DGZs			17,848
ALTERNATE 1			
Subtotal			4,930
Hawk/Hercules	909	1	909[b]
Tactical Air Bases	50	222	11,100
Total DGZs			16,939
ALTERNATE 2			
Subtotal			4,930
Hawk/Hercules	909	1	909
Tactical Air Bases	50	170	8,500
Total DGZs			14,339
ALTERNATE 3			
Subtotal			4,930
Hawk/Hercules	909	1	909
Tactical Air Bases	50	150	7,500
Total DGZs			13,339
ALTERNATE 4			
Subtotal			4,930
Hawk/Hercules	909	1	909
Tactical Air Bases	50	100	5,000
Total DGZs			10,839

SOURCE: See Appendix A.

NOTE: Each alternate includes the subtotal of 4,930 DGZs from Full Phase I (C^3, TNW, and TNW Storage). To that subtotal is added the alternative Hawk/Hercules and Air Base requirements, yielding the alternate's total DGZ number.

[a] These are the Air Defense corridor targets from NATO's Surface-to-Air Missile (SAM) belt.

[b] The same total DGZ subrequirement of 909 is compatible with different assumptions on the number of targets and DGZs per target. One might assume, for example, 303 targets at 3 DGZs apiece, imagining a more concentrated effort over a narrower axis of attack.

should, of course, be consulted if any numbers discussed are not immediately evident from the curves themselves.

Is it Plausible?

Under all the favorable assumptions built into the equations themselves, and under all the favorable assumptions made in assigning numbers to the variables in those equations, Soviet Frontal Aviation falls short of the Phase I success criterion, and each of its less demanding alternates, by a *very* wide margin.

At total destruction of 7,206 DGZs, the *more* destructive of the two attacks, Simulation I, falls 10,642 DGZs short of the Phase I criterion (17,848 DGZs), and a robust 3,633 DGZs short of its fourth, and *least* demanding alternate (10,839 DGZs).

Is it plausible, in light of all this, that Frontal Aviation has in fact acquired the capability to execute the two-phased attack of concern to the West—an attack whose first phase alone has been simulated, and one far more demanding of sustained coordination, flexibility, individual skill, and myriad other capabilities than is the Phase I operation as idealized here?

To answer in the affirmative is to commit oneself to the position (a) that our generous assumptions have been *exceedingly unfavorable* to the Soviets, and (b) that our simulation of NATO's defense has *vastly exaggerated* its capability to exploit the host of Soviet vulnerabilities documented above. One must be prepared to take and to defend this position if one is to argue the plausibility of the Frontal Air threat; this is the only position with which its plausibility is *consistent*. That the Soviets may someday acquire the capability to execute that larger two-phased campaign is a possibility. That they could today execute even its first phase—the independent air operation—though also a possibility, seems an extremely remote one.

What Level of Destruction *Is* Plausible?

To assert the implausibility of Soviet success, even in Phase I, is by no means to deny that Frontal Aviation is an object worthy of *very* serious concern. On the contrary, and in stark

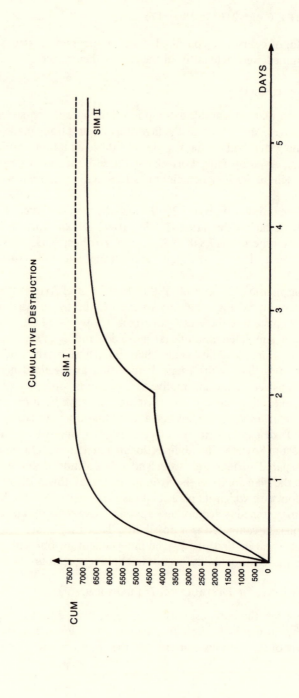

CUMULATIVE DESTRUCTION

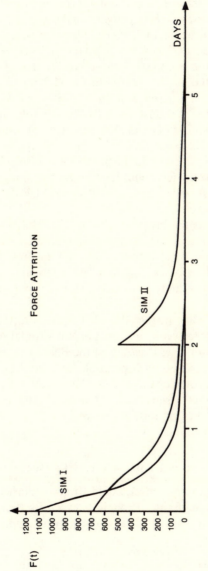

FIGURE 6.1 Cumulative Destruction and Force Attrition in Simulations I and II. (See Tables C.2 and C.3 for the data plotted in these curves.)

contrast to its defensive past, Frontal Aviation has clearly acquired an imposing offensive conventional capability. At total Simulation I destruction of 7,206 DGZs, the Soviets could destroy the significant C^3 system (1,170 DGZs) developed above while, in addition, suppressing those NATO theater nuclear missile (2,560 DGZs) and TNW storage (1,200 DGZs) facilities considered here. Even were their initial air defense corridor to represent a robust 1,818 DGZs, the total for these targets would be 6,748 DGZs. The Soviets could satisfy this with 7,206 − 6,748 = 458 DGZs to spare. At the somewhat less secure corridor expenditure of 909 DGZs (see alternates in Table 6.1), the Soviets could turn to the remaining Phase I targets (airbases) with 7,206 − 5,839 = 1,367 DGZs in their account, as it were.

Taking these as the brackets (458 to 1,367 DGZs surplus), it would appear that the Soviets could proceed to disrupt (at 100 DGZs per base) between four and, at most, thirteen NATO tactical airbases. Large-scale suppression (at 222 DGZs per base) of more than half a dozen, however, seems highly unlikely.[1]

In summary, while neither the full Phase I attack nor any of its four alternates yet seems plausible for Frontal Aviation, focused attacks on *critical subsets* of the Phase I target set lie well within its capability: it *is* plausible that, having opened a relatively secure corridor through NATO's SAM belt, Frontal Air could interdict a significant C^3 network and the above NATO theater nuclear missile group, as well as associated TNW storage facilities.

How Quickly, and with What Force Remaining?

This interdiction, moreover, could be accomplished within a very narrow time frame. Though its exact duration would, again, depend on one's air defense corridor assumptions, the

---

[1] Implicit in this discussion is a certain sequencing of Soviet targets. That is not immutable, and the reader is invited to consider the effect of changes in it (e.g., the Soviets, having opened their air defense corridor, might attempt to suppress NATO's airbases before moving on to the other targets).

echeloned Simulation II attack would require three days (assuming 909 DGZs for the corridor) to four days (assuming 1,818 DGZs for the corridor). On either corridor assumption, however, the concentrated high-intensity Simulation I attack could suppress the same critical subsets on the opening day of hostilities.

Frontal Aviation would emerge, however, with the capability to inflict only marginal damage to NATO's tactical airbase system and with virtually no capability to prosecute the Phase II operation.

IMPACT ON THE GROUND WAR

There can be no doubt that this Frontal Air attack could *disrupt* NATO's conventional defense. That such an attack would *prove devastating*, however, seems eminently unlikely. In particular, aside from its impact on that portion of NATO's C^3 system included here, and the few airbases which Frontal Air might suppress, the entire Phase I operation would appear to have little immediate bearing on the ground war.[2] Certainly, Phase II operations could have a serious impact upon it, but any concerted attempt at the nuclear-oriented Phase I attack would exhaust the Soviet force. In-theater reinforcements, lines of communication, POMCUS stocks (sets of U.S. division equipment, Prepositioned Materiel Configured to Unit Sets), the preponderance of NATO's tactical air, and large segments of NATO's C^3 net would not have been affected by Frontal Air, nor, most importantly, would engaged NATO ground forces themselves.

Whether the Soviets believe that NATO's military cohesion would be fatally undermined by that destruction of which Frontal Air *is* capable, one cannot say. What is quite clear, however, is that in prosecuting the Phase I attack, the Soviets

---

[2] The destruction of truly critical C^3 facilities, it should be stressed, could very seriously reduce the effectiveness of NATO's air and ground operations, though, for reasons pointed out in developing our target set, the wartime criticality of the *particular* C^3 system developed here is uncertain.

are likely to trade away direct Frontal Air support of the ground forces (Phase II) in exchange for this limited degradation of NATO's nuclear response capability.[3]

SENSITIVITY ANALYSIS

Even though these results indicate that the destructive potential of Frontal Aviation has expanded to significant proportions, holding at risk an array of theater nuclear and other NATO targets, some may feel that this estimate of Soviet capabilities is too low. It may be; any analysis of this sort is subject to uncertainty. The question is not *whether* uncertainty exists; but *how much* uncertainty or error can the basic conclusions tolerate? How wrong would the underlying—to my mind, conservative—assumptions *have to be* in order to call those conclusions into doubt? Very wrong.

In Appendix C, a great many runs on alternative assumptions are presented. Though the reader is invited to conduct yet more of them, *none* of the variations reviewed calls into question the basic conclusion that the full two-phased operation is implausible; the fundamental Soviet tradeoff between conventional counternuclear operations in Phase I and direct support to the ground advance in Phase II is—by that criterion at least—quite stable.

PERCEPTIONS REVISITED

While, for Western planning purposes, it is the Soviets' capabilities that are uppermost, from the point of view of deterrence, the Soviets' perception of their own capabilities also matters a great deal.

---

[3] It may be worth noting exactly how limited the degradation would be. The majority of NATO's land-based nuclear-capable tactical aircraft would survive the assault, as we have seen. In addition, NATO's nuclear artillery and untargeted Hawk/Hercules elements would remain. NATO and NATO-allocated SLBMs (Submarine Launched Ballistic Missiles), maritime TNFs (Theater Nuclear Forces), the French Plutons, and, for that matter, U.S. central strategic systems would all remain untouched by the Frontal Air assault and, *ceteris paribus*, would be available for tactical employment.

Some may feel that in the interest of prudence, still more favorable assumptions ought to be made on the Soviets' behalf. At some point, however, one must ask whether the Soviets, being prudent planners themselves, would do so. Obviously, we cannot "know" the answer; judgment is, again, unavoidable. But judgments concerning Soviet perceptions—just like those concerning Soviet capabilities—can be tested for plausibility. The above conclusions and sensitivity analyses can be recast in a way that facilitates that process of self-examination: "What am I prepared to believe the Soviets believe?"

Analysis in hand, that is, one can ask, "What alternative assumptions would the Soviets have to make in order to be confident of success in this two-phased Frontal Air campaign? Is it plausible that they would make such assumptions?"

The assumptions elaborated in Chapter V may be inaccurate; the Soviets surely have harder data than that used here. But again, accuracy is not the main issue. Rather, granting from the start that error would be likely, the effort was consistently made to ensure that error did not discriminate *against* the Soviets. Yet, under favorable assumptions (and even more favorable ones offered in Appendix C), the Soviets fall short of the mark.

No one who views the Soviets as being the slightest bit diabolical can at the same time insist that they are totally irrational and utterly inconsistent in their thinking. Let us grant, then, that the Soviet planner has not "slipped the surly bonds" of logic. On that reasonable assumption, there are some requirements for confidence on his part.

In particular, for the Soviet planner to enjoy confidence of significantly greater effectiveness than the above assessments indicate, he must make assumptions far more favorable to his own forces than those made above on his behalf. Is that plausible? To reinvoke Ivan and Sam, it is certainly not plausible that Sam would lavish on his own forces the kind or degree of analytical largesse that has been accorded Ivan's; an American planner would not make assumptions about American performance as favorable overall as those made about Soviet performance. To do so would approach "best case" planning.

Is it plausible that the Soviets are "best case" planners—that they are so much less conservative than their American counterparts? Not in my judgment.

Whether or not one concurs in that judgment (or in the view that the Soviets would, in fact, have to be less conservative) the methodological point is that technical analysis and the examination of perceptions are not at all at odds. On the contrary, one may get a better grip on even the most elusive of perceptions—the adversary's perceptions of himself—by way of analysis than one can in its absence.

MODES OF ATTACK

More interesting, perhaps, than the absolute destructive *level* of Frontal Aviation is its *relative* effectiveness under the two modes of attack simulated above. The advantages of the maximum mass/high intensity attack (Simulation I) over more measured and sustained operations (Simulation II) are evident from Figure 6.1 above (and the corresponding tables of values in Appendix C).

The Simulation I attack destroys a larger proportion of the Phase I target set in two days (7,196 DGZs) than the Simulation II echeloned attack destroys in over five (6,848 DGZs). Total cumulative destruction under Simulation I (7,206 DGZs) even further outweighs the latter's figure, and the greater result is achieved in less than half the time. Moreover, the preferability of the "maximal" attack over the approach idealized in Simulation II increases dramatically when one considers a number of constraints on the latter operation that have not been represented in this analysis.

For example, in conducting Simulation II, we have implicitly assumed a kind of perfect "dovetailing" of the two Soviet echelons. The second echelon, that is, reinforces after the first 4,338 DGZs have been hit (see Simulation II Table C.3 in Appendix C). Although the Soviets report problems in the areas of damage assessment and the transfer of ground control, in our simulation the second echelon "knows" exactly which targets have been struck, which remain, and no confusions of this sort reduce the effectiveness of second echelon sorties or inhibit their "seamless" integration into the first echelon's on-going operations.

Second, if one assumes that the second echelon deploys to austere field bases, then the Simulation II sortie rate of 3.0, favorable under any conditions, becomes questionable. Equivalently, we have assumed implicitly that the reinforcement takes place with absolutely no logistical bottlenecks or reductions in the efficiency of maintenance, whose index takes the same value as for the first echelon.

Finally, we have outfitted the second echelon with frontline ground attack aircraft exclusively. It is far from clear that this is warranted in fact.

Had the second echelon been subjected to these realistic constraints, the relative advantages of the Simulation I attack would have been even more dramatic than indicated here.

While, at the present time, neither attack succeeds in executing even Phase I of the full Frontal Air operation, it is clear that the furious Simulation I attack accomplishes more, and does so more quickly, than does the attack from lesser initial mass, sequenced out at a more measured pace over a longer period of time (Simulation II).[4]

---

[4] In addition to altering one's assumptions on Soviet success criteria and target sequencing, one can add further echelons. For example, assuming each additional echelon to be as destructive as the second echelon of Simulation II (2,386 DGZs), how many further echelons would be required, following the Simulation I attack (7,206 DGZs) to satisfy the full Phase I criterion of 17,848 DGZs? By definition, the number (n) of such additional echelons would have to satisfy the equation

$$\text{(Sim. I Total)} + n\text{(Sim. II 2nd Echelon)} = \text{Phase I Criterion.}$$

Substituting the above numbers, we have

$$7,206 + n(2,386) = 17,848.$$

Solving for n, we obtain n = 4.46, or roughly four and one-half more echelons. Clearly, if those echelons were drawn from other Soviet theaters (Far East, Southern USSR, etc.) and analyses like Simulations I and II were in hand for Soviet contingencies there, the military costs to one Soviet theater for military gains in another—the Soviet simultaneous contingency problem—might actually be assessed concretely. This seems a worthwhile goal for further research.

THE CONVERGENCE OF DOCTRINE AND DEFICIENCY

Notwithstanding its many ambiguities and internal cross-currents, the preferences manifest in Soviet doctrine would seem to be supported by that finding. "The short war" is certainly a reasonable goal if, as our analysis suggests, Soviet operations would be difficult to sustain.[5] "Mass" and "surprise," as exemplified in the Simulation I attack, yield substantially greater returns to the Soviets than the more restrained Simulation II.

At the risk of generalizing, that seemingly "micro" comparison, when combined with all the qualitative insights employed in making it, suggests a much broader relation between Soviet doctrine and Soviet capabilities.

Mass, surprise, preemption, and the short war have long been recognized as being among the pillars of Soviet theater doctrine. Whatever may be its historical bases, it is fair to say that the doctrine is *offensive*. What is disturbing, however, is that in the course of the Soviets' overall military buildup, their conventional forces seem to have come more and more into line with that doctrine: they have assumed an increasingly offensive cast.[6] Indeed, as stressed in the Introduction, Frontal Aviation is the exemplar of that offensive trend.

In a period widely characterized as one of Western military decline and Soviet ascendance, the latter's offensive theater doctrine and increasingly offensive forces are seen as harbingers of an ever-bolder, ever more confident, Soviet military. But is the convergence of Soviet doctrine and capability—in the primacy of the offensive—a clear sign of Soviet confidence?

Not judging by the accounts of the Soviet high command itself. Apparently unconvinced by the simple numerical com-

---

[5] While the Soviets have every reason to prefer a short war, it would be foolish to assume them incapable of a longer one; World War I seems unequivocal on that count. Sustainability is a necessary hedge against that very real possibility. Of course, should the Soviets prove reliant on a short war (that is, a decisive initial campaign), then the capacity first to deny it and then to outsustain them can only be the more dissuasive.

[6] See Joshua M. Epstein, "On Conventional Deterrence in Europe: Questions of Soviet Confidence," *Orbis* 26 (Spring 1982).

parisons and static assessments prevalent in the West, the Soviets themselves express profound dissatisfaction with many aspects of their forces, and with the drawbacks of ever-advancing technology—drawbacks as severe as in the ("gold-plated") American case. Indeed, seen in the light of the Soviets' own sharp self-criticism, the primacy of the offensive, in doctrine and capabilities, emerges as a rational accomodation to their most critical military shortcoming: inflexibility.

Flexibility is the capacity to change, to adjust, in the face of the unanticipated. That ability to respond swiftly and efficiently to unforeseen developments, to show decisiveness and initiative in a dynamic and *uncertain* combat environment is held in the very highest esteem by the Soviets; its inculcation is regarded by them as a primary goal of training. Military modernization itself, by increasing the tempo of war and thus the rapidity with which uncertainty may arise, has, in the Soviet view, only increased its value.

Yet, for all their defense spending, the Soviets appear to be in very short supply of that quality. Indeed the Soviets' very institutions—military, political, even cultural—seem to militate against its inculcation, at every turn stunting precisely the creativity they were meant to foster.

As a consequence, at each step in that process which is the essence of flexibility, the Soviets report deficiencies: in the detection and efficient staff analysis of unexpected developments; in the commanders' capacity for acute and timely decision-making on the basis of tactical intelligence; in the ability of combat units to execute ordered deviations from a rote and predetermined plan; and in the ability of support units to sustain advanced technology at high levels of performance.

These operational limitations create certain military incentives.

THE OFFENSIVE IMPERATIVE

In particular, *once convinced* that war with NATO was unavoidable, the Soviets would have the strongest incentive to make its *initial phase* decisive.

To do otherwise would allow NATO to mobilize forces whose suppression might require of the Soviets a sustainability that they appear to lack. NATO would have more time in which to respond and greater force with which to respond. This would only increase the likelihood of NATO's taking measures *unforeseen* by the Soviets and, in turn, would substantially increase the risk that *flexibility*, initiative, and creative decisionmaking under uncertainty would become necessary on the Soviets' part.

As long as the Soviets lack flexibility, they will have every incentive to avoid that necessity. The operation that minimizes the likelihood of its arising is precisely the crushing offensive suggested by Soviet doctrine.

A successful preemption *nips uncertainty in the bud*. It obviates the need for great flexibility by overwhelming the adversary *before* he can generate the unexpected counter, thus precluding any need to diverge from the predetermined plan or the routinized mission.[7] In turn, the Soviets know that sustained, coordinated operations are a risky proposition for them and that, if they fail to subdue NATO *at the outset*, matters may quickly go downhill. Is it not reasonable that Soviet doctrine bespeaks a preference for the "short war"?

While recognizing the Soviets' great and increasing strength, Western analysts have failed to recognize that their offensive doctrine and offensive capabilities might nevertheless converge on a host of deficiencies. The Soviets are well aware of their problems and the offensive thrust of Soviet doctrine is eminently rational in their light.[8]

[7] To the extent that all militaries share the Soviets problems, they may share their preemptive inclinations. That preemption holds out the prospect of an uncertainty-minimizing control over one's tactical environment has long been among its attractions; that is one deep source of the instability inherent in any military competition.

[8] This is not intended to imply anything about the historical development of Soviet doctrine. That is a different, and complex, question. One might put the observation here this way: if, presented with a list of the Soviets' apparent problems, one had to select a doctrine that would obviate the need for capabilities (for instance, decentralized initiative) that the Soviets lack, a very intelligent choice would be their own offensive doctrine.

THE SOVIET DILEMMA

But there is a fly in the preemptive ointment. Indeed the Soviets' deep dilemma is that the very same deep-seated problems that make a crushing preemption so attractive also cut in just the opposite direction; they make it highly risky for the Soviets to attack without prior mobilization.

Not knowing the exact criteria operative in the field evaluation of unit readiness—knowing, nonetheless, that it embodies certain distortions, "simplifications," and "indulgences" —the Soviets face uncertainty as to the *actual* readiness of their forces. And, looking with justifiable suspicion on high grades (unit ratings), they may be loath to "unleash" their forces without first taking very careful stock; this may explain why, in the postwar period, the Soviets have preceded each of their major operations with a considerable period of mobilization.

Thus, while NATO can expect the Soviets to have a great deal riding on their first—preplanned, packaged—"punch," NATO cannot know *when*, in the Soviets' mobilization, they might choose to "throw" it. Should deterrence fail, that choice will be a prerogative of the aggressor. In the face of that uncertainty—and in order that deterrence *not* fail—NATO has no choice but to adequately cover *the full spectrum of plausible threats.*

CLOSING THE CIRCLE

One thus arrives again at the beginning, with the question to which this volume has, at the most general level, been addressed: What *are* the plausible threats?

This book has shown one of the most central of Soviet threats to be implausible. It has also identified the range of lesser threats that are plausible. There is no reason why the same approach cannot be extended and applied elsewhere, contingency by contingency, theater by theater, until the global spectrum of plausible threats is constructed. The benefits—diplomatic, economic, and military—would be manifold.

But a community that worries only about "*the* Soviet threat," without bothering to assess any *specific* Soviet threats will never get there. It will miss both the forest *and* the trees. And, like Dante, it may awake to find itself "in a dark wood, where the right road was wholly lost and gone."[9]

[9] Dante, *The Divine Comedy, Cantica I: Hell* trans. Dorothy L. Sayers (Harmondsworth, England: Penguin Books, 1949), p. 71.

APPENDICES

BRIEF OVERVIEW OF THE APPENDICES

In Appendix A, numbers are estimated. In Appendix B, equations are developed. The numbers estimated (below and in Chapter V) are applied in the equations to produce the simulation results and sensitivity analyses comprising Appendix C. Numbers, equations, and then results; that is the basic structure of Appendices A–C. But the entire procedure is a special case of the completely general framework sketched in Appendix D.

SOME BASIC ACCOUNTING

The first step in the quantitative analysis, as the reader was forewarned, is accounting. An air threat without targets is, to say the least, difficult to assess. But, as discussed above, broad, unrefined categories like "NATO's C³" or "NATO's tactical air bases" are far too nonspecific to serve as bases for threat assessment. Matters must be "fleshed out" in some detail, examined, measured, and bounded if a meaningful target set is to be arrived at. In line with prevailing Western assessments, the process will begin with NATO's air defenses.

NATO HAWK AND HERCULES SYSTEMS

The variety and number of ground-based air defense systems deployed by NATO forces in the center region is remarkable. SHORAD (Short-Range Air Defense) systems (Roland, Redeye, Chaparral, Vulcan, Rapier and various 20 mm and 40 mm antiaircraft guns, for example) alone number in the thousands. They are mobile (manpacked, towed, tracked vehicle mounted, or self-propelled), difficult for an attacker to locate, and, in some cases, have sophisticated guidance systems. Presumably, while SHORAD systems would be among the targets of Frontal Air's continuing (i.e., Phase II) operations, it is unlikely that much effort would be devoted to their suppression in Phase I. The independent air operation, rather, is assumed to begin with the establishment of a "corridor" through NATO's principal SAM belt—the Hawk and Nike Hercules force.

Launchers are given in Table A.1. In line with the counting

TABLE A.1
NATO Hawk and Hercules Launchers

Country	Hawk Launchers	Hercules Launchers
U.S. (deployed in FRG)	144	144
FRG	216	216
Belgium	60	288
Denmark	96	144
Netherlands	198	144
France	162	—
Totals	876	936

SOURCES: The source for the U.S. figures is Department of the Army, *Air Defense Artillery Reference Handbook* FM44-1-2 (Washington, D.C.: 30 June 1978), pp. A-1, A-2. Abbreviating launcher as *L*, battery as *bty*, and battalion as *bn*, the Hawk launcher counting rules are:

(a) Improved Hawk: 6 L/bty × 3 bty/bn = 18 L/bn

(b) Non-Improved Hawk: 6 L/bty × 4 bty/bn = 24 L/bn.

The Hercules launcher counting rules are:

(a) 9 L/bty × 4 bty/bn = 36 L/bn, or

(b) 12 L/bty × 3 bty/bn = 36 L/bn.

As used by the IISS, a "squadron" is a battalion. The source for the European figures is *The Military Balance 1979—1980* (London: International Institute for Strategic Studies, 1979), pp. 20–29.

rules used in deriving the table (see notes), the Frontal Air targets are as follows:

Launchers

1. Each firing section of three Hawk launchers is considered to be a single target.
   Total: 876/3 = 292

2. Each firing section of three Hercules launchers is considered to be a single target.
   Total: 936/3 = 312

Command and Control

1. With each battalion of Hawks are associated two separate radar systems: the improved continuous-wave radar (ICWAR) providing low- to medium-altitude target detection, and the improved pulse acquisition radar (IPAR), providing medium- to high-altitude target detection.[1]
   Total: $876/9 = 97$
2. With each battery of nine Hercules are associated two separate radars: the low-power and high-power acquisition radars, respectively, LOPAR and HIPAR.[2]
   Total: $936/4.5 = 208$

Total Targets: $292 + 312 + 97 + 208 = 909$

The Hawk and Hercules acquisition radars are integral parts of NATO's air defense command and control network. Since NATO's C^3 is widely assumed to be within Frontal Air's Phase I target set, a portion of that larger set has been counted here. The C^3 component of the Hawk and Hercules set, it should be noted, has been constructed very conservatively. It excludes all data processing, IFF, illumination, ranging, tracking, ECCM (electronic counter-countermeasures), and weapon engagement control facilities, as well as command buildings (in the Hercules case). These are all distinct physical targets whose inclusion would expand the target set considerably. Since Western commentary merely asserts that "NATO's C^3" is within Frontal Air's target list, the inclusion of these targets would not have been inconsistent with prevailing assessments.

With little more than broad categories to guide one, assumptions are unavoidable. From the point of view of ensuring the success of subsequent air operations, the acquisition radars included above would be reasonable Soviet targets.

---

[1] Department of the Army, *Air Defense Artillery Reference Handbook* FM44-1-2 (Washington, D.C.: Government Printing Office, June 1978), pp. 4-5.

[2] Ibid., pp. 3–3 through 3–5, and 4–6.

Their elimination would be essential to ensure that suppression was sufficiently lasting to have been worth the expenditure of effort.

Coverage

While a truly detailed "fire plan" would tailor munition types to target types, we will not attempt to do so here. The meticulous planner would raise efficiency further by allocating only the required minimum number of munitions to each target. Each target must be allocated at least one munition and, although it is not likely that many would require more than three, we will adopt a coverage plan of two munitions per target. More precisely, we will assume that each target above represents two DGZs (designated ground zeros); total DGZs are thus 1,818.

The realism of this estimate depends, among other things, upon the number of attack axes one assumes for Frontal Air. Soviet doctrine, for example, praises dispersion. But, as in most other operational questions, the doctrine is ambiguous since it also stresses the primacy of mass and concentration of force. In any event, passage through the Hawk/Hercules net might well require its large-scale suppression.

As an alternate, however, we also examine a less demanding case. At one-half the success criterion specified above, its DGZ count is 909. Even the larger number of 1,818, it should be noted, is quite conservative and excludes deployed SHORAD systems of more than equal numbers, as well as NATO's alert interceptors. Untargeted SHORAD systems and alert NATO interceptors will be accounted for below in the Frontal Air penetration probability estimate.

NATO's Command, Control, and Communications (C^3)

It has become very fashionable to talk about C^3. This entity is universally assumed to be among Frontal Aviation's objects of attack. But, as noted in Chapter V, the mere term "C^3" does not identify a target set.

Moreover, the vulnerability of certain very important elements of NATO's C^3 is quite impossible to assess. For example, the extent to which "command" is actually destroyed through the elimination of high-ranking individuals depends upon the capacity of lower-ranking individuals to take over the command functions left in their wake—the capacity, that is, to rise to the occasion and exercise leadership and judgment when the necessity arises. How does one target the capacity for initiative? How does one assess the *actual* redundancy in NATO's C^3 that derives from that capacity?

Leaving aside such questions (and there are many), the physical objects that might reasonably be included in "NATO's C^3" are terribly wide ranging. However, the set constructed here will be highly selective and, it should be noted, Air Forces-oriented, since air superiority is normally assumed to take high priority among Frontal Air missions.

First, because of their mobility, size, and/or presumed hardness we will omit SHAPE (Supreme Headquarters, Allied Powers Europe), AFNORTH, AFCENT, and AFSOUTH (Allied Forces, Northern, Central, and Southern Europe) Headquarters, as well as NORTHAG and CENTAG (Northern and Central Army Groups) Headquarters, and those of the ACE (Allied Command Europe) Mobile Force, which, while designated for flanks, could be brought to bear in NATO Center.[3] Finally, AAFCE (Allied Air Forces Central Europe) Headquarters will also be omitted, along with a great many subsidiary C^3 centers. In short, we have left formal "decapitation," as it were, to forces other than Frontal Aviation.

The quite narrowly circumscribed target set we will assign Frontal Aviation is shown in Table A.2. The number of DGZs this set of targets represents will depend heavily on the attacker's goals. For example, short-term disruption of local radar operations is far less demanding than the long-term suppression of all radio activity, and/or of electronic interfaces

[3] See *The Military Balance 1979–1980,* (London: International Institute for Strategic Studies, 1979) pp. 18–19.

TABLE A.2
NATO Command, Control, and Communications Sites

COMMAND

  6 Allied Tactical Air Force Headquarters (ATAF)
  5 Allied Tactical Operations Centers (ATOC)
  8 Air Support Operations Centers (ASOC)
29 Divisional Headquarters
  8 Corps Headquarters (in Germany only)

CONTROL

  9 Major Forward Air Control Points (in Germany only)
  9 Major Control and Reporting Centers (CRCs), including missile control (again, only those in Germany).
56 Subunits of the 601st Tactical Control Wing of the USAF
  3 Sector Operations Centers (Air Control Central Region)

COMMUNICATIONS

16 407L Radar Sites (Major Air Defense)
  5 412L Radar Sites (Major Air Defense)
80 NADGE (NATO Air Defense Ground Environment) Radars

234 Total C^3 Targets

SOURCES: All command sites (except divisional headquarters), all control sites, and 407L and 412L radar sites are discussed in Dan Doyle, "C^3—The Essential Ingredient to Air Defense," *International Defense Review*, no. 6 (1978), pp. 861–862. The divisional headquarters figure from Henry Stanhope, "New Threat—or Old Fears?," *European Security: Prospect for the 1980s* ed. Derek Leebaert (Lexington, Mas.: D.C. Health and Co., 1979), p. 47. The author attributes the figure of $29\frac{2}{3}$ to Professor William Kaufmann of M.I.T. We will not target the $\frac{2}{3}$ division equivalent from Denmark that he includes in his estimate of the NATO M-Day forces (Central Region). The NADGE Radar figure is from Federal Republic of Germany, White Paper 1975/1976, *The Security of the Federal Republic of Germany and the Development of the Federal Armed Forces* (Bonn: Ministry of Defense, 20 January 1976) p. 61. See also Doyle, "C^3," pp. 862–863.

with the larger data processing and telecommunications net. Radar sites themselves may be complex targets. The 407L sites, for example, include over twenty separately targetable entities (e.g., antennae, computers, telecom, logistics, command posts), and depending upon the type and intended permanence of the suppression, the number of designated ground zeros will vary by a great deal.[4]

Designated ground zeros are force planners' numbers. Thus, the number of DGZs this set represents will also vary with the extent of Soviet knowledge concerning the technical characteristics of NATO's overall system and its subsystems. Efficient attacks do not waste sorties on inessential components or ones whose backup systems are numerous and relatively invulnerable. This author does not know which are the maximum value–minimum redundancy components, much less what the Soviets know (or think they know) concerning such targeting issues. Lacking this sort of information, we have little choice but to estimate; we will assume that each of the targets in the C^3 set represents five DGZs, for a total of 1,170 DGZs.

SELECTED NATO THEATER-BASED NUCLEAR WEAPONS AND STORAGE SITES

Since nuclear-capable aircraft are included in the tactical air base target subset below, they will be omitted here, as will European SLBM ports and the French Pluton systems. Nike-Hercules, which is nuclear-capable, is in the air defense set and will not be counted again here.[5] We will also leave aside nuclear weapons in the Howitzer family—self-propelled 8-inch M-110 155 mm, M-109 A1 155 mm, M-110 A1 203 mm, and the towed M-114 155 mm.[6] While suitable targets for Frontal Air's subsequent operations, their mobility and size would make them unsuitably time-consuming targets to locate and destroy in the initial massed attack.

---

[4] Doyle, "C^3—The Essential Ingredient to Air Defense," *International Defense Review* 6 (1978), p.862.

[5] O. Sukovic, "Tactical Nuclear Weapons in Europe," in *Tactical Nuclear Weapons: European Perspectives*, Stockholm International Peace Research Institute (London: Taylor and Francis, 1978), p. 150.

[6] Second German-American Roundtable on NATO, *The Theater Nuclear Balance* (Cambridge, Mass.: The Institute for Foreign Policy Analysis, 1978), p. 27.

Since, at the time of this writing, the final status of the Pershing II and Ground-Launched Cruise Missile (GLCM) programs had yet to be determined, neither was included. By suitable adjustments, the analysis could be expanded to include their deployment.

Subject to these counting rules, the launchers (Pershing I, Lance, and Honest John) number 320, while the storage sites number 100.[7] Since these are assumed to be very high priority targets, we will consider each launcher to represent eight DGZs and each storage site to average a dozen. The total TNW group, then, comes to 3,760 DGZs.

NATO TACTICAL AIR BASES

Tactical air bases may be exceedingly complex targets. For one, they may be very large, with main runways half a football field wide and a mile and a half long.[8] In addition, a variety of different types of assets may be present. Hangars, shelters, unsheltered aircraft, taxiways, maintenance buildings, ammunition dumps, air traffic control and other communications facilities, transportation links, and logistical (pipeline) systems are among the standard items.

Each such item has its characteristic vulnerabilities, and accordingly may be a more appropriate target for certain types of munitions than for others. The Rand Corporation's AIDA (Airbase Damage Assessment) Model, for example, is designed to accommodate twenty different target vulnerability categories, and ten different weapon types in simulations of *single* airbase attacks involving delivery of 250 munitions in total.[9]

[7] All figures other than those for storage sites are from *The Military Balance 1981–1982* pp. 104, 108. "Over 100 nuclear weapon storage sites in Europe" is the terminology used by Dr. M. Leitenberg in "Background Materials in Tactical Nuclear Weapons" in Sukovic, *Tactical Nuclear Weapons*, p. 44.

[8] See the example in D. E. Emerson, *AIDA: An Airbase Damage Assessment Model* R-1872-PR (Santa Monica, Calif.: The Rand Corporation, September 1976), p. 19.

[9] Ibid., p.v. Airbase targeting requirements are the subject of Carl Richard Neu, *Attacking Hardened Air Bases (AHAB): A Decision Analysis Aid for the Tactical Commander* R-1422-PR (Santa Monica, Calif.: The Rand Corporation, August 1974).

Requirements, again, are sensitive to the attacker's goals—the relative priority he assigns to the entire air superiority mission, as opposed to other missions, as well as the type and permanence of the airbase suppression he wants to achieve.

Finally, even in the case of runways alone, there are various approaches an attack may adopt. Some are more expensive (in total delivered munitions requirements) than others, an efficient method depending upon the precision with which certain types of weapons can be delivered and detonated, as well as upon structural characteristics of the runways.[10] We will assume that the Soviets take the classic approach of cratering in runway suppression.

Allied Command Europe "has some 3,100 tactical aircraft, based on about 200 standard NATO airfields, backed up by a system of jointly financed storage depots, fuel pipelines, and signal communications."[11] This is slightly lower than the number provided in the German Defense White Paper of 1975–1976. "The NATO Common Infrastructure Programme ... includes a network of 220 airfields with the requisite technical facilities."[12] This, then, is the largest air base set that Frontal Air might attempt to attack.

In Marine Corps testimony before the Senate Armed Services Committee, the complete suppression of the standard (approximately 4,000 ft) conventional takeoff and landing NATO runway was estimated to require 60 craters. Fifty craters, it was estimated, would reduce NATO to 20 percent

---

[10] In particular, if a runway is sufficiently reinforced and has sufficiently soft shoulders, it is possible to "insert" the munitions under the runway at a few critical points by burrowing them through the soft shoulders. Imagining a north-to-south runway, munitions detonated in the northwest and southwest corners, plus one on the eastern edge of the runway's midline, will together "lift" and twist the runway irreparably. This, however, requires a great deal of precision in both delivery and detonation if it is not to degenerate into a very inefficient form of cratering.

[11] These exclude Britain, France, Ireland, and Portugal, but include Turkey. *The Military Balance 1979-1980*, p. 18.

[12] Federal Republic of Germany, White Paper 1975/1976, *The Security of the Federal Republic of Germany and the Development of the Federal Armed Forces* (Bonn: Ministry of Defense, 20 January 1976), p. 61.

confidence in operating at 65 percent of its full mission load.[13] Considering the center of each of the required craters to be a DGZ, the suppression of NATO's standard airfields (just runways) represents $200 \times 50 = 10,000$ DGZs to $200 \times 60 = 12,000$ DGZs.

The size of the target system changes remarkably little if, instead of mere runway suppression over this implausibly large number of small (on average) airfields, Frontal Aviation attempted to conduct more thorough operations on a much smaller set of more complex airbases. Assuming, as we shall, a set of fifty such airbases, each consisting of one main runway of at least 6,000 ft in length, plus a taxiway, three hangars, and three maintenance buildings (one aircraft, one avionics, one weapons), the DGZ count still falls into the bracket above.[14] This is spelled out in Table A.3, which provides our benchmark for this element of the Frontal Air attack.

As in the air defense corridor case, Soviet capabilities will be examined over a span of mission goals (i.e., DGZ requirements), ranging from short-term disruption to long-term suppression. The 11,100 figure in Table A.3 lies toward the latter part of the spectrum, though not at its extreme. These mission goal estimates, plus four less demanding alternates for the air defense corridor and airbase suppression requirements are given in Table 6.1.

[13] Senate Committee on Armed Services, *Department of Defense Authorization for Appropriations for Fiscal Year 1979, Tactical Air: Hearings before the Committee on Armed Services on S.2571*, 95th Cong., 2nd sess., 1978, pp. 5072–5073.

[14] Fifty is the number of military airfields in the FRG alone, as reported in Sweetman and Gunston, *Soviet Air Power* pp. 14–15. Inclusion of Belgium would, according to the authors, raise the total to sixty-two. French military airfields east of Paris and north of Switzerland alone number an additional thirty. *Air Force Magazine*, March 1976, reports fourteen fields in northen Italy that have runways of 4,000 feet or more and that can accommodate military aircraft. Inclusion of Denmark, the Netherlands, Western France, and the Italian boot would raise the numbers higher still. Fifty is a number focused on Germany and the major bases in close proximity to Germany. The general description is of a medium-to-large base, though by no means in the largest category. Some of the fifty might be a little smaller than this. Many, however, would be bigger.

TABLE A.3
NATO Airbase DGZs

Item	DGZs/Item	No. Items	DGZs
Hangars	2	3	6
Runways (≥ 6000 ft)	100[a]	1	100
Taxiways (≤ 4000 ft)	50	1	50
Air Traffic Control and other C³	4	3	12[b]
Transport (rail and road)	5	2	10[c]
Unsheltered Aircraft	1	24[d]	24
Maintenance	2	3	6
POL and Ammunition[e]	4	2	8
Organic Air Defenses (ground-based)	2	3	6[f]
Subtotal			222
Multiplied by number of bases			50
Total Airbase DGZs			11,100

SOURCE: Author's estimates except where noted in the preceding text or in the citations below.

[a] "Three thousand to four thousand feet are usually the minimum requirement for use by tactical aircraft." Neu, *Attacking*, p. 31. Assuming the 4,000 foot runway requires 50 craters (see n. 13), runways between 6,000 and 8,000 feet should require roughly 100 craters, because of the way cratering is done— by slicing the runway into segments too short for takeoff. A 6,000–8,000 foot runway would require two such slices. Assuming the 50-crater figure to be a "one-slice" equivalent, the two-slice runway should represent about 100.

[b] This is roughly three penetrating Soviet aircraft, each assigned 4 DGZs, one plane for the tower and the other two on radars and other base C³.

[c] This represents an average of 5 for railroads and 5 for bridges, tunnels, and other vulnerable bottleneck points.

[d] One-third of each wing (assumed to equal aircraft on alert minus sheltered non-alert aircraft, though this may seem optimistic for NATO).

[e] POL stands for petroleum, oil, and lubricants.

[f] This is three antiaircraft emplacements at 2 DGZs each.

THE FRONTAL AVIATION INITIAL
GROUND ATTACK FORCE

Soviet Frontal Aviation is organized into sixteen air armies. Four of these are based in Eastern Europe, with the remaining twelve distributed among the twelve Military Districts of the Soviet Union. Of Soviet Frontal Aviation units deployed to Eastern Europe, by far the largest is the 16th Air Army in East Germany, with the Northern (Poland), Central (Czechoslovakia), and Southern (Hungary) Groups of Soviet forces making up the remainder. The total inventory of Soviet Frontal Aviation deployed in Eastern Europe is reported to be roughly 1,300 combat aircraft. Former Secretary of Defense Brown reports that, "about 80% of the fighter force in Frontal Aviation now consists of . . . late model MiG-21s (FISHBED), MiG-23s and 27s (FLOGGER B/G and D respectively), SU-17s (FITTER C/D/G/H), and SU-24s (FENCER)."[15]

Not all of these aircraft, however, would actually perform ground attacks. It is generally assumed that the MiG-23 Flogger B would perform fighter escort for the actual attack force of SU-17s, MiG-27 Flogger Ds and SU-24s, with late model MiG-21s and MiG-25s in the armed reconnaissance and reconnaissance/damage assessment roles, respectively.[16]

The exact percentage of the total represented by each of the above models—the mix—is not clear. There is some uncertainty, therefore, concerning the exact number of frontline aircraft deployed in Eastern Europe that are *specifically* ground attack (SU-17, MiG-27, SU-24). Even knowing this, the strong possibility would remain that a certain number—particularly, of SU-24s—would be withheld for nuclear options, or committed to Long-Range Aviation's attack on targets at the extremes of the theater or in the U.K. The latter might also be said of the MiG-23 Flogger B and other advanced Frontal Air systems whose combat radii have expanded to allow such

[15] All these figures are from Dept. of Defense, *Annual Report of the Secretary of Defense for Fiscal Year 1981*, pp. 102-103.

[16] On these assumptions see Berman, *Soviet Air Power in Transition*, pp. 71-72, and Petersen, *Soviet Air Power*, pp. 14-21.

distant roles.[17] In addition to long-range missions, one might reasonably expect local air superiority and air defense functions to absorb a further percentage of the frontline force, some of whose "number," it might be noted, are trainer versions of limited combat applicability.

Assuming that (by deception) all trainers are replaced with fully frontline systems, and giving Frontal Air's independent (Phase I) interdiction campaign the highest priority, we will assume that a mere 10 percent are otherwise allocated, leaving 1,170 aircraft of the above initial 1,300. Assuming that 85 percent of this force (5 percent higher than Secretary Brown's frontline estimate) is specifically ground attack (GA), the GA inventory is 994.

In line with the discussion of Soviet readiness in Chapter V, we assume (favorably) that 70 percent of this force is operationally available for the initial onslaught, or $(0.7)(994) = 696$ aircraft.

The total Frontal Air inventory in the three Western Military Districts (WMDs) of the Soviet Union is estimated at 900.[18] Again, subtracting 10 percent for other missions (e.g., air defense, peripheral attack, nuclear withhold) yields 810 aircraft. Assuming that 85 percent of these are specifically GA, the GA inventory is 688. Attacking from the somewhat lower availability of 60 percent (still high), the operationally ready GA force would total $(0.6)(688) = 413$ aircraft. Table A.4 summarizes the estimates above.

DIRECT MAINTENANCE PERSONNEL
PER AIRCRAFT

In Chapter I, direct U.S. maintenance personnel per TAC wing was given as 800. On a per plane basis, this yields $800/72 = 11$ direct maintenance personnel per aircraft. According to Robert Berman, U.S. Air Forces in Europe average

---

[17] Berman discusses this possibility for Flogger B in his *Soviet Air Power in Transition*, p. 72.

[18] Petersen, *Soviet Air Power*, p. 17.

TABLE A.4
The Frontal Air Attack Force

Frontal Air inventory deployed Eastern Europe	1,300
Percent *not* otherwise allocated	0.90
Percent ground attack	0.85
Readiness rate	0.70
Subtotal Ready GA	696
Frontal Air inventory in WMDs	900
Percent *not* otherwise allocated	0.90
Percent ground attack	0.85
Readiness rate	0.60
Subtotal Ready GA	413
TOTAL READY GA =	1,109

116 personnel per aircraft.[19] This figure, however, includes the aircrew, weapons handlers, indirect maintenance personnel, runway and other base maintenance personnel, logistical elements and administration. Of the total 116 support personnel per aircraft, then, the direct maintenance element, the fraction that really generates sorties, is roughly 10 percent.

Berman estimates the total support personnel per Soviet aircraft in the 16th Air Army in East Germany at sixty-seven, or 58 percent of the U.S. value.[20] This figure also includes all of the nondirect maintenance personnel mentioned above. Assuming that the Soviets' ratio of direct maintenance personnel per plane to total support personnel per plane is, like the U.S., roughly 10 percent, then the Soviets' *direct* maintenance personnel-to-aircraft ratio would be 6.7. There is reason to believe that this is rather high as an average for Frontal Air as a whole.

First, of total Soviet Air Force personnel, "about three-fourths are assigned to operational units and support forces.

[19] Berman, *Soviet Air Power in Transition*, p. 56.
[20] The Soviet figure is from ibid., p. 57.

The rest are in high command and support elements (these include Ministry of Defense), research and development, and training. Of the total in the operational Air Force units, . . . Frontal Aviation has 180,000 personnel.[21]

Total fixed wing combat aircraft is estimated at over 4,000. In addition, Frontal Air has over 3,000 helicopters and includes an organic transport force of approximately 230 aircraft.[22] In arriving at the direct maintenance personnel (DMP)-to-aircraft ratio, we must first subtract the crews (combat personnel) from the 180,000.

Given assumptions concerning crew ratios that are very favorable to the sizing of the Soviet maintenance base, total combat personnel (on-board pilots, navigators, ECM, and weapon system personnel) comes to 17,247 (see Table A.5). Subtracting this from the 180,000 Frontal Air total yields 162,753 noncombat personnel.

Ground support for Soviet Air Forces is conducted at the regimental level and is conducted by two separate services. Maintenance of aircraft is performed *solely* by the IAS (Engineering Aviation Services), while logistics, base security, and maintenance of runways and other facilities of the base infrastructure are the province of Air Technical Battalions of the Rear Services (*Sluzhba Tyla*).[23] A strict separation of functions is maintained between the IAS and Rear Services. The regimental Rear Services element is roughly equal in size to the corresponding regimental IAS element.[24] Thus, of the 162,753 noncombat personnel in Frontal Aviation, roughly half, or 81,376 are IAS personnel.

[21] Dept. of the Air Force, *Soviet Aerospace Handbook*, p. 129.

[22] Each of these figures is computed from *The Military Balance 1979-1980*, p. 11.

[23] Trapans, *Organizational Maintenance*, p. 4. That a strict separation of functions has been maintained is suggested not only by the Soviet literature itself, but by such Western analysts as Lynn Hansen. See his "The Resurgence of Soviet Frontal Aviation," *Strategic Review* (Fall 1978).

[24] Trapans, *Organizational Maintenance*, p. 8. Since 1965, there are indications that the Soviets have given more attention to logistics, particularly after the invasion of Czechoslovakia. There is not evidence, however, that direct aircraft support personnel have increased *relative to* logistics personnel.

TABLE A.5
Total Frontal Air Combat Personnel

Aircraft		Crew Size		Crew Personnel		Crew Ratio		Total Combat Personnel
60 Yak 28	×	2	=	120	×	1.0	=	120
220 SU-7 Fitter A		1		220		1.25		275
1,400 MiG-23/-27 Flogger B/D		1		1,400		1.25		1,750
1,000 MiG 21 Fishbed (J/K/L/N)		1		1,000		1.25		1,250
640 SU-17 Fitter C/D		1		640		1.25		800
230 SU-19/-24 Fencer		2		460		1.25		575
250 Beagle/Brewer		2		500		1.0		500
170 MiG-25		1		170		1.25		212
300 MiG-21 Fishbed		1		300		1.25		375
60 Brewer E		2		120		1.0		120
6 AN-12 Cub (ECM)		5		30		1.0		30
230 Transports		3		690		1.0		690
800 Mi-1/-2		1		800		1.0		800
130 Mi-4		2		260		1.0		260
470 Mi-6		5		2,350		1.0		2,350
1,470 Mi-8		3		4,410		1.0		4,410
10 Mi-10		3		30		1.0		30
540 Mi-24 Hind		4		2,160		1.25		2,700
7,976 Aircraft								17,247

SOURCES: All inventory numbers and the crew size figures for helicopers are from the IISS *Military Balance 1979–1980*. Crew sizes for the fixed wing aircraft are from Bill Sweetman and Bill Gunston, *Soviet Air Power* (New York: Crescent Books, 1978). Crew ratios are author's estimates, see Epstein, *Political Impediments*, p. 275; these are very conservative, falling far short of the A-10 (1.77) or the F-15 (1.34) *wartime* ratios cited in Chapter I. Combat troops that can be landed in helicopters are omitted because they are drawn from MTR divisions. (Department of the Army, *FM 30–40: Handbook on the Soviet Ground Forces*, 30 June 1975, pp. 6–95.)

Within the IAS, however, not all personnel perform direct flightline maintenance. A certain percentage handle and/ or maintain armaments, a certain percentage work in the regimental TECh, a further percentage perform administrative functions (senior engineers, dispatchers, and their modest staffs), and finally, some IAS personnel are assigned to depot maintenance functions. Assuming (very favorably for the Soviets) that 50 percent of all IAS personnel perform *direct* aircraft maintenance, then the total direct maintenance personnel is 40,688.

Over the 7,976 aircraft enumerated above, then, the direct maintenance personnel-to-aircraft ratio comes to 40,688/ 7,976 = 5.1. This figure is in extremely close agreement with Soviet descriptions.[25] Conservatively, the 5.1 ratio assumes Soviet crew ratios lower than the corresponding U.S. wartime values (1.34 for the F-15 and 1.77 for the A-10, see note 38 of Chapter I). A rise in Soviet crew ratios would lower the Soviet DMP-to-aircraft ratio further.

While total personnel in Frontal Aviation seems to have remained remarkably constant since the late 1960s, combat personnel has risen with force expansion. Of support forces, Western commentary suggests that increases have occurred in logistical manpower as well. While the 6.7 figure rests on the assumption that the Soviets' direct-to-indirect support ratio is, like ours, 10 percent, the evidence would suggest that, even if it was 10 percent in the late 1960s, it may have fallen since.

Our best estimate, then, will be five direct aircraft maintenance personnel per combat aircraft, while in the sensitivity analyses, radical increases are examined.

SOVIET OVERALL MAINTAINED SYSTEM RELIABILITY

We assume a *constant* overall (air vehicle and armament) maintained reliability. The constancy assumption is, if anything, favorable to the Soviets since, even under rigorous main-

---

[25] See, for example, Guk, "A Flight of Excellent Aircraft," pp. 24-29. Guk commends the *five* aircraft technicians who epitomize excellence in direct maintenance support.

tenance, failure probabilities tend to increase with time (i.e., no system has an infinite maintained lifetime). The value assigned is 0.8.[26]

DGZs Targeted Per Plane Per Sortie

The number of DGZs targeted per plane per sortie, (m), depends upon one's assumptions regarding both the type and number of munitions carried, on average, per sortie. As well, this number is sensitive to one's assumptions concerning Soviet substitution of fuel pallets and/or ECM pods for munitions. This, it might be noted, is another of those cases in which Soviet doctrinal precepts would seem to afford little direction to Soviet planners. A commitment to "mass," that is, does not answer the question, "masses of what?" Unlimited masses of everything simply cannot be squeezed out of fixed resources, no matter how big the resource base may be. So, do the Soviets intend to "mass" ECM in the hope of raising the efficiency of each sortie, or do the Soviets intend to essentially ignore ECM and "mass" munitions, hoping that some sort of economy of scale will outweigh those degradations in munition effectiveness that enemy jamming would produce? Soviet doctrine, at least in the form of commitments to such things as "mass," fails to provide any clue as to how the Soviets intend to deal with *tradeoffs*—"do I 'mass' x or do I 'mass' y?" Furthermore, tradeoffs are evident not only within each such doctrinal precept, but between such competing doctrinal elements as mass and surprise.

Tactical decisions are choices among alternatives. The doctrine does not appear to be directed at resolving such operational problems of choice. But we, as analysts, must make choices, as least to get an analysis started.

Conservatively assuming unlimited Soviet stockages of advanced air-to-surface munitions (ASMs), and giving the Soviets perfect ECM in addition, an m value of four DGZs targeted per plane per sortie seems reasonable since, given per-

[26] *The Military Balance 1981–1982*, p. 128.

fect ECM, no tradeoff between munitions and electronic countermeasures would arise to befuddle the doctrinaire. (As in the case of all the main variables, m will receive sensitivity analysis in Appendix C.)

NATO's AIR DEFENSE ENVIRONMENT

The number, N, of defensive shots to which a Frontal Air attacker would, on average, be exposed per sortie depends on the route and altitude profile of his sortie, and upon the density of NATO's air defense coverage in the sequence of sectors through which the flight path would take him.[27] What little research is available on this question strongly suggests that no sortie profile would expose the attacker to less than four shots, particularly if one allows for the possibility that at least some of NATO's interceptors would literally "rise to the occasion."[28] We will assume this estimated number, N = 4.

Needless to say, this excludes whatever number of shots the Soviets would take at their own aircraft, as determined by IFF problems. That is, we will give them perfect IFF, again to be conservative.

All of these initial Soviet estimates, plus those presented in Chapter V, are collected in Table B.1 appearing at the end of Appendix B. Listed there as well is the only numerical estimate left to be made: the virtual attrition probability parameter. That estimate will be made in Appendix B, where the equations *relating* inputs to outputs are developed.

---

[27] Defensive shots would come, for example, from short-range air defenses and alert NATO interceptors. The assumed mean kill probability per defensive shot was discussed in Chapter V.

[28] The four-shot estimate is from Congressional Budget Office, *U.S. Air and Ground Conventional Forces for NATO: Air Defense Issues* (Washington, D. C.: Government Printing Office, March 1978). See pages 9–11, Coverage of Central Region Airspace, especially.

APPENDIX B

THE SIMPLE ANALYTICS
OF INTERDICTION OPERATIONS

Sortie Rate Supply

Since supply involves the organization of ground support, and since we wish to make the equations applicable to both the U.S. and Soviet cases, it is important to recall one notable difference in their respective maintenance organizations and to agree on some nomenclature.[1]

The U.S. maintenance structure has three levels: organizational (ML_1), intermediate (ML_2), and depot (D). As was discussed in Chapter I, organizational maintenance (ML_1) in the U.S. is administered at the level of the wing, but is conducted by squadron-specific maintenance elements.

---

[1] There are more, and less, sophisticated computer simulations and mathematical models used to relate maintenance requirements, ground support resources, and sortie rates. The Air Force's Logistics Composite Model (LCOM) has proved to be among the more successful, incorporating a wide range of environmental, technical, and manpower variables in an iterative simulation that converges to an optimal set of consistently related inputs and efficiencies satisfying any specified feasible sortie requirement. LCOM is discussed concisely in Office of the Under Secretary of Defense for Research and Engineering, *Report of the Acquisition Cycle Task Force* (Washington, D.C.: Government Printing Office, March 1978), pp. 23–26, and more comprehensively in R. R. Fisher et al., *The Logistics Composite Model: An Overall View* RM-5544-PR (Santa Monica, Calif.: The Rand Corporation, May 1968). The GAO provides a general description and presents some criticism of LCOM in U.S. General Accounting Office Report LCD-77-421, *Determining Requirements for Aircraft Maintenance Personnel Could Be Improved—Peacetime and Wartime* (Washington, D.C.: Government Printing Office, May 1977), pp. 14–19. LCOM's relation to earlier methods is discussed in Senate Committee on Appropriations, *Department of Defense Appropriations for Fiscal Year 1976, Part 4—Department of the Air Force: Hearings before a subcommittee of the Senate Committee on Appropriations*, 94th Cong., 1st sess., 1975, p. 610.

The Soviet maintenance structure essentially has two levels: organizational (ML_1) and depot (D). Organizational (ML_1) maintenance is conducted at the level of the air regiment. Regimental direct maintenance personnel is the Soviet element that concerns us.

Terms such as "organizational maintenance," "direct maintenance," or "ML_1 maintenance" personnel will always denote Soviet regimental personnel responsible for aircraft maintenance in direct support of wartime sorties (analogous to U.S. wing personnel in the squadron-specific direct sortie generation units reviewed in Chapter I).

Though the discussion is strongly oriented toward the Soviets, it is important that the reader keep in the back of his or her mind the U.S. elements to which the Soviet-oriented terminology corresponds.

The key variables that determine the feasible sortie rate we define as follows:

$F(0)$ The initial attack force (readiness rate times the initial inventory of frontline ground attack aircraft). $F(t)$ will denote that force which, in expected terms, is surviving after the tth sortie. $F(0)$, the initial force, is thus the force that has survived the zeroth sortie.

$P(0)$ The initial number of direct regimental (ML_1) maintenance personnel in ground support of the attack force. The same notational convention will apply here as that which applies to $F(t)$. $P(t)$ will denote the number of personnel of the initial $P(0)$, who are available after the tth sortie.

   h   The mean workday (in hours) taken over all direct (ML_1) aircraft maintenance personnel.

   T   The mean (calculated over the total sorties flown per day) flight time (in hours) per sortie.

   M   The mean peacetime total (regimental *and* depot) maintenance manhours required per flight hour. (In the U.S. case this would be $ML_1 + ML_2 + D$ manhours per flight hour.)

   Z   The maintenance deferral rate; the fraction of M that is deferred over a given period. If the deferral rate is

0.25, then the maintenance manhours actually administered to the aircraft is given by $M(1 - Z) = 0.75M$. We assume $0 \leq Z < 1$.

SORTIE RATE SUPPLIABLE WITHOUT DEFERRAL

Suppose an aircraft flies S sorties on a given day. This represents $S \times T$ total flight hours since, by definition, T is the flight hours per sortie. If each aircraft in a force of F aircraft flies S sorties of duration T, the force's total flight hours, accordingly, becomes $F \times S \times T$. Suppose each aircraft involved requires M total maintenance manhours per flight hour. Then, in order for the sortie rate, S, to be feasible, a total of $M \times (F \times S \times T)$ maintenance manhours would be required— maintenance manhours required per flight hour (M) × total flight hours ($F \times S \times T$).

The total maintenance manhour *requirement* just derived, it should be noted, embodies maintenance peformed at *all* maintenance levels, regimental *and* depot (in the U.S. case, $ML_1 + ML_2 + D$). We will assume that for the support of generated wartime sorties, only direct, organizational manhours are available. Hence, while the manhour *requirement* (MFST) is computed including depot, the manhours available to sustain S are direct regimental manhours only. By definition, the latter quantity is hP, hours per man per day (h) times direct maintenance manpower (P).

The maintenance manhours available (hP) must be at least as great as the maintenance manhours required (MFST) if, without deferring maintenance, the specified sortie rate (S) is to be feasible; i.e.,

$$MFST \leq hP.$$

This is to say that the maximum feasible sortie rate (without deferral), which we shall denote $S^s(Z = 0)$, is given by

$$S^s(Z = 0) \leq \frac{hP}{MFT}.$$

Lending a time dependence to P and F, the basic (no deferral) sortie rate supply equation is

$$S^s(Z = 0) \le \frac{h}{MT}\left(\frac{P(t)}{F(t)}\right). \tag{1}$$

This equation, implicitly, gives the Soviets the benefit of at least one doubt. The M value in Eq. (1) embodies labor skills and technology only to be found at depot level. Personnel, $P(t)$, are assumed to be solely regimental (ML_1), and to lack depot skills and technology. In the supply equation, we should actually raise M by some increment, ΔM. Should the plane fail in a manner requiring K depot manhours, correction of that failure would likely require more than K regimental (less skilled, less equipped) manhours. To be precise, the equation should be:

$$S^s(Z = 0) \le \frac{h}{(M + \Delta M)T}\left(\frac{P(t)}{F(t)}\right).$$

In the U.S., intermediate level (ML_2) personnel could, in war, be allocated to assist organizational personnel in carrying out more sophisticated tasks than they (ML_1) would normally be called upon to perform. While the U.S. would suffer the ΔM increment, the Soviet regimental maintenance cadre lacks any cushion analogous to America's ML_2. Their ΔM would be even larger than that of the U.S.

We will give Soviet direct maintenance personnel the benefit of the (considerable) doubt and leave the M value completely unadjusted. This implicit $\Delta M = 0$ seems a significant gift.

SORTIE RATE SUPPLIABLE WITH DEFERRAL

Sometimes, in order to generate maximum sortie rates, certain types of maintenance are either left aside or are peformed less frequently than would otherwise be the case. A certain level of deferral is implicit in our decision to leave M unaltered, even though highly sophisticated depot skills are not available at the flightline.

If we agree to "homogenize" the qualitatively different man-hours available at different maintenance levels, then the deferral of certain *types* of maintenance may be represented as a simple reduction in the *number* of homogeneous manhours directly applied to the aircraft per flight hour.

That is, if Z is the fraction of the *total* M (including depot) that is deferred in war, then the maintenance manhours (here-after understood to be homogenized) applied to the aircraft are

$$(1 - Z)M.$$

Assuming that this level of deferral is not catastrophic, the maximum sortie rate suppliable rises from the no-deferral level of

$$S^s(Z = 0) \leq \frac{h}{MT}\left(\frac{P(t)}{F(t)}\right), \tag{2}$$

to

$$S^s(Z > 0) \leq \frac{h}{(1 - Z)MT}\left(\frac{P(t)}{F(t)}\right). \tag{3}$$

Since we will always speak of Z taking a value α, this latter equation is better expressed as:

$$S^s(Z = \alpha) \leq \frac{h}{(1 - \alpha)MT}\left(\frac{P(t)}{F(t)}\right). \tag{4}$$

But, by Eq. (2), this is just

$$S^s(Z = \alpha) \leq \frac{S^s(Z = 0)}{(1 - \alpha)}. \tag{5}$$

Minimum Equilibrium Deferral Rate

Suppose a sortie rate, S, is specified or simply selected at random, and suppose the maximum sortie rate suppliable without deferral to be $S^s(Z = 0)$. In addition, imagine that $S^s(Z = 0) < S$. What level of deferral, α, is necessary to raise the sortie rate supplied up to equilibrium with S? That is, what is the minimum value of α such that $S^s(Z = \alpha) = S$?

This is a simple problem. Eq. (5) was

$$S^s(Z = \alpha) \leq \frac{S^s(Z = 0)}{1 - \alpha}.$$

At the requisite deferral rate α, supply will equal S. This is what one means by the "requisite deferral rate." Substituting S for $S^s(Z = \alpha)$ on the left-hand side, the equilibrium α is readily obtained.

$$S \leq \frac{S^s(Z = 0)}{1 - \alpha},$$

$$1 - \alpha \leq \frac{S^s(Z = 0)}{S},$$

or

$$\boxed{\alpha \geq 1 - \frac{S^s(Z = 0)}{S}}. \qquad (6)$$

The reader may verify that this formula for the equilibrium α, when substituted for α in Eq. (5), yields the equality $S^s(Z = \alpha) = S$.

Thus, on the supply side, it is clear how to compute $S^s(Z=0)$ and, given any S, how to compute the equilibrium value of α. The latter plays a central role in determining the course of target destruction and force attrition. In order to discuss that role, a number of further definitions and basic equations will be required.[2]

---

[2] Eq. (6) presents α as though it were a constant. For reasons that will be given directly, we shall treat it as a constant. Technically, since $S^s(Z = 0)$ is itself time-dependent, so must be α. By Eq. (2),

$$\alpha(t) \geq 1 - \frac{h}{MTS} \left\{ \frac{P(t)}{F(t)} \right\}.$$

Mathematically, a rise in the ratio $P(t)/F(t)$ raises $S^s(Z = 0)$, reducing the equilibrium deferral rate. Various factors, however, are likely to damp the mathematical effect in practice. Assuming no attrition of personnel, it is clear that

TARGET DESTRUCTION

F(0)   The initial attack force (readiness rate times the initial inventory of frontline ground attack aircraft). F(t), as before, will denote that force which, in expected terms, is surviving after the tth sortie. F(0), the initial force, is again the force that has survived the zeroth sortie.

m   The mean (calculated over all types of ground attack aircraft and corresponding armament loadings) number of DGZs attacked per aircraft per sortie.

r   The overall maintained reliability of the weapon system (aircraft and armament) per sortie.

P_K The weapon system's kill probability against each DGZ attacked.

Assuming, as we shall, that all attrition manifests itself at the *end* of that sortie during which it "occurs," then the expected DGZs destroyed in the $(t + 1)^{st}$ sortie, $D(t + 1)$, is by

---

force attrition increases the numerical ratio. However, for the numerical change to have an effect, personnel originally assigned to now attrited planes must be shifted over to support of surviving aircraft. Even assuming that personnel initially assigned to now attrited MiG-23s are capable of maintaining surviving SU-24s, the switch would suffer some time lag, if for no other reason than that the MiG-23 attrition must be revealed before the shift would be made. That is, ground support personnel, in place at the flow-line, do not know in advance which MiG-23s will fail to return. Depending upon the degree of dispersal, any such shifting could involve further time in transportation. Moreover, the redistribution of surplus personnel through working ground support environments would require administrative resources that, at the very high sortie rates we assume, would probably already be overtaxed. When, in addition, one considers the very brief duration of the Phase I operation, very little time would appear to remain for this sort of personnel shifting. Finally, personnel would likely suffer attrition as well, reducing the net ratio increase, damped as its effects would be by such factors as those reviewed above. For these reasons, the effect will be ignored—α will be treated as a constant. While, in and of itself, the constancy assumption may seem unfavorable to the Soviets, remember that (a) the maintained reliabilities are also being held constant, and that (b) the Soviets are not being charged any increase in M for the absence of depot skills at the flightline. These, in combination with the practical impediments to its manifestation, more than compensate for the purely formal unfavorability of the constant α assumption.

definition:

$$D(t + 1) = F(t)mrP_K. \tag{7}$$

To obtain the cumulative destruction after $t + 1$ sorties, $CUM(t + 1)$, one would simply sum these terms from the zeroth sortie through the tth:

$$CUM(t + 1) = \sum_{i=0}^{t} D(i + 1) = \sum_{i=0}^{t} F(i)mrP_K. \tag{8}$$

Needless to say, not all sorties are equally destructive. As the force $F(t)$, declines, so too will aggregate destruction per sortie. Two types of attrition, virtual and actual, will be considered.

ACTUAL ATTRITION

Letting P_d stand for the mean single-shot kill probability of a NATO air defense system against a Frontal Air plane, and letting N denote the number of NATO air defense shots to which the average attacking aircraft is exposed per sortie, the average survival probability for an attacker is easily seen to be $(1 - P_d)^N$.

Taking $P(A)$ as the probability of actually attriting, the probability of *not* actually attriting is $1 - P(A)$, and we have

$$1 - P(A) = (1 - P_d)^N.$$

Thus, considering actual attrition alone,

$$F(t) = F(t - 1)(1 - P_d)^N = F(0)(1 - P_d)^{Nt}. \tag{9}$$

SURPRISE

Actual attrition, however, commences only when a defense becomes active. Surprise, as we shall idealize it here, is the number of sorties flown unopposed by a defense. For example, if surprise is achieved for the first sortie, then,

$$F(1) = F(0),$$

which is to say that for $t = 1$, $(1 - P(A))$ is held at unity.

In general, leaving virtual attrition (see below) aside,

$$F(t) = F(0)(1 - P(A))^{t-y} \qquad (10)$$

where:

$$1 - P(A) = \begin{cases} 1 & \text{for} \quad t \leq y \\ (1 - P_d)^N & \text{for} \quad t > y. \end{cases}$$

The number of surprise sorties achieved is represented by y; or equivalently, y is the sortie after which actual attrition begins. Needless to say, Eq. (10) reduces to Eq. (9) where y = 0. If, at a sortie rate of five per day the first two sorties could be executed with perfect surprise, then, at a sortie rate of ten per day, it seems reasonable to assume that four sorties could be executed with surprise. Aside from considerations of surprise, however, actual attrition is independent of the sortie *rate*. Virtual attrition, by contrast, is intimately related to the sortie rate—or, more precisely, to the duration over which its equilibrium deferral rate is sustained.

Virtual Attrition

The general topic of virtual attrition was discussed in Chapters I and V. As noted there, we are using the term in a restricted sense, as denoting only maintenance deferral-related events that effectively remove the aircraft from participation in air operations. It was argued at length that the Soviets enjoy no advantage over the United States in regard to virtual attrition; thus the imputation to the Soviets of a value plausible in the U.S. case will not bias the analysis against them.

Recalling that discussion, and the rationale given for POST's cyclicality in Chapter I, we will make the assumption that, for sophisticated U.S. aircraft (e.g., the F-15), a deferral rate of fully 50 percent ($\alpha = 0.5$), if sustained over seven *wartime* sorties, would result in a probability of virtual attrition equal to 0.75.[3]

---

[3] While this figure is varied radically in the sensitivity analyses of Appendix C (i.e. lambda, its parameter, is varied), its realism, particularly for the F-15, was attested to in interviews conducted by the author at the Engineering and Applied Sciences Division of the Rand Corporation (July–August, 1980).

Let P(V) stand for the probability of virtual attrition through sustained wartime deferral. Assume that P(V) has the exponential form:[4]

$$P(V) = 1 - e^{-(\alpha t)\lambda}. \tag{11}$$

The deferral rate is represented by α and t is the number of sorties over which it is sustained. Taking the assumed values above, we can solve for the parameter λ. With P(V) = 0.75 when $\alpha = 0.5$ and t = 7, Eq. (11) becomes:

$$0.75 = 1 - e^{-(0.5)(7)\lambda},$$

from which it follows that

$$\lambda = 0.40.$$

Substituting this value of λ back into Eq. (11), we have the equation:

$$P(V) = 1 - e^{-0.4\alpha t}. \tag{12}$$

Thus, to recall the example offered in Chapter V, an aircraft that has sustained a deferral rate of 30 percent over a total of 15 sorties would have a probability of virtual attrition equal to:

$$P(V) = 1 - e^{-0.4(0.30)15} = 0.83,$$

the same as a 15 percent deferral sustained for 30 sorties.

[4] Needless to say, the exact wartime functional relationship between maintenance deferral rates, activity levels, time, environmental stress, and the probability of virtual attrition is unknown—perhaps it cannot be known in peacetime. The negative exponential form, as a special case of the Poisson, is a sensible default, embodying (a) our definition of virtual attrition as an event catastrophic over the period in question, i.e., a "failure" with zero failures allowed in a success-or-failure (binomial) world; and (b) the assumption, lacking more information, that the rate of its occurrence is constant. On the utility of the negative exponential in engineering, under analogous scarcities of information, see Chapter 45, "Statistical Processes and Weapons Systems," in *Statistical Processes and Reliability Engineering*, Dimitris N. Chorafas (New York: Van Nostrand Co., 1960), or Chapter 6, "The Poisson Distribution and the Exponential Failure Law," in *Reliability Principles and Practices*, S. R. Calabro (New York: McGraw-Hill Book Co., 1962).

By Eq. (11), the probability of *not* virtually attriting per sortie is

$$1 - P(V) = e^{-\alpha\lambda}$$

and, considering virtual attrition alone,

$$F(t) = F(t - 1)e^{-\alpha\lambda} = F(0)e^{-\alpha\lambda t}. \tag{13}$$

Just as surprise affects the time at which actual attrition commences, various factors may forestall the onset of virtual attrition. While the exceedingly high deferral rates necessary to the Soviet attack make unlikely any significant postponement here, formally,

$$F(t) = F(0)(1 - P(V))^{t-x} \tag{14}$$

where,

$$1 - P(V) = \begin{cases} 1 & \text{for } t \leq x \\ e^{-\alpha\lambda} & \text{for } t > x. \end{cases}$$

Of course, x is the sortie after which virtual attrition sets in.[5]

THE EQUATIONS

Recovering all of the elements developed above, the six basic equations are given below.

Per sortie target destruction is as given at the outset, Eq. (7):

$$D(t + 1) = F(t)mrP_K. \tag{1}$$

Cumulative destruction as well retains its original form, Eq. (8):

$$CUM(t + 1) = \sum_{i=0}^{t} D(i + 1) = mrP_K \sum_{i=0}^{t} F(i). \tag{2}$$

However, F(t) has the trajectory

$$F(t) = F(0)\{1 - P(V)\}^{t-x}\{1 - P(A)\}^{t-y} \tag{3}$$

---

[5] The deferral rates for each simulation conducted in Appendix C are either given in the Annex of Epstein, *Political Impediments*, pp. 411–561, or, for runs conducted after that work's completion, may be obtained directly from the equations or by implementing the computer program provided in Appendix C.

where

$$1 - P(V) = \begin{cases} 1 & \text{for } t \leq x \\ e^{-\alpha\lambda} & \text{for } t > x \end{cases}$$

and

$$1 - P(A) = \begin{cases} 1 & \text{for } t \leq y \\ (1 - P_d)^N & \text{for } t > y. \end{cases}$$

The equilibrium deferral rate, α, is computed from Eq. (6):

$$\alpha \geq 1 - \frac{S^s(Z = 0)}{S}, \tag{4}$$

while

$$S^s(Z = 0) \leq \frac{h}{MT}\left(\frac{P(t)}{F(t)}\right), \tag{5}$$

with M—as developed in Chapter V—given by

$$M = M_0\left\{1 + k(1 + \delta)\left(\frac{1 - C}{C}\right)\right\}. \tag{6}$$

These are the equations used in all the simulations below. By their iterative application, one can address the central issue of the sortie rate demanded—its formal definition, the conditions of its existence, and the determination of its value.

THE SORTIE RATE DEMANDED

Given a target set of E DGZs, how does one determine the minimum sortie rate required to destroy the target set in one day of operations? All variables except α, x, and y are, of course, fixed and assumed to be known beforehand. Since $S^s(Z = 0)$ is thus determined, the higher is any postulated S, the higher will be α, and in turn, the probability of virtual attrition. This effect, however, may be opposed by the increased number of surprise sorties (y) afforded by a higher sortie rate. Damping the returns to surprise, though, is the possibility of an earlier onset of virtual attrition (a lower x) as sortie rates climb to levels precluding preventive maintenance. In general, if S is a sortie rate,

$$\frac{\Delta\alpha(S)}{\Delta S}, \quad \frac{\Delta y(S)}{\Delta S} \geq 0,$$

and

$$\frac{\Delta x(S)}{\Delta S} \leq 0.$$

The Sortie Rate Demanded, S^D, we define as the value upon which the sequence of trial S-values converges when that sequence is generated in accordance with the following procedure:

Step 1   Select any value for a trial sortie rate, S_0.

Step 2   Compute $\alpha = 1 - \dfrac{S^s(Z = 0)}{S_0}$.

Step 3   Compute $(x(S_0), y(S_0))$.

Step 4   Compute $F(t)$, $t = 0 \ldots S_0$ by the formula:

$$F(t; S_0) = F(0)\{1 - P(V)\}^{t - x(S_0)}\{1 - P(A)\}^{t - y(S_0)}$$

where,

$$1 - P(V) = \begin{cases} 1 & \text{for} \quad t \leq x(S_0) \\ e^{-\alpha\lambda} & \text{for} \quad t > x(S_0) \end{cases}$$

and,

$$1 - P(A) = \begin{cases} 1 & \text{for} \quad t \leq y(S_0) \\ (1 - P_d)^N & \text{for} \quad t > y(S_0). \end{cases}$$

Step 5   Compute cumulative DGZs destroyed,

$$CUM(S_0) = mrP_K \sum_{t=0}^{S_0} F(t; S_0).$$

Step 6   Iteration Rule:

$$IF \begin{cases} CUM(S_0) < E, \text{ choose } S_1 > S_0 \text{ and repeat steps } 2-6 \\ CUM(S_0) > E, \text{ choose } S_1 < S_0 \text{ and repeat steps } 2-6 \\ CUM(S_0) = E, S_0 = S^D. \end{cases}$$

If $S_0 \neq S^D$ and S_1 fails, one would proceed to select S_2 by the rule above, and so on, until one of two things occurs: (1)

TABLE B.1
Simulation I Numerical Assumptions

Frontal Air Inventory Deployed[a]	
Eastern Europe	= 1,300
(Western Milit. Districts)	(900)
Fraction *not* allocated	
to Long-Range Aviation (LRA)	
or Air Defense (AD)[b]	= 0.9
Fraction (of these) that are ground attack	= 0.85
Switching Rate (discussed above)	= 1.0
	(0.6)
Readiness Rate	= 0.7
	(0.6)
DMP (direct maintenance personnel-to-aircraft	
ratio)	= 5 (East. Eur. = WMDs)
h (mean hours per workday)	= 8
T (mean flight hours per sortie)	= 1.5
δ (relative adjustability factor)	= 0.15
$(1 - C)/C$ (index of technological change)	= 0.9
M_0 (MMH/FH: baseline system)	= 18
λ (virtual attrition parameter)	= 0.4
P_d (defensive single-shot kill probability)	= 0.05
N (mean defensive shots/attacker/sortie)	= 4
r (maintained ground attack weapon system	
reliability)	= 0.8
κ (virtual attrition onset point)	= 0
y (number of surprise sorties achieved)	= 1
m (mean DGZs targeted/plane/sortie)	= 4
P_K (mean offensive kill probability vs. each	
DGZ attacked per sortie)	= 0.75
S (sortie rate)	= 6

[a] For Frontal Air inventory, the upper value is the Eastern Europe deployed value; listed in parentheses beneath it is the Western Military Districts deployed value. This convention is held to for all variables where the two values are assumed to differ. Otherwise, only one value is given.

[b] In general, the values given are understood to be the fraction of inventory not otherwise allocated, as in Table A. 4.

the sequence converges, or (2) the sequence is demonstrably nonconvergent. The second possibility may quickly be tested for. Clearly, given the one-day overall time constraint, S^D (if such exists) must satisfy the relation, $S^D \leq 24/T$, where T is flight hours per sortie. If CUM $(24/T) < E$, then there is no solution. Given K days in which to destroy the target set, this criterion would simply become CUM$(24K/T) < E$. The test may easily be incorporated in the algorithm by taking $24K/T$ as S_0. In the case of Frontal Aviation, very little work along these lines need be done, as the first calculation of Appendix C (Iterations for S^D) makes clear.

All the values discussed in Chapter V, all those developed in Appendix A, and the virtual attrition parameter estimate above, are collected in Table B.1.

These are precisely the values employed in Simulation I. A few minor alterations are made in conducting Simulation II to reflect, for example, the lesser initial mass with which it confronts NATO, and the greater (by two days) mobilization time it affords the Soviet second echelon. All changes are noted under Simulation II below.

The switching rate, introduced in Table B.1, reflects the following choice. At the time of the attack, a certain fraction of the Soviets' frontline ground attack inventory will not be ready. Maintenance personnel assigned to this nonready portion of the force can be employed in bringing that force up to readiness. But they could also be "switched" to direct support of the ready attack force. Such a switch increases the wartime DMP for the ready attack force. A switching rate of 1 indicates the maximal switch, while a switching rate equal to the readiness rate of the ground attack force leaves the DMP at its peacetime value.[6] The maximum switching rate is assumed for the East European deployed force, but not for the Western Military Districts.

---

[6] P(0) = (FA invent.) × (Frac. not LRA/AD) × (Frac. ground attack)
× (Switching rate) × DMP.

F(0) = (FA invent.) × (Frac. not LRA/AD) × (Frac. ground attack)
× (Readiness rate).

SIMULATIONS AND SENSITIVITY ANALYSES

Estimates and methods finally in hand, the way is clear for our examination of the main issue: capabilities. As noted earlier, Soviet sortie rate demand is treated first, followed by the two main simulations of the analysis:

Simulation I assumes that Frontal Aviation attacks from maximum mass, operating at the very highest intensity (sortie rate) possible with the intent of completing the Phase I operation in the shortest possible time.

Simulation II addresses the question of whether the Soviets' results are improved if, instead of that furious attack from maximum mass, Frontal Air operates at a more measured pace, sustaining echeloned operations over a longer period. These are followed by extensive sensitivity analyses, with commentaries, concluding with a Soviet "high" estimate, whose plausibility is left for the reader to judge.

THE SORTIE RATE DEMANDED (S^D)

Since, at sortie rates greater than 16, a T (flight time per sortie) value of 1.5 is physically impossible, T is adjusted down at a number of points in the iteration procedure. With the exception of this variable, and of y (surprise), and S itself, all data are as listed in Table B.1 above. Following the iterative procedure developed in Appendix B, the sequence of trial sortie rate (S) values and their consequences are shown in Table C.1. Clearly, there is no solution for S^D. Even at a sortie rate of 24 per day with T = 1 (zero turnaround time), and with eight sorties of surprise, target destruction at exhaustion falls short of the *minimal* (Alternate 4 in Table 6.1) Phase I target set by almost 2,500 DGZs.

TABLE C.1
Iterations for the Sortie Rate Demanded (S^D)

Trial Sortie Rate:	$S_0 = 8$	$S_1 = 10$	$S_2 = 18$	$S_3 = 24$	$S_4 = 24$	$S_5 = 24$
x	0	0	0	0	0	0
y	1	2	3	4	6	8
T	1.5	1.5	1.33	1.0	1.0	1.0
Sorties to exhaust	15	15	15	15	16	17
Cum. DGZs	7,038	7,495	7,696	7,944	8,232	8,367

TABLE C.2
Simulation I—Target Destruction/Force Attrition Table

Time	Sortie, t	Force, F(t)	DGZs Destroyed	Cum. DGZs
D + 0	1	792[a]	2,662	
	2	461	1,901	
	3	268	1,106	
	4	156	643	
	5	91	374	
	6	53	218	
				6,904
D + 1	7	31	127	
	8	18	74	
	9	10	43	
	10	6	25	
	11	4	15	
	12	2	8	
				7,196
D + 2	13	1	5	
	14	1	3	
	15	—	2	
				7,206[b]

[a] $F(0) = 1,109$. Listed is the force *after* each sortie, attrition occurring after target destruction.

[b] In terms of the computer program offered below, this is the sum of the rounded values of DTPLUS1. The raw computer output gives a slightly lower Soviet total of 7,204.

Simulation I

This simulation assumes that Frontal Aviation attacks massively, with the intent of completing the Phase I operation—a preemptive, non-nuclear attack on NATO's nuclear response capability—in as short a time as possible.

There is no solution for S^D, and the consequences of sortie rates of 8 or greater are already clear. We will assume a sortie rate of 6.0. This, it must be reiterated, is a very high sortie rate, and, given the per sortie effectiveness (e.g., $P_K = 0.75$) we are assuming for the Soviets, it would certainly be a very admirable achievement for any of the world's air forces.

Flight time per sortie (T) is returned to its original value, as is surprise (y), so all values are exactly as given in Table B.1. Employing the six equations developed in Appendix B, target destruction and force attrition for this maximal attack are given in Table C.2.

Conclusions—Simulation I

Under all of the favorable assumptions built into the equations, and under all of the favorable assumptions made in assigning numerical values to the variables in them, Frontal Aviation falls short of destroying its Phase I target set by a very wide margin:

after one day, the shortage is $17,848 - 6,904 = 10,944$ DGZs;

after two days, the shortage is $17,848 - 7,196 = 10,652$ DGZs; and

at force exhaustion, the shortage is $17,848 - 7,206 = 10,642$ DGZs.

All of these shortages, moreover, are based on the assumption that Frontal Aviation *succeeds* in generating the sortie rate of 6.0, a significant achievement in its own right. In the minimum shortage case, Frontal Air has been assumed capable not only of generating that sortie rate, but of sustaining it with undegraded performance for two and one-half days. Had we insisted on some reduction in performance over the course of these days, the minimum shortfall would have been even great-er than 10,642 DGZs.

While the attack is not even close to fulfilling the Phase I goal, conformity even to this inadequate target destruction schedule completely exhausts the force. Not only, therefore, would the Phase I attack appear to be infeasible (regardless of the time frame), but such an attempt at the Phase I target set itself would appear to leave no aircraft surviving even to undertake Phase II. Indeed, Frontal Aviation's maximal cam-paign leaves 60 percent (in DGZs) of the Phase I set itself intact.

In summary, it seems highly implausible that Frontal Avia-tion could execute the attack of such grave concern to Western analysts. To say this is by no means to deny that Frontal Air is an object worthy of very serious concern. While even the full Phase I target set would appear to fall well outside its reach, critical NATO assets certainly fall well within it, as was discussed in Chapter VI.

Would Soviet results prove more decisive if, instead of this mode of attack, Frontal Aviation were to operate at a more measured pace, sustaining echeloned operations over a longer period of time? Simulation II addresses this question.

Simulation II

Simulation II is a more measured attack sustained in eche-lons over a longer period. The scenario is as follows.

The Frontal Air force deployed in Eastern Europe begins the assault alone. Operating at the more restrained, though still admirable sortie rate of 3.0, this force prosecutes the Phase I attack for two days, during which the forces in the USSR's Western Military Districts "stand down" and raise their readi-ness to reinforce the first echelon beginning on D + 2, the third day of operations. On D + 2, the second echelon force from the WMDs joins the initial force in the Phase I attack. The second echelon, too, operates at the sustainability-enhancing sortie rate of 3.0—half the rate generated in Simulation I.

We plot the course of events through the first six days. The issue is whether this more sustained approach is, from the Soviets' point of view, to be preferred over the more "doctrinaire" operation of Simulation I.

We will require two drawdown/target destruction profiles, one for each echelon. Each such schedule is computed exactly as in Simulation I, adding, at each sortie, the destructive contributions of each echelon. Cumulative destruction is simply the grand sum of these sortie-wise additions.

Given its two-day stand-down, the Western Military District force (the second echelon) is assumed to raise its readiness rate from its Simulation I value (0.6) to 0.7. The second echelon switching rate is assumed to rise correspondingly, from 0.6 to 0.7.

N, the mean number of active defense shots to which each attacker is exposed, has been raised modestly from 4 (Sim. I) to 5. The echeloned attack never confronts the defense with the mass of the Simulation I $F(0)$. The same defense is thus "larger" on a *per* attacker basis; i.e., N is larger.

Since the initial onslaught is more restrained in Simulation II, we will assume that a larger number of NATO's interceptors are in play; the difference is slight since the Simulation I attack does little to degrade their number. Nevertheless, their accuracy, superior to that of ground-based SHORAD systems, would raise the mean defensive kill probability. The more restrained pace of the attack itself, in addition, allows greater time for defensive target acquisition and coordination among SHORAD elements. For these reasons, the defensive kill probability is also raised, by 0.02, from its Simulation I value. For Simulation II, $P_d = 0.07$. It might be noted that increasing density contributes to the defensive kill probability in that sufficient densities in selected volumes of air space will force attackers onto unfavorable flight profiles—attackers can be "blocked," as it were, into cooperating defense systems.

These changes in the second echelon's readiness and switching rates, the defensive N and P_d values, and, of course, the sortie rate itself, are the only alterations to the values used in

TABLE C.3
Simulation II—Target Destruction/Force Attrition Table

Time	Sortie 1st Echel.	Sortie 2nd Echel.	Force 1st Echel.	Force 2nd Echel.	DGZs Destroyed 1st Echel.	DGZs Destroyed 2nd Echel.	Cum. DGZs
D + 0	1st		538[a]		1,671		
	2nd		289		1,291		
	3rd		156		694		
							3,656
D + 1	4th		84		373		
	5th		45		201		
	6th		24		108		
							4,338
D + 2	7th	1st	13	248[b]	58	1,157	
	8th	2nd	7	128	31	596	
	9th	3rd	4	66	17	307	
							6,504
D + 3	10th	4th	2	34	9	158	
	11th	5th	1	18	5	82	
	12th	6th	1	9	3	42	
							6,803
D + 4	13th	7th	—	5	1	22	
	14th	8th	—	2	—	11	
	15th	9th	—	1	—	6	
							6,843
D + 5	16th	10th	—	1	—	3	
	17th	11th	—	—	—	2	
					4,462 +	2,386 =	6,848[c]

[a] $F(0) = 696$. Listed is the force *after* each sortie, attrition occurring after target destruction
[b] $F(0) = 482$. See note a.
[c] For thoughts on the addition of further echelons, see note 4 of Chapter VI.

Simulation I. Otherwise, the values for each echelon are exactly as listed in Table B.1. This attack is charted in Table C.3.

CONCLUSION—SIMULATIONS I AND II COMPARED

The advantages of the Simulation I attack over this more measured and sustained operation are very clear.

The Simulation I attack destroys more DGZs in two days (7,196) than the Simulation II attack destroys in over five (6,848), at which point both echelons are exhausted entirely. Obviously, total cumulative destruction under Simulation I, at 7,206 DGZs, even further outweighs that achieved by the Simulation II attack. Moreover, the greater result is attained in less than half the time. Graphically, the Simulation I and II trajectories were presented in Chapter VI (see Fig. 6.1).

SENSITIVITY ANALYSES AND COMMENTARIES

Although most of the variable names used in the computer implementation of the equations have obvious meanings, some do not. To ensure the translatability of the computer results into the terminology used above, a key is provided:

FAINV $^x_{(y)}$ Frontal Air Inventory. The upper value, x, is the Eastern Europe deployed value; listed in parentheses beneath it is y, the Western Military Districts deployed value. In Tables C. 5 through C. 20, this convention is held to for all variables where the two values are assumed to differ. Otherwise, only one value is given.

NOTLRAD   The fraction of FAINV not allocated to LRA (long-range aviation), AD (air defense), or other missions.

FRACGA   The fraction of NOTLRAD that is specifically ground attack.

RRF   The readiness rate of the specifically ground attack force.

SR   The maintenance personnel switching rate; the fraction of personnel shifted from the not operationally ready force to ground support of the attack force. If the switching rate is 1.0, all personnel are shifted. If it equals RRF, then none are shifted.

DMP   The preswitching value of the regimental (direct) maintenance personnel-to-aircraft ratio.

H	As in the sortie supply equations, the mean workday.
TIME	Mean flight hours per sortie.
SELECTS	The selected Soviet sortie rate, S.
DELTA	δ, as in the MMH/FH equation.
COMIND	Commonality index, $\dfrac{1 - C(1,\,0)}{C(1,\,0)}$, as in the MMH/FH equation.
MZERO	M_0, as in the MMH/FH equation.
LAMBDA	λ, as in the virtual attrition formula.
DEFKILLP	Defensive single-shot kill probability, P_d.
N	As in the actual attrition factor $(1 - P_d)^N$.
REL	Reliability, r.
X	Sorties before virtual attrition sets in, as developed above.
SURPRIZ	Number of surprise sorties, y.
EM	m, DGZs targeted per plane per sortie.
OFFKILLP	Offensive kill probability, P_K.
SIM12P	Total direct wartime maintenance personnel, P(0).
SIM12F	The actual attack force, F(0).
MMHPERFH	Total peacetime maintenance manhours per flight hour.
ZERODEFS	$S^s(Z = 0)$, the zero deferral sortie rate.
ALPHA	Equilibrium deferral rate, α.
DTPLUS1	D(t + 1), per sortie target destruction.
STOREDT	Running cumulation of targets destroyed. The final listed value of STOREDT is cumulative destruction.
t	The sortie in question, first, second, third, etc.
FT	F(t), the Soviet force that, in expected terms, is surviving after the tth sortie.
Exhaustion Point (a, b)	The bth sortie of the ath day.

Since a rather large number of sensitivity analyses were conducted, the series for each variable is presented with only the final outputs: exhaustion point and cumulative targets destroyed. Such other information as α, $S^s(Z = 0)$, MMH/FH,

P(0), F(0), and per sortie target destruction, D(t + 1), may be recovered from the author's *Political Impediments to Military Effectiveness: The Case of Soviet Frontal Aviation* or by running the computer program in Table C. 4. The computer program, written in PL/1, merely implements the equations developed in Appendix B.

TABLE C.4
Computer Program (Source Listing)

1		0	SIMS: PROC OPTIONS (MAIN) REORDER;
			/* SIM I BEST ESTIMATE */
2	1	0	DCL FAINV (0:3) BIN FIXED INIT (0,1300,900,0),
			T FIXED BIN,
			J FIXED BIN INIT(0),
			NOTLRAD(0:3) FLOAT (16) INIT(0,.9,.9,0),
			FRACGA(0:3) FLOAT (16) INIT(0,.85,.85,0),
			SR(0:3) FLOAT (16) INIT(0,1,.6,0),
			RRF(0:3) FLOAT (16) INIT(0,.7,.6,0),
			DMP(0:3) FLOAT (16) INIT(0,5,5,0),
			PERS(0:3) FLOAT (16) INIT(0,0,0,0),
			FORCE(0:3) FLOAT (16) INIT(0,0,0,0),
			STOREDT FLOAT (16) INIT(0),
			H(0:3) FLOAT (16) INIT(8,0,0,0),
			TIME(0:3) FLOAT (16) INIT(1.5,0,0,0),
			SELECTS(0:3) FLOAT (16) INIT(6,0,0,0),
			DELTA(0:3) FLOAT (16) INIT(.15,0,0,0),
			COMIND(0:3) FLOAT (16) INIT(.90,0,0,0),
			MMHPERFH(0:3) FLOAT (16) INIT(0,0,0,0),
			MZERO(0:3) FLOAT (16) INIT(18,0,0,0),
			ALPHA(0:3) FLOAT (16) INIT(0,0,0,0),
			ZERODEFS(0:3) FLOAT (16) INIT(0,0,0,0),
			PROBNOTV(0:3) FLOAT (16) INIT(0,0,0,0),
			LAMBDA(0:3) FLOAT (16) INIT(.4,0,0,0),
			PROBNOTA(0:3) FLOAT (16) INIT(0,0,0,0),
			DEFKILLP(0:3) FLOAT (16) INIT(.05,0,0,0),
			N(0:3) FLOAT (16) INIT(4,0,0,0),
			OFFKILLP(0:3) FLOAT (16) INIT(.75,0,0,0),
			REL(0:3) FLOAT (16) INIT(.8,0,0,0),
			X(0:3) FLOAT (16) INIT(0,0,0,0),
			SURPRIZ(0:3) FLOAT (16) INIT(1,0,0,0),
			EM(0:3) FLOAT (16) INIT(4,0,0,0),

(*continued*)

TABLE C.4   (*continued*)

			FT(0:3) FLOAT (16) INIT(0,0,0,0),
			DTPLUS1(0:3) FLOAT (16) INIT(0,0,0,0),
			SIM12P FLOAT (16) INIT(0),
			SIM123P FLOAT (16) INIT(0),
			SIM12F FLOAT (16) INIT(0),
			SIM123F FLOAT (16) INIT(0);
3	1	0	DO J=1 TO 3;
4	1	1	PERS(J)=(FAINV(J)*NOTLRAD(J)*FRACGA(J)*SR(J) *DMP(J));
5	1	1	FORCE(J)=(FAINV(J)*NOTLRAD(J)*FRACGA(J) *RRF(J));
6	1	1	SIM12P=PERS(1)+PERS(2);
7	1	1	SIM12F=FORCE(1)+FORCE(2);
8	1	1	END;
			/* SIMULATION I ATTACK */
9	1	0	PUT DATA (SIM12P,SIM12F);
10	1	0	MMHPERFH(0)=MZERO(0)*(1+.95*(1+DELTA(0)) *(COMIND(0)));
11	1	0	PUT DATA (MMHPERFH(0));
12	1	0	ZERODEFS(0)=(H(0)*SIM12P/ (MMHPERFH(0)*TIME(0)*SIM12F);
13	1	0	PUT DATA (ZERODEFS(0));
14	1	0	ALPHA(0)=1-(ZERODEFS(0)/SELECTS(0));
15	1	0	PUT DATA (ALPHA(0));
16	1	0	STOREDT=0;
17	1	0	DO T=0 TO 1000 UNTIL (FT(0)<44/100);
18	1	1	IF T<=SURPRIZ(0) THEN PROBNOTA(0)=1;
19	1	1	ELSE PROBNOTA(0)=(1-DEFKILLP(0))**N(0);
20	1	1	IF T<=X(0) THEN PROBNOTV(0)=1;
21	1	1	ELSE PROBNOTV(0)=EXP((-1)*ALPHA(0) *LAMBDA(0));
22	1	1	FT(0)=SIM12F*(PROBNOTV(0)**(T-X(0))) *(PROBNOTA(0)**(T-SURPRIZ(0)));
23	1	1	DTPLUS1(0)=FT(0)*EM(0)*REL(0)*OFFKILLP(0);
24	1	1	PUT DATA(T,FT(0),DTPLUS1(0));
25	1	1	STOREDT=DTPLUS1(0)+STOREDT;
26	1	1	PUT DATA(STOREDT);
27	1	1	END;
			/*END OF PROGRAM*/
28	1	0	END;

SENSITIVITY TO FRONTAL AIR INVENTORY (FAINV)

There are three essential points to make about the celebrated beans i.e., Frontal Air Inventory. First, among the variations in Table C.5, the *smallest* Soviet force to satisfy the least demanding alternate (10,839 DGZs) to the Phase I criterion is a full 64 percent *larger* than the estimate applied in Simulations I and II. While the conclusions thus will withstand error in the 60 percent range, such large error seems especially implausible for this variable. The numbers themselves, after all, get most of the public attention and the available information is richer here than elsewhere. On the assumption that the initial estimates were reasonably accurate (if not in fact conservative, as was the intent), the Soviet inventory would have to grow by 150 percent before output (at 17,052 DGZs) verged on the full Phase I criterion of 17,848 DGZs, and it wouldn't quite make it at that, much less the entire two-phased operation.

In summary, one can quibble about the precise bean count. But, unless one can argue that the standard public sources are off by 60 percent, not even the lowest rung of the Phase I ladder seems plausible. To argue for the full Phase I criterion, one must establish error on the order of 150 percent (i.e., that the true value is two and one-half times our estimate).

The second thing to notice is that Soviet output is not, in fact, a linear function of Soviet inputs. While most of the debate makes that assumption implicitly, "twice as big" (in inputs) does not mean "twice as strong" (in output). Indeed, a doubling of the Soviet inventory falls short of doubling output by about 650 DGZs. This may bear out some of the Soviets' own trepidation concerning sheer numbers, as discussed in Chapter IV.

Third, it is interesting to compare Soviet numerical growth with other sorts of changes they might in the future undertake. For example, cutting the "force" of virtual attrition (i.e., Lambda, see sensitivity analysis below) from its Simulation I value by 75 percent would increase Soviet output almost as much as an 80 percent increase in inventory. Improvements in efficiency, that is, could easily outweigh dramatic increases in

TABLE C.5
Sensitivity to Frontal Air Inventory (FAINV)

	SIM I												
FAINV	1,300 (900)	1,500 (1,050)	1,625 (1,125)	1,700 (1,200)	1,900 (1,350)	2,100 (1,500)	2,300 (1,650)	2,600 (1,800)	3,250 (2,250)	3,900 (2,700)	4,550 (3,150)	5,200 (3,600)
NOTLRAD	0.9											
FRACGA	0.85											
SR	1.0 (0.6)											
RRF	0.7 (0.6)											
DMP[a]	5	4.33 (4.29)	4 (4)	3.82 (3.75)	3.42 (3.33)	3.10 (3.00)	2.83 (2.73)	2.50 (2.50)	2 (2)	1.67 (1.67)	1.43 (1.43)	1.25 (1.25)
H	8											
TIME	1.5											
SELECTS	6											
DELTA	0.15											

COMIND	0.9												
MZERO	18												
LAMBDA	0.4												
DEFKILLP	0.05												
N	4												
REL	0.8												
X	0												
SURPRIZ	1												
EM	4												
OFFKILLP	0.75												
SORTIES-EXHAUST	15	15	15	15	15	16	16	16	16	16	16	16	
EXHAUST POINT	(2, 3)	(2, 3)	(2, 3)	(2, 3)	(2, 3)	(2, 4)	(2, 4)	(2, 4)	(2, 4)	(2, 4)	(2, 4)	(2, 4)	
CUM DGZS	7,206	8,240	8,838	9,278	10,318	11,361	12,403	13,763	17,052	20,346	23,638	26,932	

NOTE: In this, and in all such tables that follow, a blank space means "as in Simulation I."

[a] The compensating reductions in the value of DMP are made in order that *total* direct maintenance personnel be held constant—like all other variables—as the Frontal Air inventory is raised.

the Soviet force size. But as we have seen, those improvements might require political and institutional reforms that are anathema to the Soviets. Are high numbers thus a symptom of *political* inertia? Perhaps so.

While uncertainty concerning Lambda's current value makes it hard to know where the virtual attrition and inventory curves would cross, the same comparison suggests that there is a point in the course of conflict at which NATO attacks on Soviet force "multipliers" would become more lucrative than attacks focused strictly on Soviet forces themselves. Attacks on the Soviet ground control (GCI) system, for example, might destroy fewer aircraft (actual attrition), but the same attacks might render a far greater number ineffective (virtual attrition).

Sensitivity to the Virtual Attrition Parameter (LAMBDA)

Recall that the probability of not virtually attriting per sortie is given by

$$1 - P(V) = e^{-\alpha\lambda}.$$

Force exhaustion, with x (the virtual attrition onset point) and y (surprise) equal to zero, proceeds as

$$F(t) = F(0)e^{-\alpha\lambda t}(1 - P_d)^{Nt}.$$

Exhaustion occurs at that time $\hat{t}$ such that $F(t) < 0.44$ (the largest two decimal-place number that would not be rounded up to 1); at that time $\hat{t}$, in other words, such that

$$0.44 = F(0)e^{-\alpha\lambda\hat{t}}(1 - P_d)^{N\hat{t}}.$$

Logging,

$$\ln(0.44) = \ln F(0) - \alpha\lambda\hat{t} + N\hat{t}\ln(1 - P_d),$$

which, upon some rearranging, yields

$$\hat{t} = \frac{\ln(0.44/F(0))}{N\ln(1 - P_d) - \alpha\lambda}.$$

Since, for purposes of sensitivity analysis they are fixed, let

$$\ln(0.44/F(0)) = C_1,$$

and let

$$N \ln(1 - P_d) = C_2.$$

Then,

$$\hat{t} = \frac{C_1}{C_2 - \alpha\lambda}.$$

The curve is steeper the smaller is λ and flattens out as λ increases. The sensitivity of the Simulation I estimate to variations in λ is presented in Table C.6 and Figure C.1.

As indicated by the table, the Simulation I value would have to overestimate λ by a factor of over four in order for "true" destruction to approach even the Phase I Alternate 3 (disruption) target set level. And, at $\lambda = 0.1$, even this would be achieved only after four and two-thirds days of operation. The full Phase I suppression set would still be infeasible as, of course, would be the initiation of Phase II operations.

Assuming that λ is in the neighborhood of the Simulation I value of 0.4, there are a number of important political implications for the Soviets.

Since λ is relatively high, only marginal returns in sustainability ($\hat{t}$) will result from incremental reductions—improvements—in λ. In addition, if one's λ is already high, then the penalty in sustainability for yet further increases in λ is, at the margin, hardly noticeable.

To the Soviet regimental maintenance chief (senior engineer), then, the situation might well look as follows: "Why work hard on reducing λ when my efforts will be hardly visible until I've essentially cut it in half? Moreover, why not relax even more, since the further penalty in sustainability will be even less visible?" An enforceable and compelling system of rewards focused on λ's improvement, and more importantly, an accurate system of measuring its *early* improvements— out on the flat—would be necessary to induce improvements in λ. High level involvement and a long-term commitment on

TABLE C.6
Sensitivity to the Virtual Attrition Parameter (LAMBDA)

	SIM 1								
FAINV	1,300 (900)								
NOTLRAD	0.9								
FRACGA	0.85								
SR	1 (0.6)								
RRF	0.7 (0.6)								
DMP	5								
H	8								
TIME	1.5								
SELECTS	6								
DELTA	0.15								
COMIND	0.9								
MZERO	18								
LAMBDA	0.4	0.6	0.5	0.3	0.2	0.175	0.150	0.125	0.10
DEFKILLP	0.05								
N	4								
REL	0.8								
X	0								
SURPRIZ	1								
EM	4								
OFFKILLP	0.75								
SORTIES-EXHAUST	15	12	13	18	22	23	25	26	28
EXHAUST POINT	(2, 3)	(2, 0)	(2, 1)	(3, 0)	(3, 4)	(3, 5)	(4, 1)	(4, 2)	(4, 4)

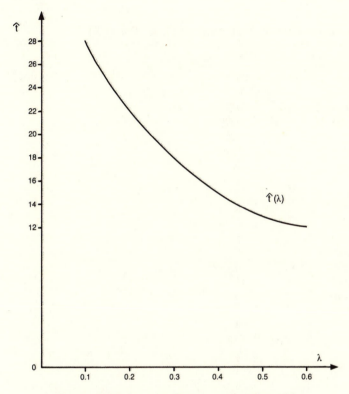

FIGURE C.1 Exhaustion Point as a Function of λ

the Soviets' part would appear to be called for if inherent incentives toward inertia are to be countered here.

SENSITIVITY TO THE VIRTUAL ATTRITION ONSET POINT (X)

Even if, once it sets in, virtual attrition proceeds at the *rate* estimated in Simulation I ($\lambda = 0.4$), there are definite returns to a delay in its onset. Both destruction and sustainability exhibit diminishing marginal returns to increases in x: $CUM(x = 4) - CUM(x = 3) = 983$, while $CUM(x = 1) - CUM(x = 0) = 1,818$. The first one counts most. (See Table C.7.)

TABLE C.7
Sensitivity to the Virtual Attrition Onset Point (X)

	SIM I				
FAINV	1,300				
	(900)				
NOTLRAD	0.9				
FRACGA	0.85				
SR	1.0				
	(0.6)				
RRF	0.7				
	(0.6)				
DMP	5				
H	8				
TIME	1.5				
SELECTS	6				
DELTA	0.15				
COMIND	0.9				
MZERO	18				
LAMBDA	0.4				
DEFKILLP	0.05				
N	4				
REL	0.8				
X	0	4	3	2	1
SURPRIZ	1				
EM	4				
OFFKILLP	0.75				
SORTIES-EXHAUST	15	18	17	17	16
EXHAUST POINT	(2, 3)	(3, 0)	(2, 5)	(2, 5)	(2, 4)
CUM DGZS	7,206	12,696	11,713	10,506	9,024

While peacetime Soviet training would appear to preclude (due to unfamiliar wartime defects, etc.) any significant forestalling of the effect, even if x were 4, destruction would still not rise to the Phase I Alternate 3 (disruption) level, even at exhaustion, though the latter would occur somewhat later, at (3, 0).

Sensitivity to Surprise (SURPRIZ)

Obviously, the role of NATO in Soviet attrition is significant. Exploitation of Soviet interoperability, GCI, and logistical problems, as well as the brittleness and apparent wartime fragility of the flow-line, are promising avenues of defense. As noted above, these operational weaknesses, among others, give the Soviets strong military incentives toward preemption, regardless of the political motivations (aggressive/defensive) that might underlie a decision to apply military force.

While it seems highly unlikely that NATO would fail to respond until after the Soviets' fourth sortie, the consequences of such a Soviet coup are worth noting, adding no fewer than 1,336 DGZs to destruction. Intermediate values are noted as well in Table C.8.

Sensitivity to the Sortie Rate (SELECTS)

For all the reasons given in discussing Soviet doctrine, the Soviets would have powerful incentives to complete Phase I and go on to direct support of the ground campaign, Phase II, as quickly as possible. That dictates a high sortie rate and we have assumed, generously, that the Soviets could execute 6 sorties per day.

But, as we have also discussed, certain penalties in sustainability are associated with such a high pace; the precipitous deferrals of maintenance necessary to achieve that sortie rate take their toll as it is sustained.

Comparing the Soviets' incentives for rapidity to its penalties reveals an intriguing dilemma. (See Table C.9.) On the one hand, they could avoid the penalties of a ferocious pace by cutting their sortie rate drastically to, say, one sortie per day. At that pace they could satisfy (with 15,548 DGZs) the second alternate (14,339 DGZs) to the full Phase I criterion. But it would take them well over a month (i.e. 36 days) to do so. They'd get over twice the output, but it would take over *fourteen* times as long. Under any but the least demanding alternates, of course, Phase II, and with it the full two-phased operation, would be infeasible regardless.

TABLE C.8
Sensitivity to Surprise (SURPRIZ)

	SIM I				
FAINV	1,300				
	(900)				
NOTLRAD	0.9				
FRACGA	0.85				
SR	1.0				
	(0.6)				
RRF	0.7				
	(0.6)				
DMP	5				
H	8				
TIME	1.5				
SELECTS	6				
DELTA	0.15				
COMIND	0.9				
MZERO	18				
LAMBDA	0.4				
DEFKILLP	0.05				
N	4				
REL	0.8				
X	0				
SURPRIZ	1	2	3	4	0
EM	4				
OFFKILLP	0.75				
SORTIES-EXHAUST	15	16	16	16	15
EXHAUST POINT	(2, 3)	(2, 4)	(2, 4)	(2, 4)	(2, 3)
CUM DGZS	7,206	7,806	8,236	8,542	6,362

But even if it were not, imagine that you are the Soviets, and you believe that Frontal Aviation's second phase is critical to the ground war. Could you afford to wait *more than a month* for Frontal Aviation to wrap up its Phase I (counternuclear) operation? The incentives for a decisive initial phase are as strong on the ground as they are in the air.

TABLE C.9
Sensitivity to the Sortie Rate (SELECTS)

	SIM 1						
FAINV	1,300						
	(900)						
NOTLRAD	0.9						
FRACGA	0.85						
SR	1.0						
	(0.6)						
RRF	0.7						
	(0.6)						
DMP	5						
H	8						
TIME	1.5						
SELECTS	6	5	4	3	2	1.5	1
DELTA	0.15						
COMIND	0.9						
MZERO	18						
LAMBDA	0.4						
DEFKILLP	0.05						
N	4						
REL	0.8						
X	0						
SURPRIZ	1						
EM	4						
OFFKILLP	0.75						
SORTIES-EXHAUST	15	16	16	17	20	23	36
EXHAUST POINT	(2, 3)	(3, 1)	(4, 0)	(5, 2)	(10, 0)	(15, 1)	(36, 0)
CUM DGZs	7,206	7,345	7,569	7,983	9,004	10,396	15,548

SENSITIVITY TO DIRECT MAINTENANCE PERSONNEL (DMP)

Reducing the force of virtual attrition (λ) and delaying its onset (x) would likely yield greater benefit to the Soviets than either manpower expansions or even certain types of aircraft performance enhancements (discussed below). Inasmuch as λ and x are measures of wartime labor efficiency, this means first that increased (wartime) productivity outweighs an expanded manpower base.

For example, an increase of the direct (preswitching ML_1) maintenance personnel-to-aircraft ratio to 15—which, if our Simulation I estimate is correct, would represent a tripling—increases cumulative destruction by 1,798. (See Table C.10.) This is less than the return to a single sortie of virtual attrition delay: $CUM(x = 1) - CUM(x = 0) = 1,818$. The tripling in DMP is even further outweighed by a halving of λ; $CUM(\lambda = 0.2) - CUM(\lambda = 0.4) = 2,671$.

Of course, our estimates for DMP, λ, and x could be off in absolute terms. Nevertheless, the above results suggest that, in their *relative* impact on destruction, λ ranks first, x second, and DMP third within this group.

SENSITIVITY TO THE MAINTENANCE WORKDAY (H)

It is hard to believe that labor efficiency would not fall were maintenance personnel pushed to work a twenty-hour day. But, not even that assumption would challenge our basic conclusions, as demonstrated in Table C.11.

SENSITIVITY TO FLIGHT TIME PER SORTIE (TIME)

Certain types of performance enhancement must also take a back seat to the virtual attrition-related variables, at least in regard to the impact of their variation upon real output. Our Simulation I assumption of a mean flight time per sortie of 1.5 hours costs the Soviets 363 DGZs more than would the assumption of 1.0 hours. (See Table C.12.) At the latter figure,

TABLE C.10
Sensitivity to Direct Maintenance Personnel (DMP)

	SIM I								
FAINV	1,300 (900)								
NOTLRAD	0.9								
FRACGA	0.85								
SR	1.0 (0.6)								
RRF	0.7 (0.6)								
DMP	5	4	6	7	8	10	12	14	15
H	8								
TIME	1.5								
SELECTS	6								
DELTA	0.15								
COMIND	0.9								
MZERO	18								
LAMBDA	0.4								
DEFKILLP	0.05								
N	4								
REL	0.8								
X	0								
SURPRIZ	1								
EM	4								
OFFKILLP	0.75								
SORTIES-EXHAUST	15	14	16	16	16	17	18	19	20
EXHAUST POINT	(2, 3)	(2, 2)	(2, 4)	(2, 4)	(2, 4)	(2, 5)	(3, 0)	(3, 1)	(3, 2)
CUM DGZs	7,206	7,070	7,345	7,493	7,647	7,983	8,357	8,775	9,004

TABLE C.11
Sensitivity to the Maintenance Workday (H)

	SIM I						
FAINV	1,300						
	(900)						
NOTLRAD	0.9						
FRACGA	0.85						
SR	1.0						
	(0.6)						
RRF	0.7						
	(0.6)						
DMP	5						
H	8	10	12	14	16	18	20
TIME	1.5						
SELECTS	6						
DELTA	0.15						
COMIND	0.9						
MZERO	18						
LAMBDA	0.4						
DEFKILLP	0.05						
N	4						
REL	0.8						
X	0						
SURPRIZ	1						
EM	4						
OFFKILLP	0.75						
SORTIES-EXHAUST	15	16	16	17	17	18	18
EXHAUST POINT	(2, 3)	(2, 4)	(2, 4)	(2, 5)	(2, 5)	(3, 0)	(3, 0)
CUM DGZS	7,206	7,381	7,569	7,770	7,983	8,212	8,456

TABLE C.12
Sensitivity to Flight Time per Sortie (TIME)

	SIM I					
FAINV	1,300 (900)					
NOTLRAD	0.9					
FRACGA	0.85					
SR	1.0 (0.6)					
RRF	0.7 (0.6)					
DMP	5					
H	8					
TIME	1.5	0.75	1.0	1.33	1.67	2.0
SELECTS	6					
DELTA	0.15					
COMIND	0.9					
MZERO	18					
LAMBDA	0.4					
DEFKILLP	0.05					
N	4					
REL	0.8					
X	0					
SURPRIZ	1					
EM	4					
OFFKILLP	0.75					
SORTIES-EXHAUST	15	17	16	16	15	15
EXHAUST POINT	(2, 3)	(2, 5)	(2, 4)	(2, 4)	(2, 3)	(2, 3)
CUM DGZs	7,206	7,983	7,569	7,294	7,135	7,038

CUM(TIME = 1.0) = 7,569 as against our CUM(TIME = 1.5) = 7,206. The variable, however, compares weakly with others as a sensitivity-driver: CUM(TIME = 0.75) − CUM(TIME = 2.0) = 945 is the complete span. Even at its lower bound, 0.75, destruction falls short of the Phase I fourth alternate (10,839) requirement by a wide margin.

SENSITIVITY TO DGZS TARGETED PER SORTIE (EM), RELIABILITY (REL), AND OFFENSIVE KILL PROBABILITY (OFFKILLP)

Other performance assumptions, however, weigh quite heavily on estimates of capability: the EM (DGZs targeted per sortie, m), REL (maintained reliability, r), and OFFKILLP (offensive P_K) estimates. These are the variables to which cumulative destruction is linearly sensitive and by which sustainability (the exhaustion point) is unaffected.

Allowing $\hat{t}$ to denote the exhaustion point, cumulative destruction is given by

$$CUM(t + 1) = \sum_{t=0}^{\hat{t}} D(t + 1) = \sum_{t=0}^{\hat{t}} F(t)mrP_K = mrP_K \sum_{t=0}^{\hat{t}} F(t).$$

Holding every variable but m constant, one may think of CUM as a function of m alone, CUM(m). Thus, for any number, k,

$$CUM(km) = (km)rP_K \sum_{t=0}^{\hat{t}} F(t).$$

The right-hand side is obviously the same as

$$k\left(mrP_K \sum_{t=0}^{\hat{t}} F(t)\right).$$

And since the parenthesized term is CUM(m), it follows that

$$CUM(km) = kCUM(m).$$

Doubling m doubles cumulative destruction; halving the former halves the latter. It is the same with (maintained) reliability, as we have used that term, and for the kill probability, P_K. None of these variables affects the exhaustion point of the

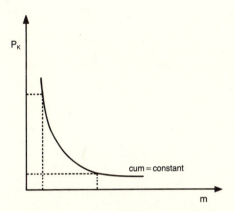

FIGURE C.2 Constant Destruction Curve

attack, since none bears either on the initial force, F(0), or upon factors responsible for its decay.

Leaving reliability aside, linearity in both P_K and m means that any pairing (P_K, m) whose product $(P_K \cdot m)$ is, as in Simulation I, 3.0, will leave cumulative destruction unaffected (see Figure C.2). Thus, while the reader might, for example, find m = 4 to be unfavorable to the Soviets, surely the same cannot be said of the Soviets' assumed wartime P_K of 0.75. The issue, from the point of view of cumulative destruction, is the product of the two. While adjustments in either may be reasonable, reasonable adjustments would be in opposite directions, producing a net difference in cumulative destruction too small to call into question our basic conclusions.

Indeed, reduction of P_K to an admirable wartime value of 0.45 (still over four times the U.S. AIM-7 Vietnam value) would wash out most of a doubling in m from 4 to 8.

$$\text{CUM}(P_K = 0.45, m = 8) = 8,647$$

$$\text{Sim. I CUM}(P_K = 0.75, m = 4) = 7,206$$

$$\text{Net increase} = 1,441$$

The consequences of variation in m, r, and P_K are illustrated in Tables C.13, C.14, and C.15.

TABLE C.13
Sensitivity to DGZs Targeted per Sortie (EM)

	SIM I							
FAINV	1,300							
	(900)							
NOTLRAD	0.9							
FRACGA	0.85							
SR	1.0							
	(0.6)							
RRF	0.7							
	(0.6)							
DMP	5							
H	8							
TIME	1.5							
SELECTS	6							
DELTA	0.15							
COMIND	0.9							
MZERO	18							
LAMBDA	0.4							
DEFKILLP	0.05							
N	4							
REL	0.8							
X	0							
SURPRIZ	1							
EM	4	6	5.5	5.0	4.5	3.5	3.0	2.5
OFFKILLP	0.75							
SORTIES-EXHAUST	15							
EXHAUST POINT	(2,3)							
CUM DGZS	7,206	10,809	9,908	9,008	8,107	6,305	5,405	4,504

TABLE C.14
Sensitivity to Maintained Reliability (REL)

	SIM I								
FAINV	1,300 (900)								
NOTLRAD	0.9								
FRACGA	0.85								
SR	1.0 (0.6)								
RRF	0.7 (0.6)								
DMP	5								
H	8								
TIME	1.5								
SELECTS	6								
DELTA	0.15								
COMIND	0.9								
MZERO	18								
LAMBDA	0.4								
DEFKILLP	0.05								
N	4								
REL	0.8	0.85	0.75	0.7	0.65	0.6	0.55	0.5	0.9
X	0								
SURPRIZ	1								
EM	4								
OFFKILLP	0.75								
SORTIES-EXHAUST	15								
EXHAUST POINT	(2, 3)								
CUM DGZS	7,206	7,656	6,756	6,305	5,855	5,405	4,954	4,504	8,107

TABLE C.15
Sensitivity to the Offensive Kill Probability (OFFKILLP)

	SIM I								
FAINV	1,300 (900)								
NOTLRAD	0.9								
FRACGA	0.85								
SR	1.0 (0.6)								
RRF	0.7 (0.6)								
DMP	5								
H	8								
TIME	1.5								
SELECTS	6								
DELTA	0.15								
COMIND	0.9								
MZERO	18								
LAMBDA	0.4								
DEFKILLP	0.05								
N	4								
REL	0.8								
X	0								
SURPRIZ	1								
EM	4								
OFFKILLP	0.75	0.8	0.7	0.65	0.60	0.55	0.50	0.45	0.40
SORTIES-EXHAUST	15								
EXHAUST POINT	(2, 3)								
CUM DGZS	7,206	7,686	6,726	6,245	5,765	5,284	4,804	4,324	3,843

Sensitivity to Variables in the Maintenance
Manhours per Flight Hour (MMHPERFH) Group

MZERO, DELTA, and COMIND are the variables that
register peacetime adjustability to technological change, as
reflected in total peacetime maintenance manhours per flight
hour. Although the effects of variation in each is recorded in
Tables C.16, C.17, and C.18, our conclusions do not appear to
be overly threatened by admissions of some inaccuracy here.
Specifically, none of the variations examined drives destruction into the Phase I requirement or any of its less demanding
alternates.

Sensitivity to the Density (N) and
Lethality (DEFKILLP) of the Defense

Last, but not least, is NATO itself. Among the classic
choices in defense analysis, the quantity vs. quality opposition
provides a context for the sensitivity analysis on the density
and lethality of NATO's defenses. (See Table C.19.)

Reduction of the Simulation I N (quantity) by one shot per
plane per sortie gives the Soviets an additional 357 DGZs,
while a reduction of NATO's defensive single-shot kill probability (quality) to 0.04 raises Soviet DGZs by 285. The former
reduction adds two sorties to the Phase I operation; the latter,
one.

However, the Simulation I estimates for NATO seem, if anything, overly conservative, as discussed above. A doubling of
NATO's density (N) reduces Phase I destruction by 932, to
6,274. A doubling of NATO's kill probability, however, reduces Soviet output by slightly more, 968, with cumulative
destruction of 6,238 DGZs at the exhaust point. This, it might
be added, occurs earlier where quality, as opposed to quantity,
is doubled.

Lacking cost data, no fully informed judgment on the preferability of quality—as against quantity—enhancement can
be made, though these relative effectiveness results are of
interest.

TABLE C.16
Sensitivity to Baseline Maintenance Manhours per Flight Hour (MZERO)

	SIM I							
FAINV	1,300 (900)							
NOTLRAD	0.9							
FRACGA	0.85							
SR	1.0 (0.6)							
RRF	0.7 (0.6)							
DMP	5							
H	8							
TIME	1.5							
SELECTS	6							
DELTA	0.15							
COMIND	0.9							
MZERO	18	14	16	20	25	30	35	40
LAMBDA	0.4							
DEFKILLP	0.05							
N	4							
REL	0.8							
X	0							
SURPRIZ	1							
EM	4							
OFFKILLP	0.75							
SORTIES-EXHAUST	15	16	16	15	15	15	15	14
EXHAUST POINT	(2, 3)	(2, 4)	(2, 4)	(2, 3)	(2, 3)	(2, 3)	(2, 3)	(2, 2)
CUM DGZS	7,206	7,407	7,292	7,136	7,019	6,943	6,890	6,850

Sensitivity to Relative Adjustability (DELTA)

	SIM I	2.0	1.5	1.0	0.5	0.0	−0.5	−1.0
FAINV	1,300 (900)							
NOTLRAD	0.9							
FRACGA	0.85							
SR	1.0 (0.6)							
RRF	0.7 (0.6)							
DMP	5							
H	8							
TIME	1.5							
SELECTS	6							
DELTA	0.15	2.0	1.5	1.0	0.5	0.0	−0.5	−1.0
COMIND	0.9							
MZERO	18							
LAMBDA	0.4							
DEFKILLP	0.05							
N	4							
REL	0.8							
X	0							
SURPRIZ	1							
EM	4							
OFFKILLP	0.75							
SORTIES-EXHAUST	15	15	15	15	15	15	16	17
EXHAUST POINT	(2, 3)	(2, 3)	(2, 3)	(2, 3)	(2, 3)	(2, 3)	(2, 4)	(2, 5)
CUM DGZs	7,206	6,916	6,963	7,026	7,116	7,252	7,484	7,968

TABLE C.18
Sensitivity to the Commonality Index (COMIND)

	SIM I					
FAINV	1,300					
	(900)					
NOTLRAD	0.9					
FRACGA	0.85					
SR	1.0					
	(0.6)					
RRF	0.7					
	(0.6)					
DMP	5					
H	8					
TIME	1.5					
SELECTS	6					
DELTA	0.15					
COMIND	0.9	0.10	0.50	1.3	1.7	2.0
MZERO	18					
LAMBDA	0.4					
DEFKILLP	0.05					
N	4					
REL	0.8					
X	0					
SURPRIZ	1					
EM	4					
OFFKILLP	0.75					
SORTIES-EXHAUST	15	17	16	15	15	15
EXHAUST POINT	(2, 3)	(2, 5)	(2, 4)	(2, 3)	(2, 3)	(2, 3)
CUM DGZS	7,206	7,801	7,405	7,083	7,002	6,957

The important point, in any event, is that neither of the reductions in N and P_d presented above substantially alters the Soviets' Phase I shortfall.

SUMMARY OF SENSITIVITY ANALYSES

Leaving aside—quite safely—counting errors in excess of 150 percent (see Table C.5), *none* of the variations reviewed will drive destruction to equality with the full Phase I criterion.

TABLE C.19
Sensitivity to the Density (N) and Lethality (DEFKILLP) of the Defense

	SIM I										
FAINV	1,300										
	(900)										
NOTLRAD	0.9										
FRACGA	0.85										
SR	1.0										
	(0.6)										
RRF	0.7										
	(0.6)										
DMP	5										
H	8										
TIME	1.5										
SELECTS	6										
DELTA	0.15										
COMIND	0.9										
MZERO	18										
LAMBDA	0.4										
DEFKILLP	0.05						0.04	0.06	0.08	0.10	0.12
N	4	3	5	6	7	8					
REL	0.8										
X	0										
SURPRIZ	1										
EM	4										
OFFKILLP	0.75										
SORTIES-EXHAUST	15	17	14	13	12	12	16	14	13	11	10
EXHAUST POINT	(2, 3)	(2, 5)	(2, 2)	(2, 1)	(2, 0)	(2, 3)	(2, 4)	(2, 2)	(2, 1)	(1, 5)	(1, 4)
CUM DGZs	7,206	7,563	6,909	6,662	6,453	6,274	7,491	6,957	6,553	6,238	5,986

Indeed, the vast preponderance of the runs offered fail—even under quantum Soviet improvements—to hoist destruction above the least demanding alternate (number 4) to the Phase I target set alone; the majority don't even cross the threshold into that destructive range. Our basic results and conclusions would seem to enjoy a certain stability.

THE SOVIET "HIGH ESTIMATE"

Inputs to whose isolated variation output is relatively insensitive, however, may vary simultaneously, compounding their individually inconsequential returns to produce significant changes in results. While the plausibility of this simultaneous variation is low, the Soviet "high" run may be considered as a case in point.

As in the Kremlinological passtime, *what if* Lenin had lived?", so too, in this case, the "ifs" are numerous. Specifically,

IF, in Simulation I, the Frontal Air inventory was underestimated by 25 percent;

IF, a sortie rate, S, of 8.0 were sustained;

IF, at that rate, and over the full duration of the campaign, kill probabilities held at the very high wartime level of 0.75;

IF, even though the higher is S, the more difficult is virtual attrition to forestall, the Soviets at once increased S by 33 percent *and* raised X;

IF, in addition to forestalling its onset, the Soviets, at the same 33 percent rise in S, were to *reduce* the probability of virtual attrition, i.e., *reduce* LAMBDA by 25 percent;

IF, the Soviets have faced not a single modernization problem more serious than the U.S. (DELTA = 0.0);

IF, in Simulation I, Soviet payloads (EM), total direct maintenance personnel, labor utilization (H), and readiness (RRF) were underestimated;

IF, in Simulation I, moreover, Soviet flight times per sortie (TIME) and baseline MMH/FH (MZERO) were overestimated;

TABLE C.20
Soviet "High Estimate"

	SIM I	
FAINV	1,300	1,625
	(900)	(1,125)
NOTLRAD	0.9	
FRACGA	0.85	
SR	1.0	1.0
	(0.6)	(0.7)
RRF	0.7	0.8
	(0.6)	(0.7)
DMP	5	4.5
H	8	9
TIME	1.5	1.33
SELECTS	6	8
DELTA	0.15	0
COMIND	0.9	
MZERO	18	16
LAMBDA	0.4	0.3
DEFKILLP	0.05	
N	4	
REL	0.8	
X	0	1
SURPRIZ	1	
EM	4	5
OFFKILLP	0.75	
SORTIES-EXHAUST	15	19
EXHAUST POINT	(2, 3)	(2, 3)
CUM DGZs	7,206	17,766

then, Soviet target destruction would fall short of the full Phase I requirement by only 82 DGZs after roughly two and one-half days of operation. Phase II, needless to say, and with it, the complete Frontal Air mission, would still be infeasible. (See Table C.20.)

A SCIENCE OF THE PLAUSIBLE
WITH THREE THEOREMS

The entire exercise recorded in this book may be seen as a special case of a far more general procedure for arriving at reasoned judgments of military plausibility. Leaving aside all sorts of technical complications (e.g., differentiability, ranges of definition), that general framework for self-examination may be set forth—here, in the context of threat assessment—as follows.

1. Required Soviet output (i.e., the criterion of Soviet success) is set as low as is plausible. Call that level $\underline{z}$.
2. Simulated Soviet output is a function of n variables, some offensive, some defensive: $(u_1, u_2, \ldots, u_n)$.
3. That function is conservative in a formal sense and is denoted by $f(u_1, u_2, \ldots, u_n)$.
4. For each i,

$$\text{If} \begin{cases} \dfrac{\partial f}{\partial u_i} \geq 0, \text{ assign } u_i \text{ the highest plausible value} \\[2ex] \dfrac{\partial f}{\partial u_i} < 0, \text{ assign } u_i \text{ the lowest plausible value.} \end{cases}$$

That is, if an increase in u_i increases Soviet output, assign u_i the highest plausible value, and if its increase reduces Soviet output, assign u_i the lowest plausible value. (The correct value of u_i, if that is known, is of course the highest and lowest plausible value.)

5. Denote the vector of values thus assigned by $(\bar{u}_1, \ldots, \bar{u}_n)$.
6. Let simulated Soviet output be denoted by $\bar{z} = f(\bar{u}_1, \ldots, \bar{u}_n)$. $\bar{z}$ is the maximum plausible Soviet output. Thus,

7. If $\bar{z} < \underline{z}$, the threat is not plausible; otherwise, the threat is plausible.
8. Sensitivity analysis examines

$$df = \sum_{i=1}^{n} \frac{\partial f}{\partial u_i} \, du_i,$$

for various choices of i and du_i.

Although it may appear to be a prescription for "worst case" threat assessment, in fact it isn't. In no way does it predetermine conclusions. But, by ensuring that conclusions are consistent with one's own judgments of plausibility, it forces one to disaggregate overall military impressions and come to grips with the problem of judgment itself.

Neither is this framework a substitute for the "art of war" or its appreciation. But it allows military intuitions and experience to be *applied* more explicitly, and critically, in assessing threats and deriving military requirements. Indeed, the general approach leads quickly to basic insights for deterrent planning.

On the Duality of Threat Bounding and Deterrent Force Planning: A Formal Critique of Mirror-Imaging

Suppose the threat is found to be plausible (i.e., $\bar{z} > \underline{z}$) and you (the defender) wish to render it implausible. Some of the u_i's are under your control. So, for expository purposes, break the u_i's up into a Soviet group (call these the x_i's) and a defensive group of y_i's that you can manipulate.

Then $(u_1, \ldots, u_n) = (x_1, \ldots, x_m; y_1, \ldots, y_k)$ with $m + k = n$, from above. Using the same formally conservative function, f, by which your threat bounding was conducted, leave all the Soviet settings at their above "maximal" values (which, of course, might be their lowest or highest plausible values, depending on the signs of partial derivatives under step 4 above). Denote those values $\bar{x}_i$.

Then, as a force planner, you seek the set of all vectors $(y_1, \ldots, y_k)$ for which the maximum plausible Soviet output is less than the minimum plausible criterion of Soviet success $\underline{z}$. Clearly, all vectors satisfying

$$f(\bar{x}_1, \ldots, \bar{x}_m; y_1, \ldots, y_k) < \underline{z} \qquad (1)$$

will meet the requirement. But, in general,

Theorem 1: $(y_1, \ldots, y_k)$ is not unique.

For a given defense problem, in general, a range of solutions exists.

Theorem 2:   Even where $k = m$, it is not in general the case that $(y_1, \ldots, y_k) = (\bar{x}_1, \ldots, \bar{x}_k)$ is among the solutions.

Mirror-imaging—matching the Soviets "tank-for-tank and gun-for-gun"—may not even address the defense problem in question.

Theorem 3:   Over the set of vectors $(y_1, \ldots, y_k)$ that satisfy (1), it is not in general the case that the mirror-image $(y_1, \ldots, y_k)$ $= (\bar{x}_1, \ldots, \bar{x}_k)$ minimizes

$$\sum_{i=1}^{k} y_i p_i,$$

where p_i is the cost per unit improvement in y_i.[1]

Even where the mirror-image is among the solutions, there is no reason to assume it is the most cost-effective solution. It might be, but nothing ensures this in general.

[1] Improvement, again, might mean reduction or increase, depending on the signs of partial derivatives under Step 4 above.

SELECTED BIBLIOGRAPHY

NOTE: Titles preceded by a single asterisk discuss the Soviet Frontal Air threat more or less specifically. Titles preceded by two asterisks are technical, and bear on the problem of mathematical simulation more generally.

"A-10 Reliability Expands Crew Training." *Aviation Week and Space Technology*, 6 February 1978.

**Abchuk, V. A., L. A. Yemel'yanov, F. A. Matveychuk, and V. G. Suzdal'. *Vvedeniye v Teoriyu Vyrabotki Resheniy* (Introduction to decision-making theory). Moscow: Military Publishing House, 1972. Translated by Joint Publications Research Service, November 1972. Distributed by National Technical Information Service, U.S. Department of Commerce (hereafter referred to as NTIS), no. JPRS 57404.

Alexander, Arthur J. *Decision-Making in Soviet Weapons Procurement*. Adelphi Papers nos. 147 and 148. London: The International Institute for Strategic Studies, Winter 1978/79.

_____. *The Process of Soviet Weapons Design*. Paper presented at Technology Trends Colloquium, U.S. Naval Academy, Annapolis, Md., March-April 1978.

_____. *R&D in Soviet Aviation*. R-589-PR. Santa Monica, Calif.: The Rand Corporation, November 1970.

_____. *Weapons Acquisition in the Soviet Union, United States, and France*. P-4989. Santa Monica, Calif.: The Rand Corporation, March 1973.

Alexander, Arthur J., Abraham S. Becker, and William E. Hoehn, Jr. *The Significance of Divergent US-USSR Military Expenditure*. N-100-AF. Santa Monica, Calif.: The Rand Corporation, February 1979.

Alexander, Arthur J., and J. R. Nelson. *Measuring Technological Change: Aircraft Turbine Engines*. R-1017-ARPA/PR. Santa Monica, Calif.: The Rand Corporation, June 1972.

Allison, Graham T., ed. *Adequacy of Current Organization: Defense and Arms Control*. Vol. 4, *Appendices*. Commission on the Organization of the Government for the Conduct of Foreign Policy, June 1975. Washington, D.C.: Government Printing Office, 1976.

Amstadter, Bertram L. *Reliability Mathematics*. New York: McGraw-Hill Book Co., 1971.

**Anderson, Lowell Bruce, Jerome Bracken, James G. Healy, Mary J. Hutzler, and Edward Kerlin. *IDA Ground-Air Model I (IDAGAM I)*. Vol. 1, *Comprehensive Description*. R-199. Arlington, Va.: Institute for Defense Analyses, Program Analysis Division, October 1974.

**Anderson, Lowell Bruce, Patricia A. Frazier, Mary J. Hutzler, and Frances Jan Smoot. *Documentation of the IDA Tactical Air Model (IDATAM) Computer Program*. IDA Paper P-1409. Arlington, Va.: Institute for Defense Analyses, Program Analysis Division, February 1979.

Anfilov, K. "Radar Repairs by Troop Personnel." *Vestnik Protivovozdushnoy Oborony*, no. 1 (1973). T3, 27 June 1973.

**Anureyev, I., and Tatarchenko, A. *Premeneniye Mathematicheskikh Metodov v Voyennom Dele* (Application of mathematical methods in military affairs). Moscow, 1967. T3, January 1973. Distributed by NTIS, no. AD-757 236. (Note: only Chapters 2, 4, and 5 are translated.)

Armstrong, Bruce E. *Avionics Data for Cost Estimating*. P-5745-1. Santa Monica, Calif.: The Rand Corporation, March 1977.

Artemov, N. "At a Field Air Base." *Znamenosets*, no. 8 (August 1978). T1, January 1979.

Babayev, Aleksandr Ivanovich. "Flight and the Combat Maneuver." *Krasnaya Zvezda*, 23 December 1976. T1, April 1977.

Bazovsky, Igor. *Reliability Theory and Practice*. Englewood Cliffs, N.J.: Prentice-Hall, 1961.

Beecher, William. "Soviets Miscalculated, Analysts Say." *The Boston Globe*, 17 February 1980.

Bell, C. F., and J. P. Stucker. *A Technique for Determining*

Maintenance Manpower Requirements for Aircraft Units. R-770-PR. Santa Monica, Calif.: The Rand Corporation, May 1971.

Berliner, Joseph S. *The Innovation Decision in Soviet Industry.* Cambridge: M.I.T. Press, 1978.

*Berman, Robert P. *Soviet Air Power in Transition.* Washington, D.C.: The Brookings Institution, 1978.

Binkin, Martin. *Support Costs in the Defense Budget—The Submerged One-Third.* Washington, D.C.: The Brookings Institution, 1972.

"Black Flag Readies Maintenance Crews." *Aviation Week and Space Technology,* 6 February 1978.

Blanchard, Benjamin S., and E. Edward Lowery. *Maintainability* New York: McGraw-Hill Book Co., 1969.

Blanco, Thomas A., George Chernowitz, James Cicotti, and Alan Lee. *Technology Trends and Maintenance Workload Requirements for the A-7, F-4, and F-14 Aircraft.* NPRDC TR 79-19. San Diego, Calif.: Navy Personnel Research and Development Center, May 1979.

*Blechman, Barry M., Robert P. Berman, Martin Binkin, Stuart E. Johnson, Robert G. Weinland, and Frederic W. Young. *The Soviet Military Buildup and U.S. Defense Spending.* Washington D.C.: The Brookings Institution, 1977.

Calabro, S. R. *Reliability Principles and Practices.* New York: McGraw-Hill Book Co., 1962.

Campbell, Heather. *Controversy in Soviet R&D: The Airship Case Study.* R-1001-PR. Santa Monica, Calif.: The Rand Corporation, October 1972.

Canby, Steven L. *The Contribution of Tactical Airpower in Countering a Blitz: European Perceptions.* Silver Spring, Md.: Technology Service Corporation, 1977.

_____. *Tactical Airpower in Europe: Airing the European View.* Santa Monica, Calif.: Technology Service Corporation, July 1976.

Carpenter-Huffman, Polly, and Bernard Rostker. *The Relevance of Training for the Maintenance of Advanced Avionics.* R-1894-AF. Santa Monica, Calif.: The Rand Corporation, December 1976.

Carpenter-Huffman, Polly, Bernard Rostker, and John Neufer. *Analysis of the Content of Advanced Avionics Maintenance Jobs.* R-2017-AF. Santa Monica, Calif.: The Rand Corporation, December 1976.

Chekmarev, R. "Work Rhythmically, with No Surges." *Tyl i Snabzheniye Sovetskikh Vooruzhennykh Sil,* no. 12 (1978). T3, 1979.

Chorafas, Dimitris N. *Statistical Processes and Reliability Engineering.* New York: Van Nostrand Co., 1960.

**Chuyev, Yu. V., P. M. Mel'nikov, S. I. Petukhov, G. F. Stepanov, and Ya. B. Shor. *Osnovy Issledovaniya Operatsiy v Voyennoy Tekhnike* (Fundamentals of operations research in combat material and weaponry). Vols. 1 and 2. Moscow: Soviet Radio, 1968. T4, March 1969. Distributed by NTIS, nos. AD-683 365 (vol. 1) and AD-683 146 (vol. 2).

Cobb, Tyrus W. "Tactical Air Defense: Soviet-U.S. Net Assessment." *Air University Review* (March–April 1979).

Crawford, Natalie W. *Low Level Attack of Armored Targets.* P-5982. Santa Monica, Calif.: The Rand Corporation, August 1977.

**Cutler, Leola, Donald E. Lewis, and Gary F. Mills. *An Improved Version of the Tactical Resources and Combat Effectiveness (TRACE) Model.* R-1733-PR. Santa Monica, Calif.: The Rand Corporation, May 1975.

*Davis, Jacquelyn K., and Robert L. Pfaltzgraff, Jr. *Soviet Theatre Strategy: Implications for NATO.* Report 78-1. Washington, D.C.: United States Strategic Institute, 1978.

DeLeon, Peter. *The Peacetime Evaluation of the Pilot Skill Factor in Air-to-Air Combat.* R-2070-PR. Santa Monica, Calif.: The Rand Corporation, January 1977.

Dertinger, E. F. "Funding Reliability Programs." In *Proceedings of the Ninth National Symposium on Reliability and Quality Control.* San Francisco: The Institute of Radio Engineers, 1963.

Doyle Dan. "C³—The Essential Ingredient to Air Defense." *International Defense Review,* no. 6 (1978).

Dubovsky, L. "Attention: Technical Monitoring Post." *Znamenosets,* no. 8 (August 1978). T1, January 1979.

Dunn, Ray A., Jr. "U.S. Air Force—Total Force Overview and General Purpose Force Manpower Requirements Issues." In *The Total Force and Its Manpower Requirements Including Overviews of Each Service.* Vol. 2. Defense Manpower Commission. Washington, D.C.: Government Printing Office, May 1976.

**Durov, V. R. *Boyevoye Primeneniye i Boyevaya Effektivnost' Istrebiteley-Perekhvatchikov* (The combat use and combat effectiveness of fighter-interceptors). Moscow: Military Publishing House, 1972. T4, July 1972. Distributed by NTIS, no. AD-751 512.

"Eastern Bloc Augments Attack Force." *Aviation Week and Space Technology,* 6 February 1978.

"Efficiency—A Demand of the Times." *Vestnik Protivovozdushnoy Oborony,* no. 4 (1978). T3, 1979.

**Emerson, D. E. *AIDA: An Airbase Damage Assessment Model.* R-1872-PR. Santa Monica, Calif.: The Rand Corporation, 1976.

**_____. *The New TAGS Theatre Air-Ground Warfare Model (Incorporating Major Ground-Combat Revisions): A Description and Operating Instructions.* R-1576-PR. Santa Monica, Calif.: The Rand Corporation, September 1974.

**_____. *TAGS-V: A Tactical Air-Ground Warfare Model.* R-1242-PR. Santa Monica, Calif.: The Rand Corporation, June 1973.

**Emerson, Donald. *TSARINA—User's Guide to a Computer Model for Damage Assessment of Complex Airbase Targets.* N-1460-AF. Santa Monica, Calif.: The Rand Corporation, July 1980.

Epstein, Joshua M. "On Conventional Deterrence in Europe: Questions of Soviet Confidence." *Orbis* 26 (Spring 1982).

_____. "Political Impediments to Military Effectiveness: The Case of Soviet Frontal Aviation." Ph.D. diss., M.I.T., 1981.

Ericson, John. "Soviet Military Operational Research: Objectives and Methods." *Strategic Review* (Spring 1978).

"F-15 Deployment to Netherlands Nears." *Aviation Week and Space Technology,* 6 February 1978.

Fallows, James. *National Defense.* New York: Random House, 1981.

Fazekas, James P. "Letter to the Editor." *Aviation Week and Space Technology,* 18 September 1978.

Federal Republic of Germany, White Paper 1975/1976. *The Security of the Federal Republic of Germany and the Development of the Federal Armed Forces.* Bonn: Ministry of Defense, 20 January 1976.

Fischer, Robert Lucas. *Defending the Central Front: The Balance of Forces.* Adelphi Paper no. 127. London: The International Institute for Strategic Studies, 1976.

Fisher, R. R., W. F. Drake, J. J. Delfausse, A. J. Clark, and A. L. Buchanan. *The Logistics Composite Model: An Overall View.* RM-5544-PR. Santa Monica, Calif.: The Rand Corporation, May 1968.

Gates, Howard P., Jr. "Electronics—X." In *Final Report of the Joint Logistics Commanders Electronic Systems Reliability Workshop.* Departments of the Army, the Navy, and the Air Force, 1 October 1975. Washington, D.C.: Government Printing Office.

Gervasi, Tom. *Arsenal of Democracy: American Weapons Available for Export.* New York: Grove Press, 1977.

*Gray, Colin. "Soviet Tactical Airpower." *Soviet Aerospace Almanac, Air Force Magazine,* March 1977.

Grinkevich, D. "Command and Control in Response to Contemporary Requirements." *Voyennyy Vestnik,* no. 4 (April 1976). T1, November 1977.

Gryakvin, G. "In Order Skillfully to Master Automated Systems of Control." *Vestnik Protivovozdushnoy Oborony,* no. 7 (1977). T3, 1978.

Guk, A. "A Flight of Excellent Aircraft." *Tekhnika i Vooruzheniye,* no. 8 (1973). T3, 19 February 1974.

Halloran, Richard. "Combat-Readiness of F-15 Questioned." *New York Times,* 11 December 1979.

*Hansen, Lynn M. "The Resurgence of Soviet Frontal Aviation." *Strategic Review* (Fall 1978).

Heiman, Leo. "Soviet Invasion Weaknesses." *Military Review* (August 1969).

Herzog, Chaim. *The Arab-Israeli Wars*. New York: Random House, 1982.

Holloway, David. *Technology, Management and the Soviet Military Establishment*. Adelphi Paper no. 67. London: The International Institute for Strategic Studies, April 1971.

Hunt, Charles. *Airfield Survivability and Post-Attack Sortie Generation*. Concept Issue Paper 80-2. Doctrine and Concepts Division, Deputy Director for Long-Range Planning, Directorate of Plans, Deputy Chief of Staff Operations, Plans, and Readiness, Headquarters, U.S. Air Force, February 1980.

"The Innovator's Relay." *Tekhnika i Vooruzheniye*, no. 6 (1978). T3, 1979.

Kirsanov, P. "Enhancing the Training of Aviators." *Tekhnika i Vooruzheniye*, no. 8 (1976). T1, November 1977.

Kiselev, A. "Incentives for Technical Creativity." *Tekhnika i Vooruzheniye*, no. 10 (1971). T3, 1972.

Kivenson, Gilbert. *Durability and Reliability in Engineering Design*. New York: Hayden Book Co., 1971.

Klass, Philip J. "Operational Procedure Shifts Yield Major Gains." *Aviation Week and Space Technology*, 6 February 1978.

Kolcum, Edward H. "Difficulty of Challenge Determines Credit in Grey Flag." *Aviation Week and Space Technology*, 6 February 1978.

Konstantinov, Anatoliy Ustinovich. "Thorough Knowledge of Affairs." *Krasnaya Zvezda*, 13 March 1977. T1, June 1977.

Koshchavko, A. "Master of Air Combat." *Vestnik Protivovozdushnoy Oborony*, no. 4 (1978). T3, April 1978.

Kunznick, Gene A. "F-15 Reliability Program Management." In *Final Report of the Joint Logistics Commanders Electronic Systems Reliability Workshop*. Departments of the Army, the Navy, and the Air Force, 1 October 1975. Washington, D.C.: Government Printing Office.

**Lanchester, Frederick William. *Aircraft in Warfare*. London: Constable and Co., 1916. The seminal chapters, 5 and 6, are reprinted as "Mathematics in Warfare" in *The World* *of Mathematics*, edited by James R. Newman, vol 4. New York: Simon and Schuster, 1956.

"Langley F-15 Group Deployed in Korea." *Aviation Week and Space Technology*, 6 February 1978.

Lawrence, Richard D., and Jeffrey Record. *U.S. Force Structure in NATO*. Washington, D.C.: The Brookings Institution, 1974.

Lee, Asher. *The Soviet Air Force*. London: Gerald Duckworth, 1961.

Leitenberg, M. "Background Materials in Tactical Nuclear Weapons." In *Tactical Nuclear Weapons: European Perspectives*, Stockholm International Peace Research Institute. London: Taylor and Francis, 1978.

**Lind, J. R. *Overview of the Air-Ground Actions Two-sided Engagement (AGATE) Simulation Model*. R-2379-AF. Santa Monica, Calif.: The Rand Corporation, April 1979.

**Louer, Philip E., and Ralph E. Johnson. *Concepts Evaluation Model V (CEM V)*. Part I, *Technical Description*. Bethesda, Md.: U.S. Army Concepts Analysis Agency, January 1980.

Marks, Kenneth E., H. Garrison Massey, and Brent D. Bradley. *An Appraisal of Models Used in Life Cycle Cost Estimation for USAF Aircraft Systems*. R-2287-AF. Santa Monica, Calif.: The Rand Corporation, October 1978.

"The Mass Character of Technical Creativity." *Tekhnika i Vooruzheniye*, no. 6 (1978). T3, 1979.

McDonnell, John A. "The Soviet Weapons Acquisition System." In *Soviet Armed Forces Review Annual*, edited by David R. Jones, vol. 3. Gulf Breeze, Fla.: Academic International Press, 1979.

Menning, F. H. "Letter to the Editor." *Aviation Week and Space Technology*, 18 September 1978.

"Military Engineer and Equipment: Efficiency—A Demand of the Times." *Vestnik Protivovozdushnoy Oborony*, no. 4 (1978). T3, 1979.

**Miller, George, ed. *The Vector-2 Theater-Level Combat Model*. Vol. 1, *User's Manual*. Ann Arbor, Mich.: Vector Research, February 1977.

Milyakhovskiiy, V. "The CP Controller and the Flight Crew." *Vestnik Protivovozdushnoy Oborony*, no. 12 (1978). T3, December 1979.

Morse, Phillip M., and George E. Kimball. "How to Hunt a Submarine." In *The World of Mathematics*, edited by James R. Newman, vol. 4. New York: Simon and Schuster, 1956.

Myers, Richard H., Kam L. Wong, and Howard Gordy. *Reliability Engineering for Electronic Systems*. New York: John Wiley & Sons, 1964.

Nekhoroshev, S. "When Friendly and Enemy Aircraft Are Airborne." *Voyennyy Vestnik*, no. 5 (May 1976). T1, November 1977.

Neu, Carl Richard. *Attacking Hardened Air Bases (AHAB): A Decision Analysis Aid for the Tactical Commander*. R-1422-PR. Santa Monica, Calif.: The Rand Corporation, August 1974.

Nosov, L. "Sudden Combat Task." *Krasnaya Zvezda*, 27 May 1976. T1, April 1977.

*Nunn, Sam, and Dewey F. Bartlett. *NATO and the New Soviet Threat*. Report to the Committee on Armed Services of the U.S. Senate. 24 January 1977. Washington, D.C.: Government Printing Office.

**Nussbaum, Israel. *Aircraft Reliability, Availability, and Maintainability (MMH/FH) Data Comparative Analysis*. St. Louis, Mo.: U.S. Army Aviation Research and Development Command, November 1978.

**Nyland, F. S. *Estimating Bomber Penetration and Weapons Effectiveness*. R-1278/1-PR. Santa Monica, Calif.: The Rand Corporation, May 1974.

Ofer, Gur. *The Opportunity Cost of the Nonmonetary Advantages of the Soviet Military R&D Effort*. R-1741-DDRE. Santa Monica, Calif.: The Rand Corporation, August 1975.

"On-the-Ground Look at an Ailing Army." *U.S. News and World Report*, 12 May 1980.

Pajak, Roger F. "Soviet Arms Transfers as an Instrument of Influence." *Survival* 23 (July/August 1981).

Pan'kin, V. "Lieutenants' Flights." *Krasnaya Zvezda*, 4 August 1976. Tl, April 1977.

Pavlov, G. "Inexhaustible Reserve." *Krasnaya Zvezda*, 4 August 1976. T1, April 1977.

Pavlovskiy, Ivan Grigor'yevich. "An Officer's Technical Culture." *Krasnaya Zvezda*, 5 February 1977. Tl, May 1977.

Perry, Robert. *Comparisons of Soviet and U.S. Technology.* R-827-PR. Santa Monica, Calif.: The Rand Corporation, June 1972.

Perry, William J. "Fallows' Fallacies." *International Security* 6 (Spring 1982).

Perry, William J., and Cynthia A. Roberts. "Winning through Sophistication: How to Meet the Soviet Military Threat." *Technology Review* 85 (July 1982).

*Petersen, Phillip A. *Soviet Air Power and the Pursuit of New Military Options.* Studies in Communist Affairs, vol. 3. Washington, D.C.: Government Printing Office, 1979.

Phillips, Samuel C. "Keynote Address." In *Final Report of the Joint Logistics Commanders Electronic Systems Reliability Workshop.* Departments of the Army, the Navy, and the Air Force, 1 October 1975. Washington, D.C.: Government Printing Office.

"The Potemkin Factory." *Time*, 25 February 1980.

"Publicity, Comparability of Results, and the Possibility of Practical Repetition of Experience." *Tekhnika i Vooruzheniye*, no. 10 (1973). T3, 10 July 1974.

Record, Jeffrey. *Sizing Up the Soviet Army.* Washington, D.C.: The Brookings Institution, 1975.

**Rehm, Allan S. *An Assessment of Military Operations Research in the USSR.* Arlington, Va.: Center for Naval Analysis, September 1973.

Robinson, Clarence A., Jr. "Future Threat Guides F-15 Advances." *Aviation Week and Space Technology, Special Report: Tactical Air Command—Modernization and Management*, 6 February 1978.

**Romanov, A. N., and G. A. Frolov. *Avtomatizatsii Sistemy Upravleniya* (Principles of automating control systems).

Moscow: Military Publishing House, 1971. T4, January 1973. Distributed by NTIS, no. AD-758 050.

Rosen, Steven J. *What a Fifth Arab-Israeli War Might Look Like: An Exercise in Crisis Forecasting.* Working Paper no. 8, Center for Arms Control and International Security. Los Angeles: University of California, November 1977.

Safranov, A. "Innovators Share Their Experience." *Tekhnika i Vooruzheniye,* no. 6 (June 1978). T3, 1979.

————. "The Creative Activity of Innovators' Thematic Contests." *Tekhnika i Vooruzheniye,* no. 11 (November 1978). T3, 1979.

Schemmer, Benjamin F. "Pentagon, White House, and Congress Concerned over Tactical Aircraft Complexity and Readiness." *Armed Forces Journal International* (May 1980).

Scott, Harriet Fast, and William F. Scott. *The Armed Forces of the USSR.* Boulder, Colo.: Westview Press, 1979.

Second German-American Roundtable on NATO. *The Theater Nuclear Balance.* Cambridge, Mass.: The Institute for Foreign Policy Analysis, 1978.

Shatokin, V. "Periodic Servicing and the Socialist Competition in the Technical-Operating *Chast'*." *Vestnik Protivovozdushnoy Oborony,* no. 5 (May 1976). T3, 1976.

Shishkin, M. "For Outstanding TECh." *Tekhnika i Vooruzheniye,* no. 5 (1975). T3, 10 December 1973.

Shlayen, P., A. Karasev, and V. Romanov. "Military Education and Psychology: Ergonomics Recommends. . . ." *Vestnik Protivovozdushnoy Oborony,* no. 2 (1977). T3, 1977.

Shlyayfert, B. "Planning Maintenance on Aviation Equipment." *Vestnik Protivovozdushnoy Oborony,* no. 5 (1976). T3, 1976.

Shpilevoy, A. "Competition Indoctrinates." *Voyennyy Vestnik,* no. 9 (1978). T3, 1979.

Sidorenko, A. A. *The Offensive.* Moscow, 1970. Translated as no. 1 of the U.S. Air Force Series *Soviet Military Thought.* Washington, D.C.: Government Printing Office.

Sigov, P., M. Vasil'yev, and V. Lysov. "When Away from Own Air Base." *Tekhnika i Vooruzheniye*, no. 10 (1974). T3, 30 August 1975.

Skibinskiy, P. "The Technical-Electrical Unit Has New Equipment." *Aviatsiya i Kosmonavtika*, no. 10 (1968). T4, 28 May 1969.

Skubilin, V. "In the Interests of Combat Readiness." *Tekhnika i Vooruzheniye*, no. 8 (1973). T3, 19 February 1974.

———. "New Equipment—New Demands." *Aviatsiya i Kosmonavtika* (July 1975). T2, October 1975.

**Solnyshkov, Yu. S. *Optimizatsiya Vybora Vooruzheniya* (Optimization of armament selection). Moscow: Military Publishing House, 1968. T4, September 1969. Distributed by the Clearinghouse for Federal Scientific and Technical Information, U.S. Department of Commerce, National Bureau of Standards, no. AD 699–629.

Stanhope, Henry. "New Threat— or Old Fears?" In *European Security: Prospects for the 1980s*, edited by Derek Leebaert. Lexington, Mass.: D. C. Heath and Co., 1979.

Stein, Kenneth J. "Forward-Looking Technology Explored." *Aviation Week and Space Technology*, January 1979.

Sukovic, O. "Tactical Nuclear Weapons in Europe." In *Tactical Nuclear Weapons: European Perspectives*, Stockholm International Peace Research Institute. London: Taylor and Francis, 1978.

Sweetman, Bill, and Bill Gunston. *Soviet Air Power*. New York: Crescent Books, 1978.

Swett, Ben H. "The Avionics Reliability Study." In *Final Report of the Joint Logistics Commanders Electronic Systems Reliability Workshop*. Departments of the Army, the Navy, and the Air Force, 1 October 1975. Washington, D.C.: Government Printing Office.

**TAC ASSESSOR Methodology Manual*. Santa Barbara, Calif.: General Research Corporation, October 1979.

Timperlake, Edward T., and Steven Leveen. *A Methodology for Estimating Comparative Aircrew Proficiency*. Arlington, Va.: The Analytic Sciences Corporation, May 1981.

**Tkachenko, P. N., L. N. Kutsev, G. A. Meshcheryakov, A. M. Chavkin, and A. D. Chebykin, *Matematicheskie Metody Modelirovaniya Boevykh Deystviy Takticheskikh Podrazdeleniy pri Pomoshchi Elektronnykh Vychislitel'nykh Mashin* (Mathematical models of combat operations. Mathematical methods for modeling combat operations in tactical units [*podrazdeleniye*] with the aid of electronic computers). Moscow: Soviet Radio, 1969. T3, April 1973. Distributed by NTIS, no. AD-764 109.

Trapans, Andris. *Organizational Maintenance in the Soviet Air Force*. RM-4382-PR. Santa Monica, Calif.: The Rand Corporation, January 1965.

Tsymbalyuk, R. "Scientific Organization of Labor and Shops." *Vestnik Protivovozdushnoy Oborony*, no. 11 (1971). T3, 27 April 1972.

U.S. Central Intelligence Agency. National Foreign Assessment Center. *Estimated Soviet Defense Spending: Trends and Prospects*. Washington, D.C.: Government Printing Office, June 1978.

*U.S. Congress. House. Committee on Armed Services. *Hearings on Military Posture and Department of Defense Authorization for Appropriations for Fiscal Year 1980. Research and Development*, Bks. 1 and 2. H.R. 1972 (H.R. 4040). 96th Cong., 1st sess., 1979. In Bk. 1, see pp. 781–782, 1210–1211. In Bk. 2, see p. 2998.

U.S. Congress. Senate. Committee on Appropriations. *Department of Defense Appropriations for Fiscal Year 1976, Part 4—Department of the Air Force: Hearings before a subcommittee of the Senate Committee on Appropriations*. 94th Cong., 1st sess., 1975.

_____. *Department of Defense Appropriations for Fiscal Year 1978, Part 4—Procurement: Hearings before a subcommittee of the Senate Committee on Appropriations on H.R. 7933*. 95th Cong., 1st sess., 1977.

_____. *Department of Defense Appropriations for Fiscal Year 1980, Part 3—Operation and Maintenance: Hearings before a subcommittee of the Committee on Appropriations*, 96th Cong., 1st sess., 1979.

_____. Committee on Armed Services. *Close Air Support: Hearings before a special subcommittee on Close Air Support of the Preparedness Investigating Subcommittee of the Senate Committee on Armed Services.* 92nd Cong., 1st sess., 1971.

*_____. *Department of Defense Authorization for Appropriations for Fiscal Year 1979. Tactical Air: Hearings before the Senate Committee on Armed Services on S.2571.* 95th Cong., 2nd sess., 1978. See especially the E-3A AWACS Test Scenario, pp. 4502–4506.

_____. *Department of Defense Authorization for Appropriations for Fiscal Year 1982, Part 5 — Preparedness: Hearings before the Senate Committee on Armed Services on S.815.* 97th Cong., 1st sess., 1981.

U.S. Congressional Budget Office. *Resources for Defense: A Review of Key Issues for Fiscal Years 1982–1986.* Washington, D.C.: Government Printing Office, January 1981.

_____. *U.S. Air and Ground Conventional Forces for NATO: Air Defense Issues.* Washington, D.C.: Government Printing Office, March 1978.

U.S. Department of the Air Force. *Soviet Aerospace Handbook.* Pamphlet 200–21. Washington, D.C.: Government Printing Office, May 1978.

_____. *U.S. Air Force Glossary of Standardized Terms.* Vol. 1. AFM 11-1. Washington, D.C.: Government Printing Office, 1973.

U.S. Department of the Army. *Air Defense Artillery Reference Handbook.* FM 44-1-2. Washington, D.C.: Government Printing Office, 30 June, 1978.

*_____. *U.S. Army Air Defense Artillery Employment.* FM 44-1. Washington, D.C.: Government Printing Office, 25 March 1976.

*_____. *U.S. Army Air Defense Artillery Employment, CHAPPARAL/VULCAN.* FM 44-3. Washington, D.C.: Government Printing Office, 30 September 1977.

U.S. Department of Defense. *Annual Report of the Secretary of Defense for Fiscal Year 1980.* Washington, D.C.: Government Printing Office, January 1979.

_____. *Annual Report of the Secretary of Defense for Fiscal Year 1981*. Washington, D.C.: Government Printing Office, 1980.

_____. *Annual Report of the Secretary of Defense for Fiscal Year 1982*. Washington, D.C.: Government Printing Office, 1981.

_____. Joint Chiefs of Staff. *United States Military Posture for Fiscal Year 1979*. Washington, D. C.: Government Printing Office, January 1978.

U.S. Executive Office of the President of the United States. *The Budget of the United States Government: Fiscal Year 1980*. Office of Management and Budget. Washington, D.C.: Government Printing Office, 1980.

_____. *The Budget of the United States Government: Fiscal Year 1980, Appendix*. Office of Management and Budget. Washington, D.C.: Government Printing Office, 1980.

U.S. General Accounting Office. *Defense Spending and Its Relationship to the Federal Budget*. Washington, D.C.: Government Printing Office, June 1983.

**_____. *Determining Requirements for Aircraft Maintenance Personnel Could Be Improved—Peacetime and Wartime*. Report to the Senate Committee on Appropriations by the Comptroller General of the United States. Report LCD-77-421. Washington, D.C.: Government Printing Office, 20 May 1977.

_____. *Productivity of Military Below-Depot Maintenance—Repairs Less Complex Than Provided at Depots—Can Be Improved*. Comptroller General of the United States. Report LCD 75-422. Washington, D.C.: Government Printing Office, July 1975.

U.S. Office of the Under Secretary of Defense for Research and Engineering. *Final Report of The Defense Science Board Task Force on V/STOL Aircraft*. Washington, D.C.: Government Printing Office, November 1979.

_____. *Report of the Acquisition Cycle Task Force*. Washington, D.C.: Government Printing Office, March 1978.

Uryzhnikov, V. A. "In a Complex Situation." *Krasnaya Zvezda*, 7 January 1977. T1, April 1977.

Vanyushkin, M. "Each Flight Is Supported Effectively." *Vestnik Protivovozdushnoy Oborony*, no. 10 (1978). T3, 1979.

"Variety of Air-Surface Weapons Studied." *Aviation Week and Space Technology*, 6 February 1978.

Vorob'yev, B. "At an Alternate Airfield." *Tyl i Snabzheniye Sovetskikh Vooruzhennykh Sil*, no. 8 (August 1977). T1, April 1978.

"Water Evacuation Equipment." *Tekhnika i Vooruzheniye*, no. 8 (1973). T3, 19 February 1974.

Welander, R. O., J. J. Herzog, and F. D. Kennedy, Jr. *The Soviet Navy Declaratory Doctrine for Theater Nuclear Warfare.* McLean, Va.: The BDM Corporation, 1977.

White, William D. *U.S. Tactical Air Power—Missions, Forces, and Costs.* Washington, D.C.: The Brookings Institution, 1974.

Wolfe, Thomas W. *Soviet Power and Europe 1945—1970.* Baltimore: The Johns Hopkins Univ. Press, 1970.

Yakushin, Viktor Zakharovich. "The Staff in the Struggle for an Effective Training Process." *Krasnaya Zvezda*, 20 April 1977. T1, August 1977.

Yarchuk, Aleksandr Grigor'yevich. "Even Though the Accident Did Not Occur." *Krasnaya Zvezda*, 26 January 1977. T1, April 1977.

Yefremov, K. "Mechanization of Labor-Intensive Work." *Tekhnika i Vooruzheniye*, no. 6 (1978). T3, 1979.

Yulin, V. "Standardization and Quality Control of the Operation of Equipment and Armament." *Vestnik Protivovozdushnoy Oborony*, no. 2 (1977). T3, 1977.

_____. "The Use of Precision Charts When Servicing Radio-Electronic Systems." *Vestnik Protivovozdushnoy Oborony*, no. 5 (1976). T3, 1979.

Zakharenko, A. "The Lessons of Coordination." *Krasnaya Zvezda*, 5 August 1977. T1, November 1977.

Zenushkin, A. "The Contribution of the Rationalizers." *Tekhnika i Vooruzheniye*, no. 6 (1978). T3, 1979.

**Zhukov, V. N., ed. *Matematika v Boyu* (Mathematics in combat). Moscow: Military Publishing House, 1965. T3, February 1972. Distributed by NTIS, no. AD-737 149.

RELATED BOOKS

Written under the Auspices of the Center for International Affairs, Harvard University

The Soviet Bloc, by Zbigniew K. Brzezinski (sponsored jointly with the Russian Research Center), 1960. Harvard University Press. Revised edition, 1967.

The Necessity for Choice, by Henry A. Kissinger, 1961. Harper & Bros.

Strategy and Arms Control, by Thomas A. Schelling and Morton H. Halperin, 1961. Twentieth Century Fund.

Communist China 1955–1959: Policy Documents with Analysis, with a foreword by Robert R. Bowie and John K. Fairbank (sponsored jointly with the East Asian Research Center), 1962. Harvard University Press.

Limited War in the Nuclear Age, by Morton H. Halperin, 1963. John Wiley & Sons.

In Search of France, by Stanley Hoffmann et al., 1963. Harvard University Press.

How Nations Negotiate, by Fred Charles Iklé, 1964. Harper & Row.

The Troubled Partnership, by Henry A. Kissinger (sponsored jointly with the Council on Foreign Relations), 1965. McGraw-Hill Book Co.

Deterrence before Hiroshima: The Airpower Background of Modern Strategy, by George H. Quester, 1966. John Wiley & Sons.

Containing the Arms Race, by Jeremy J. Stone, 1966. M.I.T. Press.

Arms and Influence, by Thomas C. Schelling, 1966. Yale University Press.

Foreign Policy and Democratic Politics, by Kenneth N. Waltz (sponsored jointly with the Institute of War and Peace Studies, Columbia University), 1967. Little, Brown & Co.

Sino-Soviet Relations and Arms Control, ed. Morton H. Halperin (sponsored jointly with the East Asian Research Center), 1967. M.I.T. Press.

Europe's Postwar Growth, by Charles P. Kindleberger, 1967. Harvard University Press.

Political Order in Changing Societies, by Samuel P. Huntington, 1968. Yale University Press.

The TFX Decision: McNamara and the Military, by Robert J. Art, 1968. Little, Brown & Co.

German Foreign Policy in Transition, by Karl Kaiser, 1968. Oxford University Press.

Nuclear Diplomacy, by George H. Quester, 1970. Dunellen.

The Logic of Images in International Relations, by Robert Jervis, 1970. Princeton University Press.

Studies in Development Planning, edited by Hollis B. Chenery, 1971. Harvard University Press.

Defense Strategy for the Seventies (revision of *Contemporary Military Strategy*) by Morton H. Halperin, 1971. Little, Brown & Co.

Transnational Relations and World Politics, edited by Robert O. Keohane and Joseph S. Nye, Jr., 1972. Harvard University Press.

The United States and West Germany 1945–1973: A Study in Alliance Politics, by Roger Morgan (sponsored jointly with the Royal Institute of International Affairs), 1974. Oxford University Press.

No Easy Choice: Political Participation in Developing Countries, by Samuel P. Huntington and Joan M. Nelson, 1976. Harvard University Press.

The Oil Crisis, edited by Raymond Vernon, 1976. W. W. Norton & Co.

Perception and Misperception in International Politics, by Robert Jervis, 1976. Princeton University Press.

Power and Interdependence, by Robert O. Keohane and Joseph S. Nye, Jr., 1977. Little, Brown & Co.

Soldiers in Politics: Military Coups and Governments, by Eric Nordlinger, 1977. Prentice-Hall.

The Military and Politics in Modern Times: On Professionals, Praetorians, and Revolutionary Soldiers, by Amos Perlmutter, 1977. Yale University Press.

Shattered Peace: The Origins of the Cold War and the National Security State, by Daniel Yergin, 1977. Houghton Mifflin.

Storm Over the Multinationals: The Real Issues, by Raymond Vernon, 1977. Harvard University Press.

Defending the National Interest: Raw Materials Investments and American Foreign Policy, by Stephen D. Krasner, 1978. Princeton University Press.

Israel: The Embattled Ally, by Nadav Safran, 1978. Harvard University Press.

Insurrection or Loyalty: The Breakdown of the Spanish American Empire, by Jorge Domínguez, 1980. Harvard University Press.

Palestinian Society and Politics, by Joel S. Migdal et al., 1980. Princeton University Press.

Energy and Security, Joseph S. Nye, Jr. and David A. Deese, eds., 1980. Ballinger Publishing Co., Cambridge.

Weak States in the International System, by Michael Handel, 1981. Frank Cass, London.

On the Autonomy of the Democratic State, by Eric A. Nordlinger, 1981. Harvard University Press.

American Politics: The Promise of Disharmony, by Samuel P. Huntington, 1981. Harvard University Press.

Bureaucrats and Politicians in Western Democracies, by Robert D. Putnam et al., 1981. Harvard University Press.

INDEX

Library of Congress Cataloging in Publication Data

Epstein, Joshua M., 1951–
Measuring military power.

"Written under the auspices of the Center for
International Affairs, Harvard University."
Bibliography: p.   Includes index.
1. Aeronautics, Military—Soviet Union.   2. Air power.
3. Soviet Union.   Voenno–Vozdushnye Sily—Tactical
aviation—Europe.
4. Europe—Defenses.   I. Harvard University.
Center for International Affairs.   II. Title.
UG635.S65E67   1984   358.4'00947   83-43070
ISBN 0-691-07671-5 (alk. paper)

Joshua M. Epstein is a Rockefeller Foundation International Relations
Fellow in residence at The Brookings Institution.